W9-CON-711

The Ermatingers

971.004973330922 Ermat -S

Stewart, W.
The Ermatingers.

MAR 2 7 2008

PRICE: $35.25 (3559/se   )

W. Brian Stewart

The Ermatingers:
A 19th-Century Ojibwa-
Canadian Family

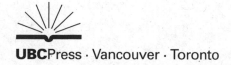
UBCPress · Vancouver · Toronto

© UBC Press 2007

All rights reserved. No part of this publication may be reproduced, stored in a
retrieval system, or transmitted, in any form or by any means, without prior written
permission of the publisher, or, in Canada, in the case of photocopying or other
reprographic copying, a licence from Access Copyright (Canadian Copyright
Licensing Agency), www.accesscopyright.ca.

16 15 14 13 12 11 10 09 08 07   5 4 3 2 1

Printed in Canada on ancient-forest-free paper (100% post-consumer recycled) that
is processed chlorine- and acid-free, with vegetable-based inks.

Library and Archives Canada Cataloguing in Publication

Stewart, W. Brian (William Brian), 1927-
   The Ermatingers : a nineteenth-century Ojibwa-Canadian family /
W. Brian Stewart.

Includes bibliographical references and index.
ISBN 978-0-7748-1233-7 (bound); 978-0-7748-1234-4 (pbk)

   1. Ermatinger family. 2. Métis – Biography. 3. Métis – Social conditions –
19th century. I. Title.

FC109.1.E75S74 2007   971.004'973330922   C2007-903166-8

Canadä

UBC Press gratefully acknowledges the financial support for our publishing
program of the Government of Canada through the Book Publishing Industry
Development Program (BPIDP), and of the Canada Council for the Arts, and the
British Columbia Arts Council.

UBC Press is grateful for the financial assistance of the Hbc History Foundation.

UBC Press
The University of British Columbia
2029 West Mall
Vancouver, BC V6T 1Z2
604.822.5959 / Fax 604.822.6083
www.ubcpress.ca

To Jenny, Bill, and Ellen

Contents

Figures

Acknowledgments

At a time in Canada's history when libraries and archives should be expanding yet funding and staffs are shrinking, I must thank those helpful people at Library and Archives Canada; at the Hudson's Bay Company Archives and the Archives of Ontario; at the Baldwin Room of the Toronto Reference Library, the Rare Books Library of the University of Toronto, the University of Western Ontario's D.B. Weldon Library, and the Mississauga Public Library; at the Eva Brook Donly Museum, Simcoe, and the Elgin Military Museum, St Thomas; and in the United Kingdom, the Public Records Office, Kew, and the National Army Museum, London.

Volunteers helping keep our history alive include the Genealogical Society of Ontario, especially the Norfolk County Branch, and the Friends of the Mount Royal Cemetery, Montreal. If libraries are shrinking, there is consolation in the Internet. I compliment the staff members of Early Canadiana Online, who are a pleasure to work with, as well as the individuals who take pride in the accuracy of their history websites.

At UBC Press I must thank the anonymous readers for their comments; Jean Wilson for her patience and persistence in shepherding the manuscript through the reading process; and Camilla Blakeley and Sarah Wight for their meticulous editing and production values, all of which greatly improved this book. Lastly I wish to thank Mr W.G. Dillabough and KPMG for the generous donation accompanying the 1998 Mississauga Literary Arts Award for my last book, *A Life on the Line*. This financed my trip to the National Army Museum in London and to the Public Records Office at Kew while researching *The Ermatingers*.

The Ermatingers

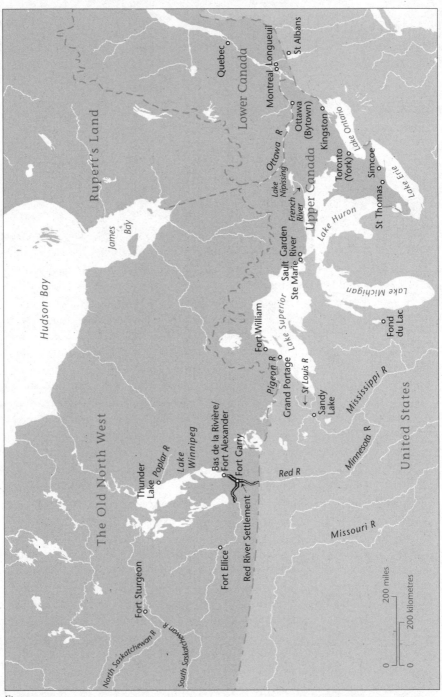

Figure 1
Ermatinger country

Introduction

About 1800, fur trader Charles Oakes Ermatinger, of Swiss-German and English descent, married, country-style, Mananowe Katawabidai, daughter of an Ojibwa chief. They had twelve children, seven of whom reached adulthood. The children spent their early years in Sault Ste Marie in contact with their Ojibwa relatives and socializing with their Métis neighbours in what John Bigsby described as "the wild man's land." The older children went to Montreal for a traditional Canadian education, and in 1828 the whole family moved there. The children lived the rest of their lives mainly in Canadian urban communities but retained ties with their Ojibwa relatives. In 1850, four Ojibwa chiefs of the Sault Ste Marie area petitioned the Canadian government that the local "half breed" families, explicitly including the Ermatingers, be given title to the lands they occupied in the area. The families deserved this because they were "the children of the sisters and the daughters of your Memorialists thus having an inheritance in the country equal to our own, and bound to it by as strong and heartfelt ties as we ourselves."[1]

In recent years, much has been written on fur trader-Indian families, usually by analyzing and generalizing over a relatively large number of cases. But Jennifer S.H. Brown writes, "More detailed family histories with time depths of three, four or five generations, could bring out important and subtle comparisons and paths of change" among the Métis. Such histories would contribute "richer perspectives, not only on individuals and families, but on Métis social history in the broadest sense."[2] The current book is such a study, showing the bicultural nature, urban Canadian and Upper Country Ojibwa, of the Ermatinger family, and the outcomes of the children's lives in urban Canada.[3] To place the family in its wider context, this introduction briefly reviews the range of outcomes of other fur trader-Indian marriages and of the lives of their progeny. It focuses on children who, like the Ermatingers, were taken out of the Upper Country and sent to urban Canada or Britain for their education.

RELATIONS BETWEEN TRADER AND NATIVE WIFE

From the first French arrivals in Canada, European traders married Indian women country-style, that is, they cohabited after no formal or religious ceremony other than a present or "bride price" to their father-in-law. These connections had more advantages for the husband than just sex and companionship. The Native wife had many skills beyond normal housekeeping. She interpreted and acted as guide, trapped small animals for food and furs, and made moccasins and snowshoes.[4] She often made life bearable and even possible for her husband: possible because he often lacked her survival skills, while family relationships with her people helped ensure a steady supply of furs. For their part, Indian women marrying white traders gained useful technology for themselves and often helped gain similar access for their sisters. "It was much easier to boil water in a metal kettle," Sylvia Van Kirk points out, "than to laboriously heat it by means of dropping hot stones into a bark container."[5] Women also increased their influence and status through intermarriage.

From a Marxist point of view, Ron Bourgeault sees marriage to a white trader as changing the Indian woman's role and status for the worse. The fur trade, he claims, transformed the primitive Indian society into a feudal society set up to extract the surplus labour of the Native people. The trader's wife lost both the equality and the decision-making powers characteristic of wives in the Indian family. Meanwhile, he alleges, traders exploited their wives politically and sexually, using them as a commodity to gain access to specific groups for trading purposes.[6]

In fact, we find wide variation in the way white traders treated their country wives.[7] At one abysmal extreme stood Frank Ermatinger, a nephew of Charles Oakes Ermatinger (see Appendix E). Affairs with Native women were, he said, compensation "to counterbalance the misery of Damned Dried Salmon." After deserting a Cree woman and daughter, an Okanagan and two children, and a Flathead and three children (sometimes with no compensation), he formally wed a young Indian-Canadian woman, Catherine Sinclair. They finally settled in St Thomas.[8] Similarly, Scottish-born fur trader Duncan Cameron warned a young relative in 1812 that he should not "let love to get the better of Reason." If he were to marry before he was properly settled, then all his future prospects would be lost: "This I too well know by dear bought experience." Cameron deserted his Ojibwa wife and family for Upper Canada and, in 1820, married Margaret McLeod. They had a daughter and three sons.[9] At the other extreme, many country marriages were successful and stable and continued for the life of the partners. For example, Alexander Ross, a Scot by birth, married an Okanagan woman, Sally. Ross said that affection for their Native wives formed the traders' attachment to the Indian country.[10]

Relatively few traders with Indian (rather than Métis) wives took them out of Indian country. Among those who did, Nor'Wester John Dugald Cameron in 1846 retired with his Native wife, Mary, and their family to Upper Canada. There, Mary adjusted well to her new environment and helped manage their farm. However, the Native wife of Allan McDonell (1776-1859) found herself "quite out of her element" in her new and elegant home in Montreal.[11]

Some fur traders who had married according to the custom of the country regularized their marriages when they took their families to the Canadas. Nor'Wester Pierre Marois considered his country marriage legal, yet on moving to Lower Canada, remarried his wife according to church and civil law. This was wise, as country-style marriages could raise legal problems. Alexander Fraser took his wife, Angélique, and their children to Lower Canada where he also fathered several children by two Canadiennes. He apparently treated all three mothers well and the children with equal affection, but left a complex legal case of legitimacy to be sorted out upon his death.[12]

THE FATHER AND HIS BICULTURAL CHILDREN

In a study of fur trade children baptized in Montreal's St Gabriel Street Presbyterian Church between 1796 and 1835, Jennifer Brown finds that boys outnumbered girls by about two to one. She concludes that anglophone trader fathers, more anxious to advance their sons than they were their daughters, personally directed the boys' education and placement.[13] Formal education, she argues, tended to affect strongly, and not always beneficially, the child's sense of identity. Often, the father wanted his children to suppress their Indian background. George Atkinson of the Hudson's Bay Company and his Indian wife, Necushin, had two sons and a daughter. Son Sneppy went to England in 1790 and was baptized as George. His father hoped this would "shake off a little of the Indian & in so doing make him exert himself like a Man."[14]

Sylvia Van Kirk concludes that to succeed in their father's world the children learned to suppress "every vestige of their Indian heritage," although racism sometimes prevented full assimilation. Fur traders often pushed mixed-blood daughters into an "increasingly passive and dependent mould" in sharp contrast to the "autonomy and self-reliance of the Indian woman."[15] Van Kirk points out that in the racist climate of North America at that time, bicultural children were often caught between two worlds, unable to see themselves as Métis but not fully accepted by whites.[16] As Elizabeth Arthur says of one mixed-blood family, "The sense of belonging to neither their father's culture nor their mother's must have been overpowering."[17] The influence of Indian or Métis mothers on their children is much less well documented than that of their fur trade fathers.

As will be shown, Charles Oakes, in his role as father, is similar in some respects to the fathers just described, but he also differs in important ways. The differences may be explained in part because most studies of dual-descent children have concerned the offspring of employees of either the

North West Company or of the Hudson's Bay Company. Though Charles Oakes Ermatinger had dealings with both those companies, he was primarily an independent trader conditioned by neither of their corporate cultures.

BICULTURAL CHILDREN OUTSIDE INDIAN COUNTRY
Brown's study also shows that between 1796 and 1835 St Gabriel Street Presbyterian Church baptized or buried eighty-nine children who came from Indian country. Ranging from infancy to thirteen years of age, almost all were partly of Indian descent. Almost one baptized child in eight died within three or four years of baptism. For Brown this mortality rate reflects the separation from one or both parents after long journeys to Montreal.[18] Those children who reached adulthood generally followed one of three life paths: they could attempt to assimilate in white, Canadian society; they could try to return to their Indian roots; or they could combine elements of both heritages in a third, or Métis, culture.

Integration with White Society
George Barnston of the Hudson's Bay Company married country-style a mixed-blood woman, Ellen Matthews. When appointed to Tadoussac in 1844, Barnston wrote that he could now give his eleven children a better education, "an object ever near to my heart."[19] He succeeded. Among his sons were a lawyer in British Columbia, a banking bookkeeper in Belleville, Upper Canada, and a clerk in Montreal. One daughter married a merchant in Colombo, Ceylon, and another the manager of an assurance company.[20] The most remarkable child was the eldest, James. After school in Red River, Manitoba, and Lachine, Lower Canada, at age twenty-one he gained his medical diploma at the University of Edinburgh and returned to Montreal to start a practice. A keen botanist, in 1857 he became the first professor of botany at McGill, though he died the following year.[21]

Alexander Ross thought "mixed bloods" were genetically inferior and he pushed his children to succeed in white society. After attending the University of Toronto, his son James returned to Red River and during the first Riel troubles spoke on behalf of the English-speaking settlers. Another son held various official positions in Assiniboia, while three daughters all married "well" into white society.[22] The Rosses, while affectionate towards, and not overtly ashamed of, their Indian mother, in private still asked defensively, "What if Mama is an Indian?"[23]

Alexander Kennedy Isbister, grandson of a Hudson's Bay Company employee and a Cree woman, was educated first in the Orkneys, birthplace of his father, and then in Red River. When he was sixteen, he joined the Hudson's Bay Company but left after four years, unhappy because he felt his Native ancestry had held up any promotion. He earned a brilliant degree at the University of Aberdeen and began a successful career in Britain as a teacher and textbook author. Though outside Métis society, he never forgot his roots and fought for the rights of his Native and Métis peoples.[24]

Integration with Indian Society
Children educated outside Indian country who returned to their Indian roots are more difficult to trace, because records of their lives were often not kept. For instance, Frank Ermatinger sent Lawrence, his son by an Okanagan, to be educated in St Thomas in Upper Canada. Lawrence, a pathetic figure later found destitute in Montreal, drifted back west to a fate unknown even to his father.[25]

The father of Ranald MacDonald was Archibald McDonald (the original family spelling), a senior officer of the Hudson's Bay Company. Ranald's mother, who died shortly after his birth in 1824, was the daughter of a major west coast Chinook chief. For a short period, Ranald's Chinook aunt looked after him, but then Archibald's second wife, Jane Klyne, probably of French-Indian descent, lovingly raised the boy along with the thirteen children she bore his father. In his youth, Ranald travelled widely around the Pacific Northwest posts with his father, but his memoirs make little reference to any contact as a youth with his Indian relatives. "I have not the remotest idea of the ceremonial dress of the Chinooks of that time," he later wrote.[26] After an education in Red River, then in St Thomas, he set out on an adventurous life at sea, including imprisonment in feudal Japan. He returned to the Canadian west coast to work on farms and various commercial ventures. He wrote that, as someone with Indian blood, he resented slurs implying any inferiority because of it.[27] In later life, Ranald registered as a member of the Lake Tribe of the Colville Indian Reservation under the name Kumkumly. Despite a limited knowledge of Chinook traditions and language, he claimed to be the chief of the Chinook nation and may have been recognized as such by the Lake Tribe.[28] The only other evidence that his Indian ancestry altered the main course of his life comes from a statement in his memoirs: "I felt, ever, and uncontrollably in my blood, the wild strain for wandering freedom; imprimis of my Highland father of Glencoe; secondly, and possibly more so (though unconsciously) of my Indian mother." Whether MacDonald himself actually wrote these words is open to considerable doubt, but they may well have expressed his sentiments.[29]

George Atkinson Jr, whose father had wished to rid him of his Indianness, returned to the fur trade with his brother and established a large family in the James Bay area. George retained his Indian sympathies, encouraging the Coast Indians to seek better payment for their furs and to refuse to hunt geese till "the Englishmen" paid them to do so. His son, George Atkinson III, was educated in England but on his return apparently went back to "his Indian mode of life." Historians Daniel Francis and Toby Morantz explain, "Full time employment with the company was an option many mixed blood, even the formally educated ones, found less appealing than the traditional life style of the Indian hunter."[30]

Integration with Métis Society

Many of the urban-educated fur trade children who rejoined the Métis society of the Prairies had French-speaking fathers. Pierre Falcon or "Pierre the Rhymer" was born near today's Swan River, Manitoba, the son of a North West Company employee and an Indian woman. Baptized in Lower Canada in 1798, he stayed there with relatives until, aged fifteen, he returned to Red River as a clerk in the North West Company. He married Mary, daughter of the Métis leader Cuthbert Grant. Sympathetic to the Métis cause during the Red River troubles, he wrote many songs about the lifestyle of voyageurs and plainsmen, which became Métis folksongs.[31]

Cuthbert Grant had been born in Saskatchewan of a Scottish fur trade father and a Métis woman. Taken to Montreal for his education, he joined the North West Company there about 1810. Two years later he was sent back to the Upper Country and rose in the company ranks. Due to his influence among his fellow Métis, Grant led the fight against the Hudson's Bay Company and the Red River settlement, including the 1816 massacre at Seven Oaks. When younger men such as Louis Riel took over as Métis leaders, Grant's influence declined and so did his importance to the company. He is nevertheless credited with an essential role in creating the concept of a Métis nation.[32]

A Fourth Path

Harriet Gorham's study of mixed-descent families in the western Great Lakes region suggests a fourth path. She finds that these families had very little shared sense of a separate Métis identity. In this region, Gorham finds "a sliding ethnic and social 'category'" wherein people of mixed descent moved back and forth between their Indian and their white backgrounds. This group functioned "as a moving bridge between the two larger societies, unencumbered by rigid ethnic identities[, and] may have been crucial to successful transactions between Indian and White interest groups." She argues that the sense of identity of such individuals may, as the social context demanded, similarly have swung back and forth between the two cultures. Billy Caldwell, for example, spent his childhood on a Mohawk reserve near Grand River, spent his adolescence among the British elite in Detroit, worked as a young man in the British Indian Department, became a fur trader at Chicago, and finished his life as a chief among Indians west of the Mississippi.[33]

PREVIOUS WORK ON THE CHARLES OAKES ERMATINGER FAMILY

Many books and articles mention members of the various branches of the Charles Oakes Ermatinger family. None, however, has looked at the cultural divide in the lives of the children of Charles and Charlotte. In her groundbreaking biography, *The Ermatinger Family*, Gladys McNeice only briefly mentions the Indian heritage of the children and, in less than a dozen pages, recounts some highlights of their lives after the death of their father.[34] In several books and articles, Elinor Senior mentions, in passing, the role of William and Charles Ermatinger in turbulent Montreal during the 1840s and 1850s, describing the two men as much loved, regardless of their Indian heritage, by the people of the city; but exploration of this theme lies beyond the purview of her work.[35] Many potted biographies and other works briefly mention the family but say little about the significance of their dual Ojibwa-Canadian heritage for the children.

The Urban Canadian Grandparents

In the spring of 1775 Lawrence Ermatinger, fur trader, prepared to send six birchbark canoes from Lachine, just above Montreal on the St Lawrence River, to Grand Portage at the head of Lake Superior. Each canoe probably carried about four tons of trading goods, men, and supplies.[1] This hazardous annual voyage along the St Lawrence, Ottawa, and French rivers, then through the Great Lakes, would take seven to eight weeks. At Grand Portage Lawrence's partner and brother-in-law, Forrest Oakes, anxiously awaited their arrival. Unfortunately, Lawrence could not find a man to put in charge of the canoes. He advised Oakes, "If in my power I'll come along with them myself." But in the next sentence he withdrew the offer: "Don't depend upon this, for I shall be once more obliged to go to England this Fall, owing to some bad usage I have met with from one of my correspondents."[2] Lawrence never did go west of Lachine. He remained very much an urban man.

THE BEGINNINGS

Lawrence, paternal grandfather to the Ojibwa-Canadian children of Charles Oakes Ermatinger, was born in the Swiss town of Schaffhausen on 29 October 1736, to Anna Maria (née Buhl) and Laurenz Ermatinger. In May 1757 Lawrence became a member of his father's guild of gunsmiths.[3] He emigrated to London and became a merchant but later went into bankruptcy.[4] On the conquest of Canada, when he was about twenty-four, he moved to Montreal. Lawrence was doing business there in early 1762 and the following year signed a partnership with an English trader named Forrest Oakes.[5]

On 2 February 1764, Lawrence was back in London and married Forrest's sister, Jemima, at St Clement Danes. They would have seven children.[6] Two of Forrest and Jemima's sisters also married immigrants from Britain. Mary married Edward Chinn, a trader on the Great Lakes; Margaret married Edward William Gray, later an influential importer, notary, militia officer, and sheriff of Montreal from 1776 to 1810.[7] The brothers-in-law developed close business associations.

THE URBAN HUSTLER

All the newly arrived anglophone merchants, whether Upper Country or urban, had to be hustlers. From London, Lawrence ordered "woolens, hosiery, stationery, shoes and leather, shot and gunpowder, hardware, glass, tobacco, Grosery and Oyl, tin, ribbons, parfumery, cordage, gloves, haberdashery, hats." From another supplier he wanted "damaged calicoes, handkerchiefs and very cheap woolen drapery or cheap linen ... articles which fetch a tolerable good price" in Montreal. He offered to buy one client land on the River St John's, probably Rivière St Jean, flowing into the Saguenay fiord on Quebec's north shore: "You may depend upon it, I shall take all necessary steps for your interest." He told another that he probably could not barter the client's wine for wheat or salt but might be able to sell the wine by auction. He sold stoves, pipes, nails, and other hardware to the officer commanding the British army post at Sorel. He tried to charter a vessel of 100 to 150 tons to carry wheat "to some part of portugall."[8] In short, Lawrence traded in anything that would bring him a profit, including slaves. He asked a colleague in Quebec to get as much as he could by selling a female slave, writing, "She cost me $130." She had neither friends nor relatives, he added, and no acquaintances to ruin her. Lawrence finally sold her for $100.[9]

Like all small Montreal traders, Lawrence was undercapitalized and constantly short of money. His excuses for not paying his bills were many and varied, especially after a fire destroyed his premises and stores in 1770. Alternatively, his canoes had just arrived from the Upper Country, which "detains me of every sou. I will have some soon." Or a ship becalmed off Montreal would make a difference to his remittance that fall. "The loss of a worthy sister who died in childbed has thrown my family in some confusion," and prevented him from paying a creditor, or a very bad hunt by "the savages" had meant one-third fewer peltries than the previous year, or the account sent by another London supplier on 1 December never came to hand; otherwise he "should not have passed it unnoticed, you may depend upon [it]."[10] Too often, Lawrence's conjuring tricks were transparent. A client in London wrote that Lawrence had promised to send money but since then had not even written: "If you fail [to send the money] you may depend upon it, I shall take measures that will be very prejudicial to you."[11]

THE UPPER COUNTRY GREAT-UNCLE

Forrest Oakes was probably born in London on 21 August 1734 to Jemima and Joseph Oakes.[12] The earliest Canadian record of Oakes and Edward Chinn (his brother-in-law) puts them in Montreal in 1762, when the town was still under martial law. A court martial charged Oakes, Chinn, and a third man named Grant with insulting and assaulting an ensign in the British army. Grant and Chinn were fined and made to "humbly" apologize to the officer before his whole regiment. Oakes spent only twenty-four hours in prison with no apology required, since the court found the insults had been reciprocated.[13]

From 1769 almost until his death in Montreal in 1783, Oakes lived and worked mainly in and around Grand Portage. Many fur traders operated from this key area at the start of the fourteen-kilometre portage from Lake Superior to the Pigeon River, which led to Lake Winnipeg and the West. The traders had built posts, usually walled, at Grand Portage when Alexander Henry passed through in 1775. He found fierce competition between traders, who were all "in a state of extreme reciprocal hostility, each pursuing his interests in such a manner as might most injure his neighbour."[14] That description would include Oakes, who, according to Lawrence's letters, was then living in the area. Oakes had at least one liaison with an Indian woman producing a son, John Meticamus Oakes.[15]

DOING BUSINESS IN THE UPPER COUNTRY

Oakes always sent his partner careful instructions for his canoes. In 1768, for example, he told Lawrence to send them as soon as possible, and not later than 6 July. They were to head for Grand Portage by South St Mary's (Sault Ste Marie, on the south shore). Oakes himself intended to travel from Grand Portage toward Michilimackinac to meet the canoes. He wanted Lawrence to engage a guide who understood Lake Superior. The canoes should then travel along the lake, firing guns whenever another canoe passed by so that Oakes would not miss them. Lawrence must get good canoes and ensure that they were filled with provisions. He must engage good winter men, fore and hind men, with specified amounts paid in advance. He should engage the men to go from Montreal to Sault Ste Marie "for one price certain," and then make a second price for the men who would continue west across Lake Superior.[16]

Business relations between Lawrence and Oakes were not always harmonious, though the men were joined in a complex and reciprocal network of debt. In 1772, Oakes accused his brother-in-law of acting extravagantly in buying tobacco on assignment. Lawrence claimed the accusation was unmerited, replying, "You may depend on its being altered if [there is] any error; for I don't want you to be my slave, nor was it my inclination to make you one, nor should I chuse that anyone should make a slave of you." Lawrence finished by saying he intended to sail for England in the fall, provided he received 40,000 livres from Oakes by return of the canoes. He added, "I have assured your creditors that you would pay them as soon as possible. If you can send Meredith something, he seems to be very angry." Two years later, Lawrence wrote, "When you are here on the spot, you may either make a connection with someone else or continue with me ... I assure you, I do all I can for your interests, as if you was present." Despite these occasional tensions, the partnership continued until the death of Oakes.[17]

Because of government restrictions on trade, eighteenth-century traders in Montreal and Quebec often skirted the law. At this time merchants could legally trade only at fortified posts and not directly at Indian villages. Merchants also had to give a security worth twice the value of their goods, to ensure that they would obey all regulations. In 1764, Lawrence received a letter from his other brother-in-law, Edward Chinn, based at St Jean, an island in Lake Superior. Chinn wrote, "This is the third letter this morning, and I am obliged to take every precaution for fear of miscarriage, for Col. Christie will seek every opportunity to hinder our work. Therefore, you must remember to get a pass for what provisions you send that it may not be stopped."[18] Apparently the local British commander had his eye on Lawrence and Chinn.

LAWRENCE'S SOCIAL VIEWS

From the first, many francophone traders of Quebec co-operated with their anglophone counterparts. Socially, the two groups of merchants mingled, and mixed marriages were quite common. Lawrence, too, spoke French and carried on commercial relations with Canadien merchants. His letters in French are as amicable as those he wrote in English. However, a letter to an English contact in Quebec hints at Lawrence's feelings towards the Canadiens. Lawrence wanted his correspondent to engage for three years a boy of about fourteen and also "a sober sprieghtly [sic] young man" to work for him in the Upper Country. The latter had to be an Englishman or a Scot who could write clearly: "It must not be a Canadian if such should offer." By "Canadian," he meant, of course, a francophone Canadien. Similarly, he warned a London correspondent against a Canadien merchant, a Monsieur Orillat: "Don't invite him for I assure you many of the French are but very indifferent correspondents."[19]

Towards Indians, Lawrence had a certain ambivalence. They were in one sense an enemy. The peoples traditionally allied with the French before the conquest often remained hostile to the English after it, and the great chief Pontiac organized an uprising against the new rulers in 1763. In 1772, mutual hostility still prevailed, and when Lawrence learned that some Indians had been killed near Niagara, he worried that retaliatory "disturbances" might imperil his canoes. A week later he wrote, "We have had no news yet from the Upper Country, how the traders have made out. All we know is that the savages have been quiet this last winter."[20] (The canoes eventually arrived unharmed.)

On the positive side, the Indians were also consumers of goods and suppliers of furs. Despite his worries about their behaviour, Lawrence included liquor and guns among the goods he traded to Indians. His 1769 outfit of two canoes and fifteen men took 160 gallons of rum and brandy, thirty-two gallons of wine, 500 pounds of gunpowder, 1,000 pounds of ball and shot, and sixteen rifles to the Upper Country trade.[21] As Lawrence told a supplier when ordering 100 North West guns and 1,000 balls, "You will know that these are absolutely necessary for the Indian trade."[22] Potential profits clearly outweighed potential dangers.

LAWRENCE AND THE TORY TRADITION

Lawrence and his fellow merchants from England were patriotic and loyal to the Crown, and they expected the Crown to uphold their rights as Englishmen. Those rights, as they saw them, implied the political, legal, and religious institutions of England, not those of New France. The Quebec Act of 1774 formalized much of what the Protestant merchants already hated: no Assembly, Roman Catholics allowed to hold political office, English law in criminal matters but the law of New France in civil matters, lack of habeas corpus, and the abolition of jury trials in civil suits. The indignation of Lawrence and his fellow English traders boiled. Petitions flowed from their coffee houses. On 12 November 1774 they wrote to King George saying they had found to their "unutterable Grief" that they had lost the protection of the English laws so universally admired. Instead they were to be subject to the laws of New France, disgraceful to them as Britons and ruinous to their properties.[23] Despite such petitions, the Quebec Act remained in force.

The real test of Lawrence's loyalty to the Crown came with the invasion of Canada during the American Revolution. By June 1775, with rebel forces holding the approaches to Montreal, Lawrence deplored "the unhappy situation the Province is in." A few weeks later he almost despaired. Trade was very dull, with no sales and no market. Indeed, nothing was stirring. "Feelings are very high. God knows what will become of us," he wrote. In late September, a defending force won a small victory against the reckless rebel Ethan Allen, whose party, when attacked, fled their camp outside Montreal. Allen himself was captured. Lawrence called it "the glorious 25th Sept." Three weeks later he was still optimistic. Montreal, he wrote, was full of Canadien *habitants* (farmers), and the invader would soon be dealt with in the manner he deserved. A rumour excited him to write, "I hope they [the rebels] will stay a little longer, for something is now preparing [for] which I hope they will remember Canada."[24]

But hopes built on "the glorious 25th" soon faded, and the British commander at Chambly surrendered. Many *habitants* and merchants lost their enthusiasm for the Loyalist cause. In October, Lawrence wrote to London his last letter for 1775. He enclosed a bill of lading and an invoice for fifteen bales of peltries and two casks of castoreum. "God grant," he wrote anxiously, "they may come to good market."[25]

Montreal, captured by the Americans in November, was guarded by a small garrison under Brigadier-General David Wooster. Wooster's actions soon alienated both merchants and *habitants*. With news of the American defeat at Quebec on 31 December, Wooster drew up a list of sixty-four prominent Montrealers recognized as good Loyalists. He sent soldiers to disarm twelve of them, including Lawrence Ermatinger and his brother-in-law Edward William Gray.[26] After Montrealers protested loudly that Wooster was violating the terms of the surrender, the Loyalists remained free for the moment. Later, Wooster rearrested Gray and three others and sent them to Chambly.[27]

Lawrence, too, went in fear of his liberty if not of his life. He would not submit to the rebel demands, he wrote later, so they had disarmed him. He had been "in great anxiety of mind." Every moment he had been threatened with jail, "which, had that been done, would have proved very fatal." However, he added, "I did stand out to the last." He also walled his goods up behind the stone wall of his house, then left town to hide in a remote part of the country. As a result, "I only lost about £200."[28] By mid-June 1776, the British had driven the invaders out of the province and Lawrence was back in business. At news of peace negotiations he wrote, "I sincerely wish matters may be adjusted, though not in such a manner as to bring disgrace on old England."[29]

JEMIMA AND HER CHILDREN

In England, Jemima Oakes' family seem to have been reasonably prosperous, and the evidence suggests she was well educated. On leaving for London in 1772, Lawrence wrote, "The business will be carried on in the same manner as usual, and under the same form, with only the addition that Mrs. Ermatinger will during my absence sign the letters, bills and any other matters which may occur ... You have her signing on foot of this."[30] Her active participation in their business affairs seemed confirmed in 1782 when an M.P. Loubet bought Lawrence's stone house on St Paul Street in Montreal. Loubet ran an advertisement in the *Quebec Gazette* saying he had bought the property from "Mr. Lawrence Ermatinger, Merchant of Montreal, and Mrs. Jemima Oakes, his wife."[31]

Because Lawrence and Jemima married in England, their marriage was subject to English common law rather than the civil code carried over from New France.[32] English common law at the time gave the husband almost total authority over the household. He could do what he wished with his wife's personal property, except sell or give away her real property, which had to go to her heirs. The famous jurist, William Blackstone, writing on the "rights of persons" and the "rights of things" under English law, argued that husband and wife were one person in law: "A man cannot grant anything to his wife ... for the grant would be to suppose her separate existence." However, "A woman indeed may be attorney for her husband; for that implies no separation from, but is rather a representation of her lord."[33] Thus Lawrence could legally make his wife his attorney. Presumably Jemima made any business decisions necessary while "her lord" was overseas.

*See Figure 4, p. 38, for the family of Charles Oakes Ermatinger.

Sources: Gladys McNeice, The Ermatinger Family of Sault Ste. Marie (Sault Ste. Marie: Sault Ste. Marie and 49th Field Regiment RCA Historical Society, 1984), 1, appendix 2; LAC, MG 19, A2, series 4, vol. 1, file 1, nos. 6477, 6478, 6481, 6482, 6483, 6487, 6495, 6499; LAC, MG 19, A2, series 2, vol. 1, part 2, no. 19, John Clowes to Edward Ermatinger.

Figure 2

THE FAMILY OF LAWRENCE AND JEMIMA ERMATINGER

Lawrence m. Jemima Oakes
1736-89

- Jemima
  1765-1840

- Anna Maria
  (aka Margaret)
  1766-1836
  =
  George Garrett

- George
  1766-1841
  =
  Mary MacDonald
  (1 child)
  =
  Catherine McKee
  (8 children)

- Lawrence Edward
  1767-1830
  =
  Italian woman
  - Edward
    1797-1876
    =
    Axie Burnham
    (7 children)
  - Francis (aka Frank)
    1798-1858
    =
    three Indian women
    (6 children?)
    =
    Catherine Sinclair
    (1 child)

- Frederick William
  1769-1827

- Forrest
  1771-72

- Charles Oakes*
  1776-1833

Jemima also had an active social conscience. In 1797, Pte. Francis McDade was court-martialled and found guilty of deserting the 5th Regiment of Foot. In a petition, he hoped that his youth (he was twenty-five) and his previous good character, would bring annulment of the death sentence. Thirty-two women, including Jemima and her two daughters, signed the petition.[34]

Jemima and Lawrence had seven children, though Forrest died as a baby (Figure 2). Little is known of the two daughters, Jemima and Anna Maria (also known as Margaret). Jemima remained single; Anna Maria married George Garrett, an army surgeon, but they had no issue. Lawrence Edward found his career in the Commissariat of the British Army, while Frederick William was a businessman and sheriff of Montreal. The remaining two brothers entered the fur trade. They both operated mainly out of Sault Ste Marie, George on the American side of the border, Charles Oakes on the Canadian side (see Appendix C). Charles, born in 1776 and the youngest in the family, married Charlotte Katawabidai and became father of the children featured in this book.

The Final Years
In the fall of 1782, Lawrence's partner, Forrest Oakes, returned to Montreal from Grand Portage. He died the next spring.[35] At that time, a great scandal of overextended government-backed credit and illegal speculation swept the province, and Quebec merchants were close to ruin.[36] None suffered more than Lawrence Ermatinger. On 1 October 1782 he sold his stone house on St Paul's Street, but this did not suffice. In August 1783, debts forced him to mortgage his remaining property to a London firm, and he then withdrew from business. On 6 October 1789, Lawrence died in Montreal, aged but fifty-three.[37] He left no will. Jemima lived another twenty years.

Lawrence, a Summing Up
Though probably no less honest than the majority of his fellow merchants, Lawrence was probably no more so. The frequency with which his creditors were assured they could "depend upon it," and then found that they could not, or at least not right now but soon, gives an eighteenth-century resonance to the phrase "Your cheque is in the mail." His bankruptcy in London, and the near-bankruptcies of 1770 and 1783, do not inspire great confidence in his business acumen.

Nevertheless, Lawrence Ermatinger had the courage to venture his small capital in a new and wild land. He had the business skill to run his Canadian operation for more than twenty years under risky and often primitive conditions, and with inadequate capital. He also brought up and educated a family who went on to make a solid contribution to the development of his adopted country. All that was no mean achievement for a man born in the very different social conditions of Switzerland.

The Upper Country
Ojibwa Grandparent

Around 1800, a Dakota war party threatened to attack a group of Ojibwa, mainly women.[1] A single Ojibwa walked into the enemy's midst and challenged a Dakota warrior to unarmed combat. The Ojibwa twice threw the Dakota to the ground. Then the two combatants, traditionally bitter enemies, smoked a pipe, and the two parties shared a camp before the Dakota returned to their home territory. Encouraged by this incident, an influential Ojibwa chief named Katawabidai (see Figure 3), father of Mananowe (later Charlotte) and grandfather of the Charles Oakes Ermatinger children, led a party to Dakota territory at the mouth of the Minnesota River. He wished to negotiate a more permanent peace, but the Dakota were already busy preparing another attack on the Ojibwa. They opened fire on the approaching canoes, and a ball tore the flag over Katawabidai's head. An influential Métis trader managed to stop the shooting and provided the Ojibwa an escort back to their own territory.[2] Katawabidai became known as a man of peace, but he lived in a warrior culture at a time of almost constant tribal war. The Ojibwa and Dakota had been fighting one another for much too long to make peace easily.

OJIBWA SOCIETY

The name "Ojibwa" subsumes a wide variety of peoples who have certain cultural themes in common. Their oral tradition says they originally lived near salt water, possibly the Gulf of St Lawrence. Over centuries they travelled west and by the 1600s had established themselves firmly on the western shores of Lake Huron, near the Sault. The Ojibwa language belongs to the Central Algonquian family of languages. Its many local dialects, which include the Saulteaux spoken around Sault Ste Marie, were not always mutually intelligible. But the Ojibwa had a sophisticated form of picture writing, with more than 200 images that allowed quite complex sentences.[3]

In summer, Ojibwa lived in domed lodges clustered into villages of 200 or 300 residents united by kinship, culture, and language. Each family had an animal totem, such as sturgeon, beaver, bear, crane, or catfish, claimed to be

Figure 3
Katawabidai, Ojibwa chief

its mythical ancestor and protector. (Katawabidai was a member of the loon totem.)[4] Marriage had no religious significance in Ojibwa society. Sometimes parents would arrange a marriage. More often, a young man would court a girl, usually within the strict view of her parents. If his hunting and other skills proved him suitable, he simply moved into her parents' lodge, slept with her as man and wife for about a year, then moved with her to their own lodge. There was no ceremony. Divorce was just as simple, with no shame or blame attaching to either party.[5]

Politically, the village was the most complex institution in Ojibwa society. No permanent confederacies allied villages, but informal groupings, usually for war purposes, were common. When Katawabidai succeeded his father as chief of the Sandy Lake band about 1805, it numbered about 350 people.[6] As hereditary civil chief of his village, Katawabidai would have had no formal powers. Typically, civil chiefs presided at band councils and spoke for their people at larger formal gatherings, especially meetings with the colonial powers. As for all such chiefs, Katawabidai's influence came from his prestige, wisdom, and ability to persuade.[7] But he was exceptional in that his influence extended far beyond Sandy Lake. An eloquent and persuasive man, he forged informal alliances with over a half-dozen other bands, including those at Leech Lake, Pokegama, Rice Lake, Fond du Lac, and Snake River. This earned him the title "emperor of Sandy Lake."[8]

In war parties, the civil chief deferred to a war chief. Distinguished by his courage, leadership, and skill in battle, the war chief called for warriors from his own and other villages. He could not compel, but the great war chiefs usually had no difficulty persuading warriors to join them. Often the civil chief joined the war party to confirm his own warrior status.[9]

In pre-Contact times, wars were fought more for revenge and glory than for territory, but this changed with the arrival of Europeans.[10] Competition for the fur trade and growing shortages of fur-bearing animals, military alliances with the French in their various wars against the British and Dutch, and the spread of guns, all radically changed the purpose of Indian warfare. The desire for new territory became a major, though by no means the only, cause for war.

Ojibwa Expansion

The Ojibwa first encountered the French near Sault Ste Marie in the 1640s, and they became middlemen in trade between the French and the more westerly Indians. Expansion began to the east when the Iroquois dispersed the Hurons in 1649 and then moved into the former Huron territory. They began blockading the trade routes, leading to conflict with the Ojibwa. After years of hostility between them, the Ojibwa defeated the Iroquois in 1655 near Sault Ste Marie and, with the Ottawa and Nipissing, defeated them again at Iroquois Point in Michigan. These defeats led to the retreat of the

Iroquois from the lakes and strengthened the French-Ojibwa alliance, with the French supplying guns.[11] Their rear secure, Ojibwa began to fan out from Sault Ste Marie. Some moved north towards Hudson Bay, some down the western shores of Lakes Michigan and Superior, and some further west as far as southern Manitoba and Saskatchewan.[12]

Lake Superior Ojibwa, with whom Charles Ermatinger would later have most contact, first clashed with Fox Indians in the early eighteenth century. Along with their French allies, they had driven the Fox out by 1734. Though for a while Dakota and Ojibwa were allied against the Fox, in 1736 a group of Dakota killed a party of French traders near Sault Ste Marie.[13] This angered the Ojibwa, and the two nations began fighting over what is now known as the Debatable Zone in the Mississippi headwaters in Minnesota. The area, rich in rice, game, and fish, was also key to controlling the western fur trade.[14] The Ojibwa, led by the great chief Bi-aus-wah, father of Katawabidai, invaded the upper Mississippi valley in the middle of the eighteenth century. William W. Warren, one of the earliest Native historians, writes that Bi-aus-wah led his warriors in their usual single file, a file so long "that a person standing on a hill could not see from one extremity [of the line] to the other." After a bloody slaughter with guns that drove the Dakota from their village at Sandy Lake, the Ojibwa settled there.[15] Ojibwa-Dakota hostilities continued for more than a century of skirmishing with only brief truces. This war, along with those against the Fox and the Iroquois, features strongly in Ojibwa oral history.

Interspersed with these intertribal battles, Ojibwa also fought with the French against the British in all four wars for European dominance of North America. Some even fought for Montcalm on the Plains of Abraham, hundreds of kilometres from home. Later, some Ojibwa joined in Pontiac's uprising against the English. Katawabidai as a boy was present when Ottawa and Ojibwa Indians captured old Fort Mackinaw in 1763 during the uprising.[16] In the War of 1812, some Ojibwa allied with the British. In short, from the mid-seventeenth century to the mid-nineteenth century, groups of Ojibwa fought a long series of wars with only intermittent and short periods of peace.

OJIBWA WARRIORS AND WARFARE

Physically, Ojibwa men were "active, generally tall, well developed and good looking ... with a bold and independent air and gait, and possessing good powers of oratory." Henry Schoolcraft, government agent at the American Sault Ste Marie, also admired their "intellectual distinction." Their legends, he said, supplied varied, never-ending traditions handed down between generations. Referring to Ojibwa picture writing, Schoolcraft wrote, "Warriors, and the bravest of warriors, they are yet an intellectual people." But success in war filled their highest aspirations. They had little interest in the arts, fixed industry, or letters. Agriculture and mechanical labours were seen as degrading compared with hunting and warfare.[17]

The traditions of the warrior and hunter were instilled early in a boy's life. Sons learned from their fathers and elders how to be brave on the battlefield using bow and arrow, war club and spear; and how to be successful in the forest using traps and snares and by learning forest lore and animal habits.[18] A boy discovered his future through a vision conjured up by taking no food, liquid, or sleep during a lonely vigil in the forest. There, his guardian spirit appeared and decided whether the boy's powers would come as warrior, huntsman, or shaman.[19] Boys were killing birds by the age of three; a few years later they were laying traps, then hunting with their father. By their early teens, they had their own hunting grounds.[20]

Schoolcraft described Ojibwa men as "pre-eminently expert and brave warriors, and woodsmen, and foresters."[21] Other nineteenth-century observers also described heroism in battle as the source of status. George Copway, himself Ojibwa, wrote that as soon as Ojibwa children were old enough to handle a bow they learned to shoot at images of the enemy. Old men told them of deeds of bravery while mothers taught them, even before leaving the breast, to hate their enemies.[22] Peter Jones, who was part Ojibwa, said that the more scalps the civil chiefs took, the more they were revered and consulted by their tribe.[23] According to William Warren, the Ojibwa warrior fought for glory and the desire "to wipe the paint of mourning from his face" for the death of some near relative.[24] Modern historians concur. Ojibwa expansion, they hold, was motivated not just by economic reasons but by the old values of revenge and the social status that came to young warriors who could boast of their prowess and victories on the field.[25]

Despite their strong warrior ethic, and unlike, say, the Dakota, Ojibwa generally avoided armed conflict with Europeans – unless allied with one white nation against another. One theory holds that credit extended by white traders for the Ojibwa to buy traps, ammunition, and so forth created a symbiotic relationship. The Indians could not escape it without destroying an important economic resource. Further, traders and government officials took on the role of a father figure towards whom hostility could be expressed only verbally, not in violent action.[26]

For the Ojibwa male, highly decorative clothing signified that a guardian spirit was guiding the hunter/warrior.[27] Summer garments for men were a breechcloth, leggings, and moccasins decorated with notches or coloured beadwork, plus a blanket. Men were very careful in the way they wore their blanket, folding it stylishly over one shoulder and under the other arm. Both men and women decorated their costumes and persons. Men wore braids of sweetgrass and painted their faces with coloured earth mixed with grease. They sometimes painted their bodies in stripes or zigzag lines. The young men proudly wore their black hair long and shining with grease, often applied by their sisters.[28]

In warfare, neither Ojibwa nor their Indian enemies saw any reason to stand, European style, in brightly uniformed rows to be shot down. They preferred ambushes, surprise attacks, and night raids seldom lasting more than a few minutes. If regular pitched battles occurred, they used trees or other cover to fire on the enemy.[29] The battle of Crow Wing River provides a good example.[30]

About 1768, according to William Warren, the Dakota decided to reconquer the territories around Sandy Lake taken from them by Chief Bi-aus-wah. Now armed with guns, they felt equal to their enemies. A war party of nearly 500 Dakota canoed to the headwaters of the Mississippi and descended the river to attack Sandy Lake. They killed a few Ojibwa on the way and captured a party of women who were picking huckleberries. Two Ojibwa men saw the approaching party and rushed to warn the villagers. Many of the men were drunk, but those sober enough prepared the defences. When the Dakota attacked, the Ojibwa who were still on their feet put up a stout defence while the women poured cold water over the others to bring them to their senses. Finally, they drove off the attackers who, honour achieved, took captives with them as they canoed home.[31]

Unfortunately for the Dakota, a party of sixty Sandy Lake Ojibwa were returning on foot from an unsuccessful raid into Dakota territory. They heard of the raid on their own village and, although outnumbered at least six to one, they prepared an ambush where the Crow Wing and Mississippi rivers join. They dug a series of holes in the riverbank, each hole holding ten men invisible to the enemy that would canoe by. They waited.[32]

Upstream, just out of range of Ojibwa fire, the Dakota came ashore to prepare a meal and celebrate with scalp dancing. The Ojibwa leader had to restrain his younger hotheads from attacking right there. The Dakota re-embarked in their fleet of canoes, scalps dangling from poles, pipes passing from one canoe to the next. Their war chiefs with their war ensigns of feathers led in the front canoes. The drums beat. The warriors sang. The Ojibwa struck. Dakota died. They died from arrows and bullets, or they drowned when their canoes overturned. Many of the captive Ojibwa women escaped.[33]

The surviving Dakota, still outnumbering their enemy, rallied and courageously counterattacked the entrenched ambushers. The Ojibwa held them off till night fell. Next morning the Dakota attacked again, this time more cautiously. When their ammunition failed, they too dug holes, and both sides were reduced to heaving rocks at one another. Some fought hand to hand with knives and clubs. Finally the Dakota withdrew, and the Ojibwa had won the battle of Crow Wing. Exact losses are unknown, but they were said to be heavier among the Dakota. Next spring an Ojibwa war party went to avenge the raid on Sandy Lake. They attacked a well-defended Dakota village and returned home with many scalps.[34]

Such killing, especially of women and children, helped mould a nineteenth-century view that Indians were innately (today, genetically) warlike savages whose nature could not be changed. Historian Francis Parkman (1823-93) saw the Ojibwa as "a ferocious horde and likely to remain so."[35] By this reasoning, one must assume that the Europeans and North Americans who in wartime have been killing men, women, and children for countless generations are also genetically wired to do so. Whether collateral damage is deliberate or allegedly accidental, its victims suffer equally.

OJIBWA ECONOMY

In the 1700s, lakes and rivers covered the country of the Mississippi headwaters. They abounded with whitefish and trout, while wild rice grew in many of the lakes. Pine, sugar maple, and birch lined their banks. Moose, deer, bear, and beaver were plentiful.[36] The seasons set the pattern for Ojibwa economic activity. In the fall, individual families or small groups dispersed across the region. They first hunted duck, then in winter hunted game or trapped for the fur trade. The scattered camps of the families forced fur traders to travel from camp to camp to make their purchases. In spring, families tapped maple trees to make sugar, often used as seasoning or preservative. Then the Ojibwa families rejoined each other at major fishing sites for a round of social events. Throughout the summer and early fall they fished using baited hooks and nets, and spear-fished by torchlight. They also collected berries. In some areas, the Ojibwa grew a small amount of corn. Late summer and fall brought wild rice, collected by men and women in canoes. With winter in sight, the social events ended, the larger groups split up, and once again the individual families left for the winter hunt. This economy was efficient and adaptive to changes in the ecology that came with the fur trade.[37]

In the Ojibwa socioeconomic system, mutual gift giving was central, binding giver and recipient in a social as well as economic relationship. Parents looked after their young children and adult children looked after aged parents; relatives supplied food to relatives in time of need, knowing it would be returned; village members exchanged gifts among themselves. The bonds thus established were as strong as a written contract in European society. Ojibwa extended this behaviour to their relationship with fur traders and with government representatives.[38] For example, in 1816 Katawabidai told army officers at Drummond Island, "I come from a great distance and have waited patiently in hopes of getting some of your milk."[39] This language drew on the symbolism of the first gift a child ever gets: milk from its mother. In this case, of course, the "milk" was rum.

OJIBWA RELIGION

The Ojibwa believed in the "Great Spirit of good." Nothing equalled the veneration with which they regarded this unseen being. He was the creator and master of life, and from him flowed all power.[40] In everyday life, however, he did not have much effect for good or for evil. More influential were many lesser spirits usually taking the form of animals or other natural phenomena, from Thunderbirds to the Great Serpent.[41]

Members of a secret society called the Midewiwin played an essential role in the spiritual lives of the Ojibwa. They held the oral history and myths of their people and preserved knowledge of herbs useful in prolonging life. They were less concerned with worshipping than with prolonging life by right living.[42] But Ojibwa also often darkly perceived Midewiwin practitioners as sorcerers. Midewiwin ceremonies often accompanied great social gatherings, especially the annual congregations at major fishing locations. Ceremonies included stories of the creation and of Ojibwa history, often with a moral on the right way to live.[43] American government agent Henry Schoolcraft said Midewiwin members opposed Christianity, believing it would reduce their natural freedom.[44] Nevertheless, by the 1830s and 1840s many Ojibwa were converting to Christianity.

Ojibwa Women

An Ojibwa girl was very close to her mother. From her, she learned how to make wigwams; to cook and make birchbark vessels; to find herbs used in medicine and make maple sugar used in preserving food; to harvest berries and rice; to dress skins and make clothing from them; and to birth children.[45] Ideally, though not always in practice, she burned cedar boughs in the lodges to purify the air. She aired the bedding daily in summer and spread it on the snow in winter. She dried damp clothing over a smoky fire to prevent vermin. For cleaning, she used lye made from hardwood ashes.[46]

These were the in-house duties of the wife, but the contribution of women was much greater. Towards the end of the 1700s, large game were beginning to get more scare in the Mississippi headwaters. By equating the loss of large game hunting (a male occupation) with near starvation, historians have shown a gender bias. In the new economy, gathering wild rice and maple syrup, trapping small game and fishing, and cultivating corn and potatoes were increasingly important — and these were all mainly female skills.[47]

European travellers often deplored the lives of Indian women as brutally hard, and saw Indian husbands as slave masters. Anthropologist Albert Ernest Jenks described children playing house. The little boy, Ji-shib, arrived at the wigwam dragging a puppy by its hind leg. He left it at the door, sat down with dignity, and lisped in baby talk, "Squaw, I just killed a great big bear; go skin him, I am hungry."[48] Edward Allen Talbot described the wife as obediently strapping to her back the deer killed by her husband and carrying it three or four miles home. There, she skinned and dressed it while "her lazy lord" reclined on his bearskin.[49]

Schoolcraft took a different view. He held that the duties of Indian life were shared equally by husband and wife. The man took responsibility for concerns outside the lodge; the woman mainly for those inside, though as discussed earlier, she also worked at lighter outside jobs. Men had the hard business of hunting, "for this is an *employment* and not a *pastime.*" As well, they had to keep away intruders and enemies, prepare canoes for travel, and maintain the arms and implements of war – more hard, often dangerous work. Certainly a woman's work was laborious, often brutal. But she also had much autonomy, given entire care and control of the lodge and all its utensils and apparatus.[50]

When giving birth, Indian women usually squatted or knelt over a receptacle of some kind, thus apparently easing the pain and duration of labour.[51] Travellers and traders often remarked that a woman had her babies quickly and easily, by herself or with only her husband present. But John West noted that while women in a wholly Indian setting had few birthing problems, they had many more problems when living with white men and giving birth by European practices.[52]

KATAWABIDAI

Katawabidai (in English known as Broken-Tooth and in French as DeBreche), the son of Bi-aus-wah, was born about 1750 and died in 1828. Schoolcraft described Katawabidai's lodge: "He was noted for the spaciousness and neatness of his wigwam. On his mat table he used the knives, forks and dishes of the whites. He also kept his liquor case, which was ever well supplied, and from which he indulged but sparingly; occasionally enjoying with his friends 'a good comfortable smoke.'"[53]

Katawabidai was popular with the whites precisely because he was an exception to the warrior culture of his people. Another contemporary of the chief, Thomas L. McKenney, paints a glowing portrait of him as a man of peace whose courage was never questioned. He was "expert and ready in debate, his speeches were marked by shrewdness, ingenuity, and subtlety of argument, and by a simple brevity and force of expression ... A sensible, prudent, politic man, who was revered by his own people, and looked up to as a safe counsellor by the surrounding villages."[54]

He was, said Schoolcraft, a "warm friend to the whites" and the traders of the country loved him. They sent clerks with presents to Sandy Lake and the Mississippi, where Katawabidai distributed them to the hunters.[55] Katawabidai wanted to keep peace with both the British and American governments, the agent conceded. But he believed the chief should have been, and was not, using his influence to persuade the Indians of the values of the American system of government. The chief failed to make them see the importance of strictly complying with the American intercourse laws banning foreign traders. In that he favoured the British.[56]

At his death in 1828, Katawabidai's family by his own request hung the body in the air on a scaffolding. This became the family's custom with the dead.[57] Though he was himself a man of peace, he failed to establish any widespread and long-lasting peace between the Ojibwa and the Dakota. In the ten years from 1835 to 1844, Rev. S.W. Pond, minister to the Dakota, kept a record of the battles and skirmishes between the Dakota of Minnesota and the Ojibwa. In twenty-five incidents he found that some 215 Ojibwa and Dakota (many of them women and children) were killed. Some of these were single killings. Other incidents occurred on a much larger scale, with revenge killing countered by revenge killing.[58]

"LET ME DRAW NEAR YOUR BREAST"

Katawabidai's 1816 speech to the military at Drummond Island illustrates much about the chief and his people, and their relationships with the British. Katawabidai starts by giving thanks for past aid: "Father ... had you not given us the ammunition we received, some of your children would have perished." He then establishes his credentials. After last year's "kind treatment" he has come again to listen to his father's voice. He has no medal with him yet he is from a great family, "good and faithful children to you redcoats." So far, the address has been respectful, even humble. Now resentment appears, albeit gently phrased: "Father, I came from a great distance and have waited patiently in hopes of getting some of your milk to drink but I find you do not seem inclined to let me draw near your breast." The metaphoric language of "milk" and "draw near your breast" was possibly a good way for the Ojibwa leaders to get what they wanted yet still insult Europeans by implying they were women.[59]

The traders, Katawabidai says, usually supply him with from ten to thirty drams of rum. But since his arrival, "I have not tasted a drop." Much of that liquor he would have redistributed among his people in the traditional Ojibwa manner, and its loss probably meant loss of prestige. In a gentle reminder of past services to the Crown, his side of the sharing relationship, Katawabidai says he has given several flags to tribes of Indians to stop them warring against each other. He has also erected a flag at the grave of his eldest son, whose death several years previously he still mourns. His only remaining, and favourite, flag he had forgetfully left at Sault Ste Marie.[60]

Lieutenant-Colonel McKay then replies, "My child. I have paid attention to your discourse." He promises to provide the Ojibwa every reasonable assistance that year. In return, Katawabidai and his people must observe the peace. Historians have debated the "Father/My Child" addresses in common use in the 1800s and earlier. For the Ojibwa, the parent-child terminology may have simply reflected the sharing relationship of a parent looking after a young child and an adult child looking after an aging parent.

McKay then instructs Katawabidai that it is "absolutely necessary" for his people to "preserve your various avocations" and, by industry, assist their families. In effect, they must not rely on the white man's presents. McKay is now cooling the sharing relationship, hence the chief's resentment. McKay also wants Katawabidai and his people to be on friendly terms with all the whites. Then comes the sting: he has withheld rum from the Ojibwa because "they most shamefully have been stabbing, wounding and killing each other." At this point, the script has many illegible words.[61] Katawabidai seems to be asserting that the Indians McKay alluded to come from another part of the country, and that his own people had acted quite differently.

The chief then talks of the attack on the Red River settlement.[62] North West Company traders had asked him to have his young men attack the settlers there. On one occasion they promised him and his people all the goods and rum at Fort William, and on another occasion two kegs of rum and two carrots of tobacco. The chief refused both requests. As they are meant to, Katawabidai's words please Lieutenant-Colonel McKay. He is happy the chief did not take the advice of those who wanted to lead him astray but behaved as "an obedient child." He hopes that Katawabidai and his people will continue to be friendly with the English merchants and traders as well as the settlers.

Overall, Katawabidai's speech illustrates the reluctance of the Ojibwa to take up arms, or to express open hostility, against the whites. The resentment bubbled up, however, when the military damaged that relationship by refusing rum. Perhaps Katawabidai also sensed another threat in McKay's insistence that the Ojibwa, by their own industry, take care of their families. This hints that in future, as the importance of Ojibwa presents to the whites diminished, so the value of the their presents to the Ojibwa would lessen. Despite their key role in defending Canada in the War of 1812, the partnership-in-arms of the Indians with one or another of the European empires in North America was fast disappearing. And with it disappeared, in European eyes, the importance and power of the Native peoples.

KATAWABIDAI'S CHILDREN

Katawabidai had at least seven children. A son, Mang'osid or Loons-Foot, who lived at Fond du Lac in what is now Minnesota, was chief of the Lake Superior Ojibwa.[63] Mang'osid was especially influential as a practitioner of Midewiwin who first accepted but later rejected Christianity.[64] Some local Ojibwa feared he was too ready to cede lands to the United States.[65] Another son, Kahnindumawinjo, was chief of the Sandy Lake Ojibwa in the United States from 1837 to 1852. A third son was as a child taken prisoner at Cross Lake by the Dakota and was still living with them in 1852. Details about the eldest son Katawabidai mourned in 1816 are unknown. One daughter married an Ojibwa warrior and chief called Hole-in-the-Sky while another married fur trader Samuel Ashmun, described by Schoolcraft as a very respectable resident of Sault Ste Marie.[66] Mananowe or Charlotte, the eldest child, married Charles Oakes Ermatinger.

Charles Sr's Fur Trade Career

One spring morning in 1798, twenty-one-year-old Charles Ermatinger took the fourteen-kilometre dirt track from Montreal to Lachine, bypassing the St Lawrence rapids. At Lachine he joined a small fleet of birchbark canoes, probably those of a trader named L'Etang who may have been a member of the New North West Company, known as the XY Company.[1] They began the long, dangerous journey up the St Lawrence River, up the Ottawa River, across waterways to Lake Nipissing, down the French River into Lake Huron, and then to the head of Lake Superior and the Upper Country (*le pays d'en haut*).

Just why Charles chose the fur trade is not known. In prosperity, his father had sent two of his sons, Frederick William and Lawrence Edward, to London for their schooling. By 1782, he was under financial strain and brought them home. Charles and George must have received their education in Montreal. Later evidence suggests that education was a good one.[2] Charles could probably have chosen a profession in Montreal, where his uncle Edward William Gray was sheriff and his elder brother Frederick was also a businessman. Perhaps the example of his maternal uncle Forrest Oakes drew him to the Upper Country. Whatever the reason, by late September of 1798 L'Etang and Charles, with two canoes, had reached the area near Fort Sturgeon where the Sturgeon River joins the North Saskatchewan. Unfortunately, the Indians had already left the place so the two traders secured less than two packs of furs.[3]

The north bank of the North Saskatchewan River, where Charles started trading, was dangerous country, covered with pine, brushwood, swamps, and muskeg – almost impossible country for horses.[4] In late December Charles and another trader named Papin went hunting in this wild country and got lost. Sixteen days later Charles found his way back to safety, but his companion had disappeared in the wilderness. Alexander Mackenzie of the North West Company wrote laconically that Papin "never returned. No account of his end." None has since been found.[5]

CHARLES AND CHARLOTTE MARRY "COUNTRY STYLE"

In 1799, the Indians in the upper part of the St Louis River were expecting a trader to winter with them, but Charles was having a problem finding canoes to get there. "If Ermatinger should not be able to get in for want of Canoes," wrote Mackenzie, always anxious to outdo a competitor, "would it not be advisable to send [someone else] there with a small assortment?"[6]

The area in question was some two days' march from Sandy Lake, home of Chief Katawabidai. Charles did travel there, and it was probably during this winter that he married Mananowe, Katawabidai's daughter. He was twenty-two years old, she about fifteen.[7] He was the educated son of a Swiss merchant living in Montreal, she the illiterate daughter of an Ojibwa chief living in the Upper Country. Unlike his friend George Nelson, who agonized before taking an Indian wife, Charles did not hesitate to cohabit with an Indian woman.[8] Whether Chief Katawabidai suggested the liaison or Charles initiated the matter, her father's agreement was essential. The marriage, following Ojibwa tradition, would have had no formal or religious ceremony. Charles probably gave his father-in-law some gifts, in effect a bride price, and perhaps smoked a ceremonial pipe.[9] Then Charles took Mananowe, later called Charlotte, to bed. Their first child, Anne, was born in 1800. For over thirty years they would live together as husband and wife, producing another eleven children.

CHARLES JOINS THE NORTH WEST COMPANY

At some point, Charles left L'Etang to work with John Ogilvy, another bitter rival of the North West Company. Ogilvy and his people were of "such pityfull an appearance" that Alexander Mackenzie believed Charles would be sorry he had made a deal with them; others who had done so had come to regret it. Mackenzie's prediction proved true. In the summer of 1800 another Nor'Wester, William McGillivray, wrote, "Ogilvy's haughty and imperious conduct has deprived him of all his clerks. Mr. Ermatinger has joined us."[10] Clearly McGillivray considered Charles an acquisition.

Any problems of loyalty for Charles would later solve themselves when the North West Company absorbed the XY Company in an agreement of 5 November 1804, signed in the presence of Edward Gray and Frederick W. Ermatinger. Charles had influential relatives.[11]

TRADING RELATIONS WITH THE INDIANS

Little is known of his early years with the North West Company, but company documents show that by 1806 Charles was stationed at Bas de la Rivière.[12] (An earlier sighting of him came in 1805.)

Even by the 1790s, traders had complained that overhunting had depopulated the beaver and large game from this area around Lake Winnipeg. This led to intense competition to harvest what was left. The Indians also found it increasingly difficult to survive and in 1806 began leaving the area, which meant loss of furs for the traders.[13] Charles had a solution; he planted fifteen or sixteen kegs of potatoes, turnips, and barley. With these crops and a newly found fishery, local Indians began to prosper and stayed. Charles prospered along with them. In the spring of 1806, he "got a fine house raised in the English fashion," It had two stores eighteen metres long. That winter he also got two horses from Red River.[14]

Charles was not content to wait for Indians to come to his post. He and his men combed the area for furs. When Charles was wintering at Bas de la Rivière, he asked Nelson to accompany him on a visit to his Indian clients, who were dispersed over a large circuit in the environs of the Red River. Nelson jumped at the chance to spend three weeks exploring a large area he did not know. One previous autumn, the company had stationed Charles at Thunder Lake, on the upper Poplar River, a very difficult country indeed. Charles had had to "exert the utmost prudence, foresight and economy," to survive, wrote Nelson. It was out of the question to lay up a stock of provisions, and difficult even to procure enough for subsistence. He managed so well, however, that "he had a tolerably good winter of it." Nelson called Charles a prudent and far-sighted man, capable of providing well for his family where many could not even survive.[15]

Curiously, Nelson makes no mention of Charlotte, despite the fact that she must have played an essential role in this wilderness family. Other visitors to the Ermatinger household repeated this omission.

CHARLES LEAVES THE NORTH WEST COMPANY

Charles was a successful trader, and in 1806 the proprietors of the North West Company agreed that he and two other clerks should in 1808 become partners in the concern. But when the canoes arrived from Montreal in mid-December 1807, Nelson heard disturbing news: "Mr Ermatinger, who I have reason to remember with kindness and respect, had also 'gone to Montreal', an equivalent, in our vocabulary, to disgrace which he certainly, for many reasons, did not deserve." Years later, Nelson expanded on this. Charles "too, poor fellow, had severely writhed" under slanderous accusations.[16]

Nelson had experienced his own scandal when he formed a liaison with a young Indian woman in 1803. He was severely reprimanded for this relationship and for management weaknesses in controlling his men.[17] In its early years, the North West Company had encouraged trader-Indian liaisons, but from 1800 on the urban partners grew hostile to them, claiming that the families cost the company money. In July 1806, the annual meeting banned any partner, clerk, or engagé "henceforth" from taking an Indian woman to live with him.[18] Charles' marriage must have long been known, so in itself could hardly cause a scandal. But perhaps, as with Nelson, the slander concerned Charles' relationships with his Ojibwa relatives. Indian fathers-in-law expected that traders who prospered by marrying their daughters should reciprocate in kind.[19] Reciprocity was the Ojibwa way. Maybe the company felt that Charles was too generous in his trading with Katawabidai. Or perhaps Charles found the new climate of hostility in the company unacceptable.

Whatever the reason, in 1807 he left the company. He was given £600, while promising not to compete at the expense of his former employer for seven years.[20] Had the scandal involved misappropriation of funds or theft, the company surely would not have allowed Charles that money. No company records making charges against him, or explaining his departure, have been found.

The Family Goes to Sault Ste Marie

In 1807 or 1808 Charles settled in Sault Ste Marie with his wife and four, possibly five, children. He built his first establishment about two and a half kilometres below the rapids where the North West Company had its post. His brother Frederick William now acted as his agent in Montreal. Frederick's accounts show that on 27 July 1808, he paid a bill (£7/14/–) drawn on a draft from Charles in Sault Ste Marie.[21] Their fraternal and business relationship remained close for twenty years, much as their father Lawrence had acted as Montreal agent for Forrest Oakes but without their mutual recriminations. In 1817, for example, Charles and Frederick outfitted a "joint adventure" costing £389/10/10 and employing sixty French Canadians, Indians, and Métis.[22]

At Sault Ste Marie Charles found immediate success. Even in his first year he had at least three men working for him. By 1812, he had fifty.[23] His former bosses in the North West Company were not known for tolerating competitors, yet Charles had set up shop near the company's post. Apparently, the company did not object to the apparent contravention of his agreement, again suggesting that any earlier troubles were not of a business nature. But little is known of Charles' early years in Sault Ste Marie.

Charles and the War of 1812

The United States declared war on Britain in June 1812. One month later, a British force under a Captain Roberts landed quietly in the middle of the night on Michilimackinac, an American island south of Sault Ste Marie in Lake Huron. The force consisted of less than 50 regulars, some 189 local volunteers, and about 300 Indians, mainly Ojibwa. The volunteers were formed into three militia companies with a colonel, a major, three captains, and four French Canadian lieutenants.[24] Charles, one of the captains, brought his fifty employees with him.[25]

A garrison of only sixty-one officers and men commanded by a young officer, Lieutenant Porter Hanks, manned the American fort. In the early morning of 16 July, the British dragged a cannon onto a hill dominating the American log fort, then silently evacuated all civilians from a nearby settlement. At dawn, Captain Roberts sent two American civilians to the fort to warn the commander of the cannon, of 1,000 troops standing to, and of hundreds of Indians who, if resistance were offered, would massacre every American they could find. Roberts exaggerated only the number of troops – the threat of a massacre was very real – and the young American commander surrendered almost immediately. The British had secured a strategic fort, and captured many guns along with their ammunition, but the real value of the expedition lay in rallying the Indians to the British cause.[26] Describing the affair, Roberts warmly thanked his own officers and "the Gentlemen of St Joseph's and St Mary's." In a district general order, General Brock also thanked "those gentlemen etc. in the neighborhood who so honorably contributed" to the victory. Roberts and Brock also commented that due to the generous counsel of the Britons, the Indians had spared the enemy from annihilation.[27] Charles no doubt played a role in calming his kinsmen.

Two years later, the Americans tried to take back Fort Michilimackinac and failed. Two frustrated American gunboats then raided Sault Ste Marie. As they approached, Charles and his men buried bundles of furs. Soon looting Americans had gutted the North West Company post and burned the company schooner and its sawmill. A traveller who arrived soon after the raid, Gabriel Franchère, reported that the houses, warehouses, and sawmill of the North West Company were still smoking.[28] Virtually every British resident had fled or gone to fight at Michilimackinac, except Charles. When the American commander questioned why he stayed, he said he was simply an honest man, trying to make a living while minding his own business. At that, the Americans let him go.[29]

The Americans also spared his buildings but burned those of the trader John Johnston, at that stage still a British citizen but living in American Sault Ste Marie.[30] With about 100 voyageurs and engagés, he had slipped through the American fleet to help defend Fort Michilimackinac. This time, Charles had stayed behind. When the war finished, Charles immediately resumed trading. In 1816, a government appointment as justice of the peace confirmed his status in the community.

CHARLES AND THE AMERICAN TRADERS

After the War of 1812, the 1816 Exclusion Act banned foreigners from trading with Indians on US soil. This act had been preceded by the Non-Intercourse Act of 1809 forbidding importation of British goods into the United States. A three-way battle began for control of the fur trade on the American side of the Great Lakes. First, US government officials in charge of fortified "factories" were responsible for supervising trade with the Indians, and for "civilizing" them. Typical was Major William Henry Puthuff, government factor at Michilimackinac. Second, the American Fur Company under John Jacob Astor wanted a monopoly in the Indian trade, with no government interference. Third, the Canadians, Charles Ermatinger prominent among them, were determined to continue trading with their old Indian allies in America despite US laws.

Over time, alliances formed and dissolved among these three competing factions. At one point Puthuff strongly opposed Charles' working in the United States, but later he was even more opposed to the policies of Astor and the American Fur Company. He then made friends with Charles, sometimes giving him a licence to trade with the Indians. In 1818, however, Puthuff was cashiered and Charles lost his licences.[31]

Charles then tried several techniques to get around the law. When it suited them both, he and the American Fur Company representatives allied: for instance, Charles held an interest in a Fond du Lac business in partnership with the company.[32] He also tried to use his father-in-law, Katawabidai, to import liquor into the States. But American agent Henry Schoolcraft turned down Katawabidai's request to do so.[33] Charles also failed in his attempt to work through his brother, George, who was trading in the American Sault Ste Marie. He had more success in 1819, when he bought out Jean Baptiste Nolin, a trader in the American Sault Ste Marie since 1780.[34] Charles used this post to continue trading in the United States.

CHARLES AND THE OJIBWA

Both Charles and Katawabidai travelled by canoe throughout their trading areas and must have often met in a mutually profitable business relationship. Katawabidai certainly visited Sault Ste Marie in both 1816 and 1822 on his way to meet the military at Drummond Island, and again in 1828, not long before he died. On one occasion the chief gave Charles a French flag captured during the wars with France. Schoolcraft said that Charles took it to Montreal.[35] Many years later, Charlotte presented Lord Elgin, then the Canadian governor general, with a French flag she said she had inherited from her father, which was probably the same flag (see Chapter 7).

Charles had more than Ojibwa family connections working in his favour. During the Ojibwa winter hunt he sent his men on buying trips called by the French, and later by the Nor'Westers, "derouines."[36] These visits to their hunting sites helped bind the Indians to him through the credit he extended them, the usual method of trading in the Great Lakes area. Every summer, he himself made a canoe trip to Michilimackinac and Drummond Island. He bought furs on promissory notes for "value received," to be redeemed on 10 October of that year. For 1817, brother Frederick's papers contain such notes for nine transactions totalling £1,062. A typical sale of Charles' pelts by Henry and Bethune included "27 deer (£2/5/–), 47 otters (£11/3/3), 23 bears (£2/6/–), 108 martins (£–/11/4), 10 buffaloes (£8/7/6), 1 buffalo dressed (£–/12/6). Total: £35/18/3." Mostly Charles sent his furs to Montreal, and brought his trade goods back, by canoe. But at least occasionally he sent packets of fur down the Great Lakes by schooner, once by the schooner *Elizabeth*.[37]

Charles was allegedly capable of using devious means to persuade Ojibwa not to trade with Americans. Schoolcraft said that Charles told one man, Bisconaosh, not to go south of the border as "the Americans would cause him to be whipped, with other idle stuff of that sort."[38]

As it was for his father, alcohol constituted an important trade item for Charles. An invoice book shows that he imported much liquor. One invoice dated 1 May 1822 says, "By the lake, under the care of his son Charles, viz 1 keg ten gallons West Indian Madeira wine," while another canoe carried two barrels of best Spanish wine, two gallons of brandy, and one keg of L.P. Tenerife.[39] Brandy, rum, and wine, always watered down, were popular trade items with the Indians. In 1826, Charles sold the Hudson's Bay Company 350 gallons of wine for trade in the Lake Huron and Lake Superior districts.[40] Just after Charles retired, the American Fur Company offered to give up trading liquor in the area if the Hudson's Bay Company would do so, but the trade continued.[41]

LORD SELKIRK AND THE HUDSON'S BAY COMPANY

Lord Selkirk, the major shareholder in the Hudson's Bay Company, arrived in Montreal in 1815 to oversee the Company's affairs. He was especially interested in his beloved Red River settlement, an area of 300,000 square kilometres where he was settling Scottish farmers, driven from their highland homes.[42] Charles began to act as Selkirk's agent. Among many activities, he helped establish a winter express between York and Hudson's Bay posts with Sault Ste Marie as a relay point; he received instructions from Selkirk about the route to be taken by bearers of despatches; and he supplied the Red River settlement with fresh meat, hens, and ducks. In an 1816 letter, Charles advised Selkirk of the loss of a canoe with nine people including two Hudson's Bay Company employees, two soldiers, and five Iroquois (the fur trade was still a dangerous occupation).[43]

On 16 June, Métis allies of the Nor'Westers killed twenty-one of a Hudson's Bay Company party at Seven Oaks. Lord Selkirk, on his way to Red River from Montreal, was staying at Charles' home when word of the Seven Oaks massacre arrived. Selkirk had with him his voyageurs, a group of soldiers, and more settlers. He decided to go to Fort William and bring the perpetrators to justice. Fearing that he would be perceived as biased, Selkirk asked Charles and another local justice of the peace to join him in this quasi-military expedition. "Their avocations did not permit them to undertake this duty," wrote Selkirk.[44]

In October 1818, when Selkirk initiated a series of prosecutions for murder against certain Nor'Westers, he asked Charles to attend the trials in Upper Canada. Charles did not do so, though Selkirk usually paid his witnesses' expenses.[45] Caution was probably Charles' motive. By now, murderous assaults by Nor'Westers on Hudson's Bay Company employees were common, and Charles would not want to identify himself too strongly and publicly with either side in the bitter dispute. Selkirk apparently bore no grudge. He suggested Charles be paid for his services as agent in Hudson's Bay Company stocks.[46] The relationship between Charles and the company continued after Selkirk's return to England (see Appendix C).

FINANCIAL PROBLEMS

At least until 1820, Charles' business seemed to be thriving. He was still trading with the Indians south of the border, evading US restrictions through the property bought from Nolin in the American Sault. He had a profitable arrangement with the Hudson's Bay Company. His store at Sault Ste Marie was busy and presumably also profitable. He was building an imposing stone house on the Canadian side of the river, begun shortly after the War of 1812. The stone house, which cost the large sum of £2,000, would become famous in the 1820s for the parties and dinners given by Charles (see Chapter 5). He also built a windmill for irrigation, hoping it would lead other inhabitants, mainly French Canadian boatmen married to Indian women, to grow more grain than they had hitherto.[47] This last initiative was reminiscent of his days at Bas de la Rivière.

Despite this apparent prosperity, ominous signs were appearing. After the merger of the North West and the Hudson's Bay companies in 1820, the new Hudson's Bay Company installed its own manager in Sault Ste Marie, Angus Bethune. He saw Charles as competition that cost him lucrative contracts, though the relationship remained friendly: in 1824, Bethune reported that Charles had returned the scow that he had borrowed earlier.[48] Unfortunately for Charles, as civilization moved closer to *le pays d'en haut,* the American army moved in and more rigorously applied the law. In 1822, the military wanted to build a fort at Sault Ste Marie, Michigan. Troops took over Charles' property there, and he had to transfer his American operations to the Canadian side.[49] This made trade with his Ojibwa relatives much more difficult.

Even worse, by the 1820s Sault Ste Marie, never a major fur centre, was declining rapidly in importance. George Keith, a Hudson's Bay Company agent, in 1828 referred to the exhausted state of the country in fur-bearing animals.[50] As well, amalgamation of the Hudson's Bay and North West companies had reduced the importance of the old voyageur route via Sault Ste Marie. Now, the new company used the traditional Hudson's Bay Company routes, tracking south and west from its bases at Fort York and the mouths of rivers flowing into the bay. Still another sign of frontier taming came with the arrival of the first Canadian customs officer to be stationed at the Sault. Bethune described him as "a gentleman of no great reputation. He annoys the inhabitants a good deal. We shall have to pay a duty on all we purchase from the American side." But the customs official gave Bethune and his company power to seize all property imported from the United States without payment of Canadian duties, including canoes, boats, horses, dogs, and a few other items. Bethune told his agents, "I shall caution Mr. Ermatinger to give certificates to those whom he may have occasion to send onto the Lake, on producing which you are not to seize any property from them."[51]

Despite difficulties, co-operation continued with the American Fur Company. For example, the company's representative at Michilimackinac wrote to Charles in 1822 offering to buy all the muskrats he had at 35 cents each. Alternatively, if the bad rats and kittens were thrown out he would buy the remainder, say 45 lots, at 37½ cents. He made "this extraordinary offer" to keep some control over the market, "and," he concluded, "I hope you have no objection to keeping up their values."[52]

By 1825 financial troubles were compounding. Bethune said Charles' collections, including whatever he had picked up in trips to the south side of Lake Superior, amounted to £700. But he made no profits since his mode of trading (sending agents around the Indians' winter camps) was enormously expensive. He added, "The only way in which Mr. Ermatinger makes money is by selling his goods to the private traders on the south side of Lake Superior," and that was becoming much harder to do. The following year Bethune heard that unless things improved, Charles would sell out his interests on the south shore to the American Fur Company because he was having so much trouble with their agents.[53] A final blow came in 1828 when he lost his Drummond Island post because Britain gave the island back to the United States. Charles' only claim to his land there was permission for a building lot signed in 1816 by the officer commanding at the time, Major James Winniet.[54] Charles sold the post to the American Fur Company, whose local agent wrote, "Ermatinger has resigned to us all his interest in the Superior trade."[55]

On the Canadian side of the border, Charles' title to his land at Sault Ste Marie had always been in doubt because the government had reached no general land settlement with the local Ojibwa. He was, in effect, a squatter with only a certificate signed in 1821, again by Major Winniet, permitting occupation of "a lot of land on the River St Mary at present in his possession and to the following extent: with three acres in front facing the river and on as prolonged a line perpendicular from that front as may suit his purpose."[56] In 1825, Charles petitioned the government of Upper Canada for a deed to the land, citing his contribution to the capture of Michilimackinac in the War of 1812. His local knowledge of the country, he said, and his advice to the officers who commanded His Majesty's troops at Michilimackinac and St Joseph during the rest of the war, were acknowledged to be of great service to the military. Charles maintained that these services had entitled him to a share in the prize money for the capture of the fort, which he had never claimed. He applied for a patent deed for the 200 acres of land he now

Figure 4
THE FAMILY OF CHARLES AND CHARLOTTE ERMATINGER

Charles Oakes = Charlotte (Mananowe) Katawabidai
(1776-1833)   (c. 1785-1850)

Children of Charles Oakes and Charlotte:

- Anne 1800-17
- Charles Oakes Jr 1802-57
- Frances 1804-84
  = Francis Perry (3 children)
  = James H. McVey (1 child)
- George 1806-22
- Jemima 1808-38
  = Thomas C. Cameron (1 child)
- (Frederick) William 1811-69
  = Caroline-Elisa Juchereau Duchesnay (1819-90)
- Edward ?-1822
- James 1815-90
  = Mary Isabella Fraser
- John 1817
- Anna Maria (aka Anne) 1818-89
  = Carl Becherer
- Jane 1824-75
  = James R. MacDonald
- Lawrence ?-1822

Children of (Frederick) William and Caroline-Elisa Juchereau Duchesnay:

- William Roch Daly 1846-70
- Charles Henry Catawabiddy 1848-?
- Edward Juchereau 1851-91
  = Mary Josephine Alger
- Edmund Monk Tancred 1855-?
- Wilhelmina 1857-1905
  = P.E. Smith
- P.T. Hildebrand 1858-92
  = Fanny Bruneau

Sources: LAC, MG 19, A2, series 4, vol. 1, file 1, 6484, 6485, 6486, 6488, 6489, 6490, 6491, 6492, 6493, 6494, 6496, 6497, 6501, 6502, 6510, and Deed of Tutorship; Gladys McNeice, *The Ermatinger Family of Sault Ste. Marie* (Sault Ste. Marie: Sault Ste. Marie and 49th Field Regiment RCA Historical Society, 1984), 22, 51, 52, 68-69, appendix 2; Pierre-Georges Roy, *La Famille Juchereau Duchesnay* (Lévis, QC, 1903), 353, 356-57; Ontario Genealogical Society, Oakwood Cemetery, book 1, 2 May 1890-11 March 1932; St. John's Anglican Church, Woodhous, Upper Canada, Parish Register, 1830-1851, 1885-1948, 35.

occupied. He had lived there for nineteen years, he said, cleared much of it, and built a house that cost him upwards of £2,000.[57] But the petition failed.

CHARLES RETIRES

On the death of his brother Frederick in 1827, Charles inherited both money and substantial property on the Island of Montreal. For him, the fur trade struggle had gone on long enough. He decided to retire, and did so the following year at age fifty-two. His retirement excited little reference in the known correspondence of the Hudson's Bay Company. Nonetheless, Robert Stuart of the American Fur Company, often a bitter rival, wrote to Charles wishing him "health and pleasant winters" in Montreal.[58]

Years before, Charles had written a letter to his nephew Edward Ermatinger, a young clerk in the Hudson's Bay Company whose relationship with Charles Oakes and family are discussed in Appendix E. "Connections formed in the [Indian] country," wrote Charles, "should, if possible, be avoided by you." Steering clear of a country marriage "will always keep you independent, and enable you to leave it [the Indian country] at a future period, when you may have realized a competency, without regrets."[59]

Happily, Frederick's legacy had allowed Charles another option. Unlike many other fur traders, Charles now took his wife and family to Montreal. As early as 1820, Frederick had paid £500 on account for a farm at Longue Pointe, Montreal Island.[60] There, in a pastoral setting close to the city, Charles and Charlotte lived out the remainder of their lives with their bicultural family. Although they had twelve children, five had died before this move east (see Figure 4). The lives of the remaining seven occupy Chapters 5 through 12.[61]

Charles and Charlotte in Montreal

When, in the summer of 1828, Charles moved his family to their new home in Montreal, its size and furnishings showed that the family could expect to host dinners and parties on the scale of their Sault Ste Marie days. The two-storey house, also built of stone but much larger than the old establishment, contained twelve rooms plus a kitchen and pantry. Besides the dining and living rooms, the house had four, possibly five bedrooms; a room with a camera obscura and an optical machine; a library with 340 volumes; an amusement room with card tables and a bagatelle board; and a music room with a small hand organ and guitar. The rooms were curtained, carpeted, and heavy with mahogany – mahogany chairs, armchairs, sideboards, beds, and tables. A succession of bills for materials and repairs shows a great deal of work completed on the house and farm. One bill alone lists three tradesmen and two labourers spending 101 days on the house.[1]

Charles brought much of the furniture from Sault Ste Marie, but a flurry of shopping in Montreal followed the family's arrival. Among dozens of purchases were a horse, carriage, and sleigh; five bedsteads, two of them mahogany; three chests of drawers, one mahogany; one dressing table; three washstands; a mahogany sideboard; three tables including a rosewood work table; a cherrywood secretary; eight Windsor chairs; twenty-seven yards of fine carpeting; two little window curtains; one foot mat and five table mats; tin kettles and tureens, a colander, four tumblers, a teapot, milk strainer, gravy strainer, pepper box, two tin candlesticks, six spoons, two oval tin tart pans, tin mug, two tin funnels, and a tin dusting pan. Their expected entertaining required an additional four dozen plates, eight dishes, and one dozen each of tumblers, wine glasses, and cups and saucers.[2]

Despite the opulence of the home, in its early days Longue Pointe saw few if any caribou dinners or grand parties. Charles was soon nostalgic for the Montreal of his youth. A letter to his married daughter, Jemima, sadly contrasted the "hospitable" people of York, where she lived, with a "much changed" Montreal. Here, he said, the Ermatingers knew little of local society and had been to few parties.[3]

Charles was not alone in this view of retirement in Montreal. Years earlier, Alexander Henry had written, "I find myself in a strange country, hundreds who I do not know or ever heard of, I meet in church and other places, both male and female."[4] They were, he complained, mainly merchants, mostly Americans, and little French was spoken. In those years, Henry had the solace of old friends in the Beaver Club, the highly convivial social club whose only members were those who had wintered in the Upper Country. Charles would have qualified for membership, but by the time of his retirement the club was dead along with all its original members, many of them his friends.

All this contrasted with his early memories of Montreal. In 1771 his father, Lawrence, had described the winter's entertainment in the city to a London merchant from whom he imported goods:

> [The fine weather] has afforded great pleasure to those who are fond of carioling, many parties have been in the country; and a concert in one week, and an assembly in the other, make things very agreeable. However, I would have you to import a cargo of pistols and swords. They are much in want, and very lucky [that] it is a scarce article, for quarrels [about] who dances last and which of the ladies should be handed into the room first, has occasioned some disturbance and occasioned a duel, the parties fixed with [illegible, possibly "candlesticks"] but lucky nobody was sided.

Lawrence then added casually, "Bindon got himself a wife. He married Mrs Wigans, Jacob's daughter-in-law. There are no ladies left to marry."[5]

Reading was a part of the Ermatingers' lives. Frederick had had a subscription to the Montreal Library, and Charles kept it up. The family in 1829 was fined seven shillings and one penny for books overdue for seventeen days. Charles also subscribed to several newspapers, including at least one in French, *L'Ami du Peuple*. The church, too, played a role in their lives. In 1818, Frederick had given £10 for the salary of an evening lecturer in the Protestant Episcopal Church, and subscribed £5 a year for Pew 81 in the same church. Charles kept up these payments.[6]

The lack of social activities apparently did not result from prejudice against the old Indian trader and his Ojibwa-Canadian family. The Montreal business elite trusted Charles. In 1829 John Molson and his partners gave him power of attorney to investigate a firm while he was visiting London, and to take any action necessary to collect money owed the Molsons. In a dense legal argument that Charles took back to Montreal, the London lawyers offered only limited hope that the Molsons could win their case.[7] While Charles was in London, his brother Lawrence Edward died there. Charles attended to the funeral arrangements.[8]

FURTHER FINANCIAL PROBLEMS

On the death of his brother Frederick in 1827, Charles had inherited the bulk of that active businessman's estate, though it is not known how much it totalled. Charles also had property of his own. As early as 1821, he was a shareholder in the newly formed Bank of Montreal along with Frederick and an aunt.[9] On 1 June 1832, he had seven shares in the bank, and by 1 December he had 103 shares, suggesting he was doing well financially. He also owned ten shares in the Quebec Fire Assurance Co., probably among other investments.[10] The various Ermatinger farms, mainly inherited from Frederick, also seem to have been doing well enough. In 1831, Charles Jr wrote, "All our crops are in some time ago. We cannot complain much of them, the wheat rather worse than last year."[11]

Signs of financial troubles were beginning to appear, however. Astonishingly, they sprang from the affairs of the late Frederick, epitome of a businessman. In an 1830 public notice, Charles announced that unanticipated demands for many hundreds of pounds had been made against him due to his inheritance from his brother. To meet these claims, Charles had to collect without delay any sums due Frederick's estate.[12] Those demands seem to have arisen at least in part from an allegedly wrongful seizure and sale by Frederick, as sheriff of Montreal, of some real property.[13] Charles had to take a number of cases to court to get the money to pay off the inherited debts. In 1829 he won a suit against David Handyside for £31/19/11, the amount of a promissory note plus costs. In 1831 he made a loan to a man named John D. Campbell. When it was not paid back, he demanded a draft on the trustees of an estate that, he had heard, owed Campbell money. These among others in a series of legal affairs required the advice of Samuel Gale, his lawyer.[14]

CHARLES AS A FATHER

At this time all of the Ermatinger children were living at home except for Jemima, who was married to a Lieutenant Thomas C. Cameron of the British Army and living in Kingston. A series of letters written mainly to Jemima in these retirement years sketch out more of Charles Sr's character and relationships with his family.[15] The letters contain quiet but deep expressions of affection. The man hitherto seen only through the eyes of others comes into focus as a loving father and family man. For example:

> I was extremely happy to be favoured with a letter from you, and I can almost say, undeservedly, as I did not answer your former one. But believe me, it was not for want of affection, and although recovered from my former illness, I still continue to be unwell … We shall be extremely disappointed in not being favoured with a visit from you, as we had reason at first to anticipate, but as the distance will now become greater between us owing to your future destination [the Camerons were transferring from Kingston to York], … evidently we cannot expect to see you as often we would wish.[16]

Charles was also happy to read in Jemima's letter that her little boy's health had so much improved. He wrote that though the family would have found much pleasure in seeing him and his mother at Longue Pointe that summer, they would all the more eagerly await a visit the following spring.

Much of the content of these letters concerns Jemima's farm, which Charles was managing for her (as discussed in Chapter 12), but his worries went beyond that. In early summer 1832, despite quarantine measures on Grosse Île in the St Lawrence River, cases of Asian cholera had spread from Europe to Quebec, then to Montreal, and finally to Upper Canada. By the time the epidemic had finished in September, some 6,000 people had died of it. Charles wrote Jemima thanking Almighty God that he and his family had been spared the mighty ravages of the cholera outbreak. He assured Jemima that, by living temperately and in an army location with close medical assistance, "above all, in your state you have nothing to apprehend." Jemima must then have been pregnant, though how this would protect her from cholera is not clear. In December he wrote that they must thank God cholera had not attacked the family. The dreadful disease continued to lurk about but he hoped its greatest effects had passed.[17]

Charles' compassion reached beyond his own family. He wrote that Jemima must not be alarmed by the disease, as the only people in danger were the intemperate and those poor who lived where every kind of filth accumulated. The poor immigrants were particularly unfortunate, many of them lying outside, exposed by day to the sun and at night to cold with scarcely any covering. "However, I am happy to find the town has taken their deplorable case into consideration": buildings for the poor immigrants were being erected and that would, he was sure, alleviate great mishap.[18]

CHARLOTTE

In the fall of 1814, long before his retirement, Charles had taken most of his family to Montreal on a visit. When passing through Lake of Two Mountains, some kilometres west of Montreal, Charles left Charlotte there. He and the rest of the family arrived in the city some time before 22 November, when his brother Frederick invited friends for dinner to meet Charles.[19]

In Lake of Two Mountains, on 1 February 1815, Charles and Charlotte's son James was born.[20] This provokes the question: why did Charlotte stay here to have her baby? The area, now called Oka, has long been known as an Iroquois region. Ojibwa and Iroquois speak different languages and the two were often mutually hostile. The Iroquois would not have created a welcoming climate for an Ojibwa mother-to-be. In the early 1800s, however, the Hudson's Bay Company representative there, John McLean, described two groups of Native people living side by side, albeit uneasily. They were Iroquois *and* a small group of Ojibwa. The Iroquois cultivated the soil, said McLean, and acted as voyageurs, while the Ojibwa "lived by the chase." Since their languages were mutually unintelligible, they communicated little.[21] Charlotte must have had her earlier babies in the traditional Indian manner, since she and Charles lived far from European midwives or doctors. Indian women bearing children under European rather than traditional methods had a more difficult time of it. Plausibly, Charlotte may have preferred to stay with her own people and give birth in the traditional Ojibwa manner rather than travelling to alien white Montreal and there trusting herself and her baby to a European midwife. It is also possible that Charlotte stayed in one of the local fur trade households with Indian wives.

While the family was in Montreal in 1815, George Jenkins, chaplain to the armed forces, baptized five of the children at the Garrison Anglican Church. The baptism records identify the children as those of "Charles Oakes Ermatinger Esq. and Charlotte Mannanowe." Two years later, the burial certificate for John Ermatinger, just one month old, was signed by J. Somerville, of St Gabriel Street Presbyterian Church. The Presbyterian and Anglican records differ in one interesting respect. The Anglican record gave Charlotte her names, English and Ojibwa, as mother of the children. The Presbyterian record cold-bloodedly recorded John as the son of "Charles Ermatinger Esquire, Indian Trader, by a woman of the Indian country."[22] Such a designation of Indian wives is quite usual in church records, Anglican or Presbyterian.

In 1815, Charles made a will before he left Montreal to return to the Sault. He left all his property to be "divided between and among his natural children by an Indian woman." His brother Frederick was to be guardian of the children and of their funds until each came of age. Charlotte merited nothing, not even being named as the mother.[23] Even if ministers and lawyers were responsible for omitting Charlotte's name, Charles was either not conscious of the slight to his wife, or not willing to kick against custom.

By the time they returned to Montreal, Charles and Charlotte had had twelve children. Just before his retirement, Charles received a letter from his old friend and lawyer, Samuel Gale, warning him that he must make another will. Otherwise, neither his children nor their mother would be entitled to any of Charles' inherited or acquired property.[24] To protect the surviving seven children, Charles signed a second will in 1828, and then a third in 1831, two years before his death. The third set aside £1,000 in a trust fund. Interest of £60 a year was to go in half-yearly instalments to "Charlotte who hath resided with me as my wife for upwards of thirty years ... [and is] the mother of all my children."[25] The balance of the money and property went to the children. Note that this phrasing is significantly different from the 1815 will in that it gave Charlotte both a bequest and her name.

Probably to safeguard the inheritance further, and to avoid the legal problems left by Alexander Fraser (mentioned in the Introduction), Charles took another step. On 6 September 1832, he and Charlotte were formally married.[26] They could have performed the ceremony quietly at home. Instead, they married according to Anglican rites in Montreal's Christ Church, the most upscale of the city's Protestant churches and later to be the cathedral. One admirer described the church as "one of the handsomest specimens of modern architecture in the province." It had a front of stone cut in the Doric style, and shining tin covered its steeple and spire, which carried a weathervane and a four-dialled clock.[27] The children of Charles and Charlotte attended the marriage ceremony at this impressive site, with Charles Jr, his sister Frances Perry, and her husband Frank acting as witnesses. Unashamedly, the bride's European first name and what is apparently a variant of her Ojibwa name were used on the licence: Charlotte Cattoonalieté. Here, there was no attempt to hide her origins.

Charles' mother had died in 1809, and it is unlikely she could have met her daughter-in-law, who probably first visited Montreal in 1815. Jemima Ermatinger, née Oakes, an urban woman, probably had the educational and other advantages of a childhood in a prosperous middle-class family in England; Charlotte Mananowe, daughter of an Ojibwa chief and a child of the Upper Country, was illiterate. But they did have in common their womanhood and their marriages in an era when those factors alone determined at least one aspect of their lives: Jemima had eight children, the first three born in under three years and one dying in infancy; Charlotte had twelve children, the first five born in eight years, five dying before reaching adulthood. But the contrast between these women showed markedly during their husbands' absences. When Lawrence went to Britain, he left his wife as attorney with power to sign business documents; in contrast, when Charles died, Charlotte lost control of her children. According to an 1833 Deed of Tutorship, "Being unacquainted with the management of affairs, she is unable to manage the property left to her minor children." She petitioned that tutors be appointed for her three youngest children, James, eighteen, Anna Maria, fifteen, and Jane, nine. The court appointed their brother Charles and brother-in-law Francis Perry as tutors.[28]

In existing documents Charlotte does not emerge as an identifiable figure, and her role in the family is still not clear. She is never mentioned in Charles' social rounds, and travellers who recorded their visits to the Ermatingers at Sault Ste Marie had described the house and sometimes the children, but never their mother. John Bigsby, writing that daughter Frances "seemed mosquito-proof and did the honours of her home with kindness and grace," made no mention at all of Charlotte.[29] Thomas L. McKenney in 1821 was equally impressed with Frances but again mentioned only that Charles had an Indian wife, giving no details. This is especially puzzling because McKenney was entertained and impressed by the Ojibwa wife of the Irish trader John Johnston, with whom he stayed on the south side of the river.[30]

Why then the lack of any description of her by guests to the stone house?

The simplest and most plausible reason is that she probably had little English. She would have had none when, aged fifteen, she married Charles. We know from George Nelson that for the next eight years in various North West Company posts she had no stimulus to learn the language, since French and Indian languages were usually spoken but very little English.[31] We know she was illiterate. And when, aged twenty-three, she moved to Sault Ste Marie, she could certainly have filled her role as housekeeper and mother in the Ojibwa language, the language she taught her children. It would not be surprising if a shy, unilingual woman preferred that her confident, trilingual daughter, Frances, play hostess to the grand earl of Selkirk, to the snobbish Englishman John Bigsby, and to the formidable head of American Indian Affairs, Thomas L. McKenney. McKenney, after all, in formal meetings would refer to Charlotte's father as "my child" and her father would in return call McKenney "father." Charlotte may well have felt herself wanting in the role of hostess to such men.

Certainly, her family regarded Charlotte with affection. Writing to his daughter, Jemima Cameron, after the birth of her first child, Charles wrote, "Your mother thanks you kindly for the lock of your little boy's hair, with the measure of his little wrists. It gives us pleasure, and Jane thought of nothing else the whole day." In another letter, he wrote, "Your mother begs particularly to be remembered to you and feels much disappointed in not seeing you down here this summer and begs of you to take special care of your health." And again, "Your mother and little Jane join with me in wishing you a happy Christmas." And yet again, "Your mother joins me in wishing you every happiness and begs particularly to be remembered to Mr. Cameron."[32]

Two more letters confirm that affectionate relationship. To his nephew Edward, Charles wrote, "At Long Point, I am sure you will meet with a grateful reception, and particularly from the mother who begs to be remembered to you." Edward, writing to his brother, Frank, on the death of their own father, compared their family life with that of the Ermatinger children: "We were never nursed by a fond mother, nor has our interest been continually watched by a kind father."[33]

Some Indian-Canadian children, however, were wholly affectionate to their mothers in private, but, like the Rosses, asked the defensive question "What if Mama is an Indian?" This suggested some discomfort with public opinion.[34] The evidence does not confirm a similar attitude among the Ermatingers. Though early documents refer to her only as "an Indian woman" (in the 1815 will), and "a woman of the Indian country" (in her son John's death certificate), this language was probably the doing of clerks and lawyers. Later references include the name "Charlotte" in the 1831 will and then "Charlotte Cattoonalieté" in the 1832 marriage certificate. In 1850, her death certificate read "Charlotte Kattawabide," presumably so designated by her children.[35] The Ojibwa name in these public documents, and the fact that in their later lives Charlotte's sons and daughters acknowledged their Ojibwa heritage in other public documents, suggests they felt no shame in being her children.

By the numbers, Charlotte fits the Marxist thesis discussed in the Introduction that she was exploited sexually (twelve children, many more than she probably would have had were she married to an Ojibwa);[36] and exploited again in that through her, Charles gained trading access to Ojibwa trading partners. She certainly worked hard as the mother of a large household. Yet viewed as a mother loved by her children, with a husband apparently faithful for thirty years, and living in relative comfort, it is difficult for the non-Marxist to see her as any more exploited than most European wives at that time.

DEATH OF CHARLES SR

By 1830 Charles' correspondence shows him in steadily declining health. In April he told Jemima that, although recovered from his former illness, he still felt unwell.[37] Next February Jemima wrote to her cousin Edward that Charles had been much better. The last accounts had not been so favourable but she trusted it was nothing.[38] Later that year, the governor general's representative wrote asking Charles to take on the duties of a magistrate in Montreal. Charles expressed his thanks but replied, "My state of health is such as to render me unable to assume" that duty. The next year, he wrote to his friend Louis Gugy that health had forced him to reduce his affairs as much as possible. When Gugy next came to Montreal, would he substitute another of his friends as one of his sureties?[39] These letters also illustrate Charles' acceptance by the elite of Montreal.

On 4 September 1833, Charles died at Montreal, aged fifty-seven. Charlotte remained on the Longue Pointe farm until her death in July 1850, aged about sixty-five.[40] Nephew Edward had earlier paid a fulsome tribute to his uncle. He wrote his brother, Frank, "Living in this family as I do, I know the worth of our uncle to his children, and the irreparable loss his death would be to them, and I am confident I would feel it as much, if not more than, I did the death of our own father." Charles Jr also wrote affectionately after his father's death: "To dwell on the melancholy event would only lacerate wounds which time alone and a resignation to the divine will can cure, but never to be forgotten so excellent and indulgent a father. You can imagine the loss, affliction and [illegible] in our family."[41]

CHARLES SR, A SUMMING UP

The Upper Country fur trade was never a career for the timid. Charles was a shrewd trader, a hard worker, and an adventurous man. He had the reputation of being generous, outgoing, and fond of entertaining. So far as we know, he remained faithful to his country wife at a time when sexual adventures were common in the fur trade. His letters show him as an affectionate and wise father.

Charles was at least trilingual in English, French, and Ojibwa.[42] Unlike two of his elder brothers, he had not gone to Britain for his education, but on the evidence of George Nelson he was well read: "I passed this summer [1806] with [Charles] and am indebted to him for the little reading I may have. He pitied my recklessness and in a true fatherly manner insisted on my reading at least, and would frequently ask me questions of those portions of history I had been reading. This gave me a taste for this truly delightful employment which I have ever since strongly held."[43] The books presumably came from Charles' library. The "fatherly" Charles at this time was no more than thirty years old.

The "illegality" of Charles' trading in America has been seen as a possible blemish on his moral character.[44] Although, in a strict sense, he was acting illegally, the correspondence between all the parties suggests that in *le pays d'en haut* the old rules of out-and-out competition and devil-take-the-hindmost still applied. Charles, the American Fur Company, and possibly William Puthuff were happy to claim the benefit of the law when it suited them, and equally happy to forget the law when it did not.

A more serious charge, moral as well as a legal, is the sale of alcohol to the Indians, forbidden by American law. Both the Hudson's Bay Company and the North West Company constantly traded liquor, and the American Fur Company insisted it must also do so as long as its opponents did. "Little does the spirit of commerce care how many Indians die inebriates, if it can be assured of beaver skins," wrote Henry Schoolcraft.[45]

The euphoria of liquor may have played a role in some Indian ceremonies but the evidence suggests that Indians, genetically, are no different from Europeans in their ability to handle liquor. But liquor and the destruction of Indian communities often went hand in hand. The question is, which came first? European expansionism caused immense problems for the Indians of the eighteenth and nineteenth centuries. Many successfully adapted. Many, like their counterparts faced with the Industrial Revolution in nineteenth-century English cities, found the quickest way out of their misery in a gin bottle. Official attempts to restrict the liquor trade with the Indians in the United States and Canada met with little success. It is difficult to see how Charles Ermatinger could have refused liquor to his father-in-law and his people while still managing to trade successfully, whether married to Charlotte or not.

The undefined scandal mentioned but not believed by George Nelson, and an allegation Charles had acted unethically against the Hudson's Bay Company (see Appendix D), run contrary to what we know of the man. In contrast, we have John Bigsby's judgment that Charles was "every inch a trader, public-spirited, skilful, sanguine and indefatigable."[46] That judgment is much more representative of the views of Charles' friends from George Nelson, of the very early days, through to John Molson and other Montreal businessmen who trusted him as their attorney, as well as the governor general who offered him a post as a Montreal magistrate.

A Wild Man's Land
and a World of Virgil

Indians had lived by the St Marys River perhaps for as long as 9,000 years, according to archaeological records.[1] Every summer long before Europeans arrived, Cree and Ojibwa travelled hundreds of kilometres to the Sault for great gatherings where they celebrated religious ceremonies or built friendships between the many different bands. Catching whitefish played an essential role in these festivals. The Ojibwa fishermen launched their two-man canoes into the savage whitewater rapids, some 450 metres wide and 1.2 kilometres long. They steered miraculously from rock to rock as the bow man of each tossing canoe used a scoop at the end of a three-metre pole to net the magnificent whitefish. In the 1760s, Alexander Henry reported that a skilful fisherman in autumn could take 500 fish in two hours.[2] Fish remained a staple food in the 1820s for Indians, Europeans, and Métis in the area. In 1824, with sixty casks of fish already salted, Hudson's Bay Company fishermen caught 300 more fish one day and 200 more the next.[3]

One of the oldest known maps of Canada, drawn by Samuel de Champlain in 1632, shows an Indian village in the area of Sault Ste Marie.[4] In 1761, Alexander Henry reported four houses at the Sault, occupied by Jean Baptiste Cadotte and his part-Ojibwa family. By 1777 there was a small fort and about ten log houses of English and French traders. The North West Company first built a post on the south side of the St Marys River, but when Jay's Treaty of 1794 gave this shore to the Americans, the company moved to the Canadian side. There, at the top of the rapids, it built houses, a sawmill, and a canal to carry the larger canoes around the rapids. In 1821, with the amalgamation of the North West and Hudson's Bay Companies, the latter company took over the post (Figure 5).

Alexander Henry wrote that in the summer "the weather was sometimes exceedingly hot. Mosquitoes and black flies were so numerous as to be a heavy counterpoise to the pleasure of hunting. Pigeons were in great plenty; the stream supplied our drink; and sickness was unknown."[5] In the early

Figure 5
Sault Ste Marie in the 1820s, by George Catlin

1820s, Nicholas Garry saw great beauty in the area. The dark green of the "magnificent" forest growing on the banks and on ten islands in the river, along with the lighter green of the long grass, contrasted with the "snowy whiteness and bright foam" of the rapids. "The number of Indian tents, the Villages on each side, the canoes fishing in the middle of the Rapid form, united, the most beautiful romantic scenery," he wrote. He described the Ojibwa playing lacrosse or baggatiway, their cheeks painted with vermilion and their bodies with the most fantastic colours. The posts of the opposing teams, he said, were a mile or more apart.[6]

About the same time, artist George Catlin, visiting Sault Ste Marie, described "a great concourse of Indians [who] had assembled to witness an Indian regatta or canoe race which went off with great excitement, firing of guns, yelping, etc." The Ojibwa birchbark canoes were exceedingly light "and propelled with wonderful velocity"[7] (Figure 6).

All this made John Bigsby, a British traveller in the 1820s, feel "I was near the wild man's land." He found his view confirmed when he met a handsome white woman in the village wearing a broad silver plate on her head where she had been scalped. Bigsby described the Canadian Sault Ste Marie as "a straggling line of fifteen log huts on marshy ground, with, at its lower end, the comfortable dwelling of Mr. Ermatinger."[8] Many in the population here were families of mixed descent. They worked as traders, interpreters, or Indian agents, the wives helping their husbands in their work. Most were Catholic and French speaking.[9]

Figure 6
An Ojibwa regatta, by George Catlin

THE ERMATINGER CHILDREN

The Ermatinger children fit very well into the Sault Ste Marie scene. Charlotte must have played an important role in their early years. To the older four, born in the Lake Winnipeg area, their young mother certainly spoke in Ojibwa to them before they learned much English. George Nelson, Charles' friend from the days near Lake Winnipeg, years later wrote that the languages in use there were entirely Indian and French except for a few days in June and September, just before and just after the Indian winter hunt. Then the white traders of the North West Company met to prepare for and wind up the season. At those times they occasionally spoke English.[10] All the later children were also fluent in their mother's tongue.

Charles' children would have met Katawabidai during his several visits to Sault Ste Marie. The children must have spent their childhood playing with their Métis neighbours and their Indian cousins, establishing relationships, and learning Indian and Métis ways. Charles and William would both return to the Sault after going to school in Montreal, Charles for six years and William possibly for two. As young men, they hunted with their Indian friends and relatives, and traded with them on the traplines or at remote trading posts. They emerged as accomplished canoeists – in 1823 Charles canoed from Montreal back to the Sault with supplies – and they remained avid hunters all their lives.[11] Of the Ermatinger children, George Nelson wrote, "The girls, I am told, have turned out to be fine women, which I can easily believe. – The boys I am told are wild fellows."[12] The British traveller John

Bigsby, however, gives us much more detailed insight into the upbringing of the Ermatinger children.

JOURNAL OF DR JOHN BIGSBY

John Bigsby in 1821-23 travelled around Lakes Huron and Superior. Volume 1 of his journal, *Shoe and Canoe,* published in 1850, describes how, in 1822 at the Portage La Talon on the Ottawa River, he met a vision: "I had a great surprise at the Portage Talon. Picking my steps carefully as I passed over the rugged ground, laden with things personal and culinary, I suddenly stumbled upon a pleasing young lady, sitting alone under a bush, in a green riding habit, and white beaver bonnet. Transfixed with a sight so out of place in the land of the eagle and the cataract I seriously thought it was a vision of – 'One of those fairy shepherds and shepherdesses / Who hereabouts live on simplicity and watercresses.'" Bigsby paid his respects in some confusion that very much amused her. He learned that she was Charles' daughter Frances, on her way to the Sault. Her father was then at the other end of the portage. "A fortnight afterwards," Bigsby wrote, "I partook of the cordialities of her Indian home, and bear willing witness to the excellence of her tea and pleasantness of the evening."[13]

In volume 2, Bigsby describes an 1823 trip he made with the Canada-USA Boundary Commission. On this trip, the survey party passed rapidly through Sault Ste Marie but he begs the reader's permission to break the continuity of his narrative "to assemble in one chapter all our proceedings in, and remarks upon, Lake Huron." (See Appendix A for the full extract from Bigsby's journal.) After a description of the two Saults he describes his previous visit, when he had been entertained at the homes of Charles Ermatinger and John Johnston.[14] He describes the children of both households. At this time in 1822, four Ermatinger sons and three daughters were at home: Charles, twenty; Frances, eighteen; Edward, something over seven; James, seven; Lawrence, something under seven; Anna Maria, four; and Jane, a baby. George, sixteen, Jemima, fourteen, and William, eleven, were all in Montreal.

Bigsby was not greatly impressed by the intellect of the Sault Ste Marie residents. There were "a few loftier minds, driven into hiding-places by misfortune" but "not enough of the fine gold of English society to make a public impression." He advised only the "uneasy classes" of Britain to emigrate to Canada, but strenuously advised "the easy classes" just to visit. He describes social life in the Sault: "The style, manners and conversational topics, both here [at Johnston's] and at Mr. Ermatinger's, were remarkable, and quite distinct from those of the cities we had left behind us." Some of the guests had "the unsettled postures, dark hue, and wandering black eye of the Indian ... and the perfect gipsy face." Although William Ermatinger did not meet Bigsby on this visit, records show that his son had black eyes, presumably a family trait inherited from Charlotte.[15] "Their English was good, and without the disagreeable nasality of the American," writes Bigsby. They all ate very quickly and in silence, but when finished, "we were very merry, in spite of an abundance of mosquitoes." The talk was "uncourtly but not uncourteous." They "wasted no words upon civilised man" but "dilated upon the prospects of the fishery, of the wild-rice harvest, the furs of the last winter's hunt, the rumoured incursions of the Sioux and other Indians upon the quieter tribes, the massacre of the whites at Red River, then recent."[16]

Though Charles Jr was probably the only Ermatinger youth present and old enough to contribute much to the "uncourtly but not uncourteous" conversation, the atmosphere in which the younger children were growing up is very clear. Like their Ojibwa cousins, by age seven or eight the Ermatinger boys were already hunting with their father, or more probably with their elder brother Charles.

The sons of traders usually worked for their fathers, according to Bigsby. The principal winter occupation of the young men of Sault Ste Marie lay in following the Indians to their hunting grounds to the south and west of Lake Superior, and buying their furs almost as soon as ready. This ensured repayment of the usual autumn advances made to the Indians. "In summer, my friends performed the functions of country gentlemen. They farmed, fished and sported." He adds, no doubt with some exaggeration, "The young men of this neighbourhood were brave fellows, who could steer the canoe and point the rifle, and would ask nothing better than a roving war-commission at the head of their Indian friends to kill and be killed at ten shillings a day for all time."[17] The influence of the Ojibwa cult of the warrior seems obvious.

Ojibwa love for style and adornment, especially of their hair, also fits the patronizing description by Bigsby of the appearance of the Ermatinger and Johnston children. He would not be so ungallant as to describe the dress of the ladies, fashions ten years old, "although no obsoleteness in dress can hide goodness and intelligence." But he smiled inwardly at the garb of the young men with their vast coat collars "a la régent," and "waists so high that the coats were all skirts. Their pantaloons were slit up outside, and adorned with a profusion of bullet-headed brass buttons; while, in imitation of the Mexican rancheros and the English dragoons in Spain, these good people, who never crossed a horse, made the inner parts of this nameless garment almost wholly of leather."[18] He "envied the masses of long black hair which rested upon the shoulders of my friends. They had enough hair to make perukes for twenty duchesses."[19] Style and even dandyness, traits of the Ojibwa, would stay with at least some of the Ermatingers all their lives.

THE ERMATINGER STONE HOUSE
Even in the wild man's land of the Sault amid their Ojibwa relatives and friends, however, the Ermatinger children learned the other side of their bicultural heritage, one that would help them cope with their later move

to Montreal. The Hudson's Bay Company agent in Sault Ste Marie, John Siveright, in 1821 described Charles' "New Elegant Mansion" as quite an asset. This showed only on the outside as the inside would take at least another couple of years to finish. It was all on a grand scale, said Siveright, and did much credit to Charles' good taste.[20] The house, measuring roughly fourteen by ten metres, overlooked the waterfront. The walls were mainly of split, reddish granite fieldstones, some of them coarse red sandstone, built on foundations of fieldstone and lime mortar seventy-five centimetres thick. Cedar logs, thirty to thirty-eight centimetres in diameter, supported the floor. The large central hall had a broad staircase leading to the second floor. Four downstairs rooms, one small and one large on either side of the hall, were replicated upstairs, plus an extra bedroom over the front door. All the downstairs rooms had fireplaces. The house also had a loft and a basement. Outbuildings included a barn kitchen, grist mill, and stables.[21]

An 1836 watercolour by George Catlin shows the stone house and its outbuildings in a forest clearing. The fields behind, fenced by rock walls, are cultivated. Along the river bank, nine small residences stretch west in a line that disappears behind a rocky point. Across the river, the fort at the American Sault Ste Marie flies the Stars and Stripes. In the far distance, the river fades into the vast haunting spaces of the west.[22]

A statement by John Bigsby concerning his visit to the stone house in 1822 is curious: "Save two rooms, his whole dwelling was a warehouse."[23] At that time, Charles and Charlotte lived in the house with seven of their children. Presumably, the rooms were not so filled with trade goods that the family could not live and sleep there. Bigsby says of Frances, "Her boudoir was full of little tokens of Atlantic city education," suggesting she had a room of her own. In 1826 Thomas McKenney described the house as "large and commodious" with no mention of its interior looking like a warehouse.[24] Presumably the 1822 household clutter was temporary since Siveright said in 1821 that it would take a few years to finish the inside.

Life in the stone house was one of great hospitality. The Ermatinger children met many distinguished visitors from outside – Lord Selkirk, Bigsby, McKenney, and Franchère among them – and dined with them at caribou dinners served on mulberry-printed plates and in blue painted bowls, with wine in cut glasses.[25] At New Year's 1826, Charles and family entertained forty-seven men, thirty women, and seventy-five children.[26] John Bigsby gave a different picture of dining in Sault Ste Marie. They lived, he said, almost solely on whitefish. Rich and delicately flavoured as it was, he grew to loathe it.[27]

According to Schoolcraft's diary, the American agent and Charles did a great deal of partying during the 1822-23 winter. On 28 December 1822, they both attended a party at the home of John Siveright, of the Hudson's Bay Company, with most of the officers of the American garrison and other traders. On 14 January 1823, he dined at Charles', a gentleman "who, from small beginnings, has accumulated a considerable property by the Indian trade, and has a numerous Anglo-Ojibway family." Ten days later he was one of sixteen who dined with Charles: "I here first tasted the flesh of the cariboo which is a fine flavored venison. I do not recollect any wise or merry remark made during dinner which is worth recording." On 31 January, he dined with Charles and his son (presumably Charles Jr, aged twenty or possibly twenty-one) and others at Colonel Lawrence's. By 4 February, the parties had palled for the scholarly Schoolcraft. While reading Plutarch's *Life of Marcellus,* he refused an invitation from Charles, telling himself he would not renege on a previous resolution to abstain from "one mode of evening's amusement." Whatever that mode was, probably either drinking or gambling, it did not sour the American completely on Charles. On 10 February, he wrote, "At four I went to dine with Mr. Ermatinger on the British shore."[28]

John Siveright wrote that the Ermatingers that season were not as socially active as usual. In 1822, son George, studying in Montreal, had died, and that fall and winter, Edward and Lawrence had died of dysentery at home. These deaths, Siveright wrote, "prevented the usual Winter Amusement further than a game of Whist now and then."[29] Given Schoolcraft's description of his social activities, "the usual Winter Amusements" must have been extensive indeed.[30] But in all this entertainment, no one makes mention of Charlotte as hostess in the stone house, or as accompanying her husband to other households.

THE CHILDREN'S FORMAL EDUCATION

The children received their earliest formal education from their father. According to George Nelson, writing of the Lake Winnipeg days, Charles "taught his children the English language and they could read and write it, according to their ages, very well indeed."[31] Nothing beyond that is known of the children's early education. Charles followed the pattern of many traders with multicultural children by sending the children to Montreal for their higher education. He also broke the general pattern by educating his daughters as well as his sons.

In the fall of 1814, he took most of the family to Montreal. When Charles and Charlotte returned to Sault Ste Marie, probably in the fall of 1815 for the start of the winter fur hunt, the family split. Anne, aged fifteen, Charles Jr, thirteen, and George, nine, who had all attended school there since February, stayed in the city under the care of their uncle Frederick. Frances had joined them by 1818, aged fourteen. William followed in 1821, aged ten, and James in 1825, also at ten.[32] Jemima, eighteen, was living with her uncle Frederick in 1826.[33] Jane and Anna Maria apparently started schooling in Montreal only when their father retired there in 1828, when they were twelve and nine years old.

Charles Jr finished his schooling when he was seventeen and returned to the Sault to work for his father in May 1819. Charles Sr paid him £6/5/– for bringing a new canoe back with him. For the winter of 1820-21, Charles Jr returned to Montreal, apparently to improve his French, and boarded with Edward Parkins. He returned to Sault Ste Marie in charge of canoes carrying liquor for his father.[34] In 1822, Frances returned home, meeting Bigsby on the way. William finished his schooling and probably returned home in 1826. James was still at school in Montreal when his father retired. Meanwhile, the eldest daughter, Anne, had died in Montreal in 1817 aged seventeen. George had also died in Montreal in 1822 aged sixteen, while studying for the Anglican priesthood.[35]

In Montreal, the Ermatinger children had to cope with a bewildering parade of schools and lodgings, as shown by Frederick's accounts. In 1815 P.I. Gill of Montreal provided tuition for Charles and George from 25 February to 30 June, when Thomas Porteous provided board and schooling at Terrebonne. They travelled by steamer to Trois Rivières for further education and apparently stayed there until November 1818, when they transferred to Ste Catherines, Montreal. In 1819 the Rev. Glenn took over their education at St Eustache. In 1822, bills arrived from Edward Parkins at Chambly for board, education, and sundries for George. The sundries included books, haircuts, a straw hat with band, a tailor's bill, and pocket money. That year William studied under A. Urquhart but boarded with his uncle Frederick. By 1824, William was at the Montreal Academical Institution at a cost of £3/8/1½ with another 15/– for three months' French instruction. In 1825 and 1826, bills arrived from Benjamin Workman for instructing James. Later, James joined William at the Montreal Academical Institute, with William still taking extra French. William's school bills stopped in May 1826 when presumably he went home to Sault Ste Marie. James continued in school until 1830.[36]

The bills paid by Frederick offer glimpses of the content of the children's education. Clearly, French was a major subject but not the only language they learned. Frederick bought for Charles a French grammar, a French dictionary, and four volumes of Gil Blas in French; a Latin grammar, and works of Julius Caesar, the Roman historian Sallust, and Virgil, all in Latin; and Euclid's geometry. Other books included French and Latin exercises, a set of books for "Merchants' Accts.," Murray's English grammar, Johnson's dictionary, and Goldsmith's geography. An 1815 bill for tuition of Charles and George includes two English testaments, one English grammar, one arithmetic book, and a slate. An 1822 bill for William included instruction in French, a book for "cyphering," and Clarke's Latin exercises. James' books included A. Ewing's *Principles of Elocution*, a catechism of ancient geography, and a catechism of mythology.[37]

If Hudson's Bay Company fathers gave their mixed-blood daughters much education, it tended to be a genteel one to fit them for the drawing room.[38] Certainly, the education of the Ermatinger daughters contained such elements. In 1824, Frederick paid a bill of 15/– for six riding lessons for "Miss Armintinger [sic]." Bills in 1833 for Anna Maria and Jane included pianoforte and drawing lessons at the Montreal Academy of Fine Arts. That year, Jane also had lessons in "English, sewing, etc.," plus music and drawing. These were obviously subjects considered suitable for a genteel woman of the period. But taken alone, they probably misrepresent the education Charles gave his daughters. Books bought for Jane and Anna Maria included a German history book, two grammars, a dictionary, and an ancient history (it is not clear whether the grammars were in German or English). In 1835, a Mrs Felton was providing board and tuition for "the Misses Ermatinger." She billed £25/–/– plus the cost of "two theme books," one French phraseology, and two geography. The last bill from Mrs Felton, for Jane in 1837, included the cost of another ancient history book.[39]

The family estate papers include Frances' exercise book with "Fanny" scribbled on the inside cover plus some neat figures. Among many "Exercises in Parsing" was this sentence: "Many men mistake the love for the practice of virtue and are not so much good men as the friends of goodness." Frances, using abbreviations, then parsed each word:

> *Many*: Adjective positive state belonging to sub[ject] men
> *men*: Com[plex] sub[ject] mas[culine] gen[der] plu[ral] num[ber] nom[inative] case.
> *mistake*: 3 pers[on] plu[perfect] pres[ent] of the verb to mistake agreeing with the nom[inative] men
> *the*: definite article
> *love*: Com[plex] sub[ject] neu[ter] gen[der] sin[gular] num[ber] obj[ective] case gov[erned] by the act[ive] verb mistake

Grammar, of course, also taught virtue and prudence. The sixty-four handwritten pages of Fanny's parsing contained such gems as "Think not, when all your scanty stores offered at once upon the sparing board is spread, think not when worn the homely robe appears, while the howling tempest bears on the roof, what shall this feeble life sustain farther, and what again shall clothe these shivering limbs."[40] These worthy sentiments she parsed, word by word.

The moral code and social etiquette that Charles expected of his children comes through in two letters. The first he wrote to his nephew Edward, who was working with the Hudson's Bay Company, but its message would undoubtedly apply to his own sons:

> [Your welfare] can only be attainable by a most strict attention and obedience [to your superior]. I do not mean that kind of unnecessary servility used by many and which you may frequently meet in the country, but a strict sense of duty you owe him as being one of the principals of your employers, not forgetting a close attention to his private character and making every allowance of any little deficiency, at least they should never

be the subject of complaint, not even to your most intimate friends particularly if they do not personally regard you, this I merely hint to you to put you on your guard. Many young men have inadvertently fallen into this error, to their great disparagement.[41]

In 1832 the fourteen-year-old Anna Maria, known as Anne, was visiting her married sister, Jemima, in York. Their father wrote to Jemima, "I was happy to hear that Anne was attentive to her learning and obedient to you and her aunt. She by this attention will fully reap the benefits of your kindness towards her." He asked Jemima to notify him of any expenses Anna Maria incurred, adding, "I do not think there can be any impropriety in her going out when invited." She might not always get such opportunities, which might give her "some idea of the propriety of good manners when absent from home and in company."[42]

For the Ermatinger boys and girls the difference between the wild man's land and the world of Virgil, between life in the Sault stone house and life in a Montreal boarding school or even their uncle Frederick's home, must have come as a near traumatic shock. Perhaps the culture shock had some influence on the early deaths of Anne and George, both of whom died in Montreal in their teens from unstated causes. As discussed in the Introduction, a high proportion of the younger children transplanted from the Upper Country to Montreal died early. Unlike some fur trade parents, however, Charles Sr showed no signs of stressing his children by forcing them to deny their Indian heritage. The rest of the Ermatinger family seem to have adapted to their new urban conditions relatively quickly.

Farmer and Cavalryman

On retiring from Sault Ste Marie to Longue Pointe in 1828, Charles Oakes made his eldest son, Charles Jr, manager of the store. Young Charles ran it for some months. By this time, the closure of the American frontier and the long-past shift of the fur trade centre further west must have restricted Charles mainly to a shopkeeping business, a far cry from the roving expeditions of earlier years to visit his father's Ojibwa clients. Storekeeping was certainly not one of the activities prized by Ojibwa men, however vital a role it played in the life of Charles' paternal grandfather, Lawrence. Charles was also probably lonely without his parents and noisy siblings. Whatever the reason, he closed down the store, abandoned the old stone house, and joined his family in Montreal later that year.[1]

MONTREAL

The future must have seemed exciting for Charles and his siblings when they moved to the city. The Longue Pointe farm lay just five kilometres east of Montreal, which had a population of more than 27,000. Cultural and social activities including theatre, sports, churches, and patriotic societies were booming in the town that commercially dominated the two Canadas. The family expected to have an active social life. However, the most exciting thing mentioned in family correspondence during the winter of 1831 was a bazaar. "Montreal has not been so gay this winter," wrote Jemima, in York, to her cousin Edward. "As usual they had a bazaar which has given nearly £700."[2]

The fall of 1831 did see another social event. Charles Jr wrote to Edward saying he would describe the most important and striking coincidence ever recorded in the annals of history. Charles Sr was building a pigsty, young Charles wrote, large enough to contain twenty pigs. He continued, "Maria has got married. If you had been here to have seen the sweet sister go by with ten other carriages in the gay trappings of a bridal day the very horses snort to the air with scorn [when] passing by the house as if to say how lived the base deceiver who slited our happy bride." Would she have married without the pigsty being built? "Undoubted not. She required something corresponding the event whence to date her unexpected change."[3]

Five years earlier in 1826, Charles' aunt Anna Maria, by then in her sixties, and George Garrett, a surgeon with the 70th Regiment of Foot, had signed a marriage agreement. But apparently the marriage did not take place until 1831. Why not? What did the pigsty have to do with anything? Why did the horses "snort the air with scorn" as the bridal party passed by? Who was the base deceiver? It is a minor historical mystery. Sadly, the bride did not have many years of marriage. She died in 1836.[4]

In 1832, a gloomy Charles Jr wrote his cousin Edward, who, it appears, had recently stayed with them, that they all enjoyed good health but visitors seldom interrupted the harmony and peace of the house: "Judge if the charm of the country can overbalance such privations, particularly in winter." They greatly missed Edward's agreeable society and the sweet sound of his flute and violin: "Indeed, scarcely a person to speak to. Pitiable state you must allow. I must not dwell too long on this dull subject the bare mention of it makes me fancy my room filling with the blue vapours."[5]

Slowly, the family's social life began to improve. Like his uncle and father before him, Charles Jr continued to support the Montreal Library. He subscribed to the Montreal Music Society's four-month season for 1833. He was a member of the German Society and attended the society's dinner in 1836. He also became an active member of the Montreal Turf Club, remaining so for most of his life.[6] In 1841 a steeplechase started at the Ermatingers' farm at Longue Pointe, but "neither the weather nor the condition of the ground were favourable, and there were several spills."[7] In 1848, Charles was elected to the club's Committee to Collect Transient Subscriptions.[8]

Charles Jr's Ideal Woman

The attitudes of the male Ermatingers towards women ran the gamut. Grandfather Lawrence and father Charles Oakes seemed to have been faithful to, happy enough with, and – judging from the number of children – sexually active with their wives. Brother James was married for nearly fifty years but had no children. Cousin Edward, who was a strict and religious man, was miserable with though probably faithful to his wife, Axie.[9] They had several children. Edward's brother, Frank, showed little but contempt for the Indian women in his life and indifference to all of his children but the last.

Unlike his relatives, Charles Jr was a hopelessly romantic bachelor. When he was thirty years old he wrote to Edward,

> I begin to think the life of single blessedness not to mean what the words would seem to imply. Quite the reverse. Would not even a prison appear a paradise? How sweet woman is to be with, one whom you love with true affection, and mingle your soul with hers in the enjoyment of each other. The thought is bewitching. Oh could I but find one such

as my imagination pictures. Delusive thought. Why distract one with images never to be realized. Such a being seldom exists or only in the wild vision of the romantic and poet. I scarcely know what I have been writing all this while. I dare not look it over with the fear it may induce me to consign these sheets to the flames. But such has been the train of my reasonings since I seated myself to write.

It was, indeed, a delusive thought. Charles never would find one such as his imagination pictured. But he asked Edward to stop being a stoic and admit the truth about love: "The God of Nature has implanted it in the breast of all living beings. Why then are we living in perpetual warfare with passions, the gifts from above? Do not mistake my meaning and think I extend my views beyond the pale of morality. I am certain you will do me the justice to think differently."[10]

Charles Jr Becomes Family Head

At the time of Charles Sr's death in 1833, his estate journal showed 102 shares in the Bank of Montreal worth £5,100 with a dividend of £510, plus ten shares in the Quebec Fire Assurance Co.[11] It is not known what other monies belonged to the estate, though in addition to their residence, the family owned at least four farms on the Island of Montreal, along the south shore. Charles Jr inherited the houses and lands at Sault Ste Marie, plus land on the south side of the St Lawrence River opposite Longue Pointe. Charlotte inherited £1,000, William £1,500, and James £1,500. The daughters received various farms. All the children, except Jemima and Frances who had property from their uncle Frederick, shared the residue of the estate.[12]

Despite the apparent wealth, all was not well following Charles Sr's death. After a visit to Edward in St Thomas, Upper Canada, in 1833, Charles wrote congratulating his cousin on his marriage. (He also sent two dollars that he owed Edward's driver for his trip from London to Port Stanley. He had known the man owed money to Edward, so Charles had decided to withhold the fare and pay it to his cousin.) The letter, written just weeks after Charles assumed his inheritance, says, "I find it necessary to limit my expenses within my means. I therefore have to request you to discontinue my subscription to the St Thomas Journal ... The H.B. [Hudson's Bay Company] canoes have arrived at Lachine a few days ago. I have not heard any news yet from that quarter."[13] The reference to the "H.B. canoes" shows that Charles was still involved in the Upper Country trade, no doubt through his Ojibwa relatives.

Charles was having, at best, a cash flow problem. Available records show that he was not the manager his father was. Charles Sr had kept careful accounts on all the financial aspects of his business, his farms, and his family. Accounts for the various farms were kept in an estate book until 1833, the year that he died. But for 1834, this estate book has only a couple of entries.

Charles Jr seems to have kept no systematic accounts. All that remains is his "blotter book" listing various household expenses:

Self: 55 lbs beef; buttons & red ink; other household goods.

A. Ermatinger: prayer book.

Mother: snuff.

James Ermatinger: cash for gloves.

Miss J. A. Ermatinger: Cash for Fire Assurance Company on the house and furniture.

A. Ermatinger: cash for woman serving for her. (Same for Jane.)

A & I Ermatinger: Cash.

Mother: 4 yards of ribbon.

Mother: Cash.

James Ermatinger: cash.

Mother: Cash for pins.[14]

Charles' ignorance of, and perhaps contempt for, European-style bookkeeping was consistent with the culture of his Ojibwa mother. The traditions set by his grandfather and father with their laborious and detailed accounting apparently had little influence on him.

Money constantly dripped away. Records do not show what came in, but by 1837 Charles was clearly in financial difficulties. A constant and dismal succession of notes fell due. He owed money to City Bank (four notes due in July, October, and December totalling £350); the People's Bank (four notes due in March, June, and July totalling £209); and the Bank of Montreal (four notes due in May, July, and September totalling £755). The same year, he also signed many notes to merchants: Gibb & Co. (£87/1/–); Alexis Pinet (three notes totalling £141/10/–); S.T. Francis, MD (£50); [illegible] (£22/5/9); A. Ferguson (£39); George McKenzie (£220); Louis Compte (£66/14/11); John Atkinson (£50); Dr Arnoldi (£32/15/–); and Cunningham and Buchan (£49/14/6).[15]

There may be some duplication in this list, since banks sometimes bought up the notes of merchants. But Charles owed over £2,000 to banks and merchants at various times during the year. One merchant protested nonpayment of £66/14/11 in November 1837. Others too had to wait for their money. In January 1838, Charles paid his tailor a bill for repairs to a suit William had bought in 1836, plus two years' interest, and for a suit bought for James, plus interest for one year and three months. In 1838, James Carswell sold to Seraphino Geraldi a note from Charles for goods Carswell had sold and delivered to him; Carswell had already instituted action against Charles for £63/12/11 plus 19/6 interest and £8/7/6 costs. Bills were also coming in from Europe, where William had gone to fight in Spain with the British Legion: four in 1837-38 totalling £134.[16]

Despite these obligations, Charles managed to fit in some travelling. In August 1833, he spent seven days in Detroit; in June 1834 and again in January 1836 he stayed five days in the American Hotel, New York. He also won some financial battles. With Anna Maria and Jane, he successfully sued Patrick Quinn for £71/16/5¼ for rent and damage to a farm Quinn had rented from them. They won various smaller sums as well, plus the return of cattle and other goods. And Charles found £2,400 for the final payment on a series of purchases of shares in the Bank of Montreal.[17]

Charles also engaged in a confusing series of property transactions. Before his death Charles Sr had apparently paid £1,000 to build a house in Montreal. Three years later, Charles Jr took out insurance on a stone house on Notre Dame Street occupied by Messrs Meade & Co. He renewed the insurance in 1835. About 1837 Charles was trying to sell "a lot of sand" in the Scarborough area of Upper Canada. In 1834, a John Cliff billed Charles £3/15/–, "To a set of plans and specifications for a country house." Charles must have changed his mind, because in 1837 Frances Dufresne billed him £391/18/7 for cut stone and mason work to the Longue Pointe house.[18] In fact he continued to make his base there at least until his mother died in 1850.

In the Upper Country, the Ermatinger efforts to get compensation from the US government for lost property in the American Sault Ste Marie and Drummond Island dragged on for years. In 1829, Charles Jr appointed a Montreal advocate to take action against the American government for compensation.[19] But it was not until 1847, some fourteen years after the death of Charles Sr, that the Americans paid full compensation to his heirs.[20]

Meanwhile, on the Canadian side, the old stone house stood empty from 1828 to 1833. In that year, a young Church of England missionary lived and preached in the house. Charles Jr petitioned the government for a deed in 1835, but failed, like his father previously.[21] The situation would remain cloudy for another fifteen years. Meanwhile, the missionary left the house in 1842, and another tenant occupied it until 1844. The Hudson's Bay Company representative in Sault Ste Marie, John Ballenden, then wrote Charles that unless considerable repairs were made to the roof and gutters, the walls would soon fall in. Cracks in the walls and leaks in the roof meant not one habitable room in the house. The sad litany continued: the kitchen had burned down, one of the outbuildings had fallen down the previous summer, and the other probably would in the spring. Even $4,000 would not be enough to restore the house.[22] The old stone house where the Ermatingers had lavishly entertained seemed to be crumbling away.

John Ballenden's letter would have made dismal reading for Charles, and all the bookkeeping, real estate and farming activities on Montreal island must have been irksome for him. Fortunately, more glorious activities distracted him.

THE LIBERATOR

"General" James H. Dickson (also known as the Liberator, or Montezuma II), often wore a scarlet uniform with gold braid; sometimes he wore a false beard.

This apparel suited a magnificent dream. Possibly the son of a Sioux woman by an English fur trader, Robert Dickson, the Liberator decided in 1836 to travel from Montreal to Red River, collecting an army of Indians and Métis on the way. His objectives are obscure. In one account, he intended to fight with the Texans for their liberation from Mexico; in another, he intended to move down to California and there liberate the Native peoples of North America by establishing an Indian kingdom. The latter seems the more likely version. An expedition member, Martin McLeod, wrote that Dickson seemed somewhat visionary in his views: "God only knows where and when it may end. Dickson seems quite sanguine of success." He added, "No matter. I wish to go north and westward, and will embrace the opportunity, but must look before I leap."[23] McLeod, the only expedition member to have no Indian blood, joined it for personal not ideological reasons.

In Montreal, the Liberator recruited a party of about thirty men, mainly sons of fur traders and their Indian wives. Governor Simpson of the Hudson's Bay Company described them as "wild thoughtless young men of good education and daring character, half breed sons of gentlemen lately and now engaged in the fur trade."[24] At least some of that description fits Charles. A file in Library and Archives Canada in Ottawa contains a certificate with a scroll that reads:

The LIBERATOR OF THE INDIAN NATIONS
[sketch of an eagle on a mountaintop]

To all who shall see these presents greeting: Know ye that reposing special trust and confidence in the patriotism, valor, fidelity and abilities of Charles Ermatinger, I have nominated and do appoint him Secretary of Foreign Affairs and Relations in the service of the LIBERATOR. to rank as such from the first day of July, 1836. He is therefore carefully and diligently to discharge the duty of Secretary of Foreign Affairs and Relations, by doing and performing all manner of things there unto belonging.

And I do strictly charge and require all Officers and Soldiers under his command to be obedient to his orders as Secretary of Foreign Affairs and Relations. And he is to observe and follow such orders and directions from time to time as he shall receive from me, the LIBERATOR, according to the rules and discipline of war. This commission to continue in force during the pleasure of me, the LIBERATOR.

Given under my hand at New York, this first day of July in the year of our Lord, one thousand eight hundred and thirty-six.

By the LIBERATOR: James H. Dickson
Witnessed: John George McKenzie, Secretary of War.

[coat of arms inscribed "Fortes fortuna juvat"][25]

Later in July, the Liberator arrived in Montreal. The certificate appointing Charles was signed in New York before Dickson's arrival in Montreal, so presumably Charles had been in touch with him in June or earlier. When the Liberator and his army left Montreal in late July, however, Charles was not with them. He had other things on his mind. The Montreal *Gazette* wrote that some young Montrealers had been "induced by flattering and tempting offers of future rank and fortune to leave the quiet and steady routine of duty of a Canadian life, and to proceed to Texas as volunteers against the Mexicans." The paper saw little hope for the Mexicans in their fight against the Texans. Two months later, the *Gazette* described the Dickson supporters as "fired with military ardour, and willing to 'mortalise' themselves in the field of Mars." They were headed for Texas via Buffalo, "where they displayed the brilliant uniforms." According to a story reprinted from a Detroit paper, they were arrested somewhere on the St Clair River as pirates but later released.[26]

The Dickson party passed through Buffalo in August 1836, leaving there by boat for Red River. Martin McLeod wrote on 11 September at Sault Ste Marie that during their stay in the village, they were treated with great kindness by Mr. Ermatinger and family. "Mr E. is an old Indian trader," he wrote. This was George Ermatinger, Charles Sr's brother.[27] At this time, George wrote to his son James on the River Onatonagon, Michigan, describing Dickson's party as a fine set of gentlemen: "Charles and [illegible] are appointed Major Generals. Charles will be here early in the spring to join General Dickson. I will go likewise. Doctor Bell says your mother's brother and Thomas W. are to be here in the spring with about four hundred Indians." Perhaps Dickson worked his charms most effectively on George's wife, Catherine. She asked her son to assist General Dickson "all in your power as they are a glorious cause for the good of mankind at large." They were fine young men, she thought: "If he wants anything, dear James, let him have it for our sakes. You will never loose [sic] by the good attention and kindness you may show them all."[28]

In the event, neither Charles nor any other Ermatinger joined the expedition, which was just as well. On leaving the Sault, the "army" was shipwrecked on Lake Superior, then made a long painful journey to Red River. Some members were lost or died of starvation and cold; others just left the expedition. At Red River the authorities, fearing some sort of Métis restlessness, arrested the Liberator. The grand new Indian kingdom would never be. After a period at Red River where he was generally feted as a character, General Dickson disappeared from history.[29]

Charles' attraction to the romantic idea of somehow restoring the rights of his mother's people is quite consistent with his romanticism about women. But by 1836 it was clear that principles Charles had inherited from his father's people also needed defending.

CHARLES AND THE LOWER CANADA REBELLION

In 1831, reporting on a successful harvest, Charles wrote, "I speak of our farm only, the crops elsewhere seem very poor."[30] Indeed, farming problems and overpopulation were causing economic distress throughout the St Lawrence valley. Immigration exacerbated hostility between anglophone Loyalists and francophone Patriotes, the latter wanting more political power through constitutional reforms, the former resisting such change. The threat of rebellion and counter-rebellion hung over the St Lawrence valley.

Quebec anglophones, Charles among them, wanted no constitutional reforms. On 21 December 1835, the Montreal *Gazette* carried a report of a meeting called to form the British Rifle Corps. This corps of 800 volunteers would help preserve the connection between Great Britain and Lower Canada, and maintain unimpaired the rights and privileges given them by the Constitution. Catholics saw the corps as an Orange plot against their religion. *The Vindicator* said that the British Rifle Corps "assumed the sacred garb of charity to conceal their dark and real designs." The paper referred to the hypocrites in the St Andrew's, St George's, and German Societies, whose sole aim was political power, and threatened to fight them.[31] Charles was a member of the German Society.

The new governor general, Lord Gosford, at first conciliatory to the Canadiens, declared the volunteer corps to be "illegal and unconstitutional" and forced its dissolution. He said it was not warranted as no rights were endangered, and the corps would be harmful to public tranquility.[32] A few weeks later, the *Gazette* reported on a second meeting of the proposed British Rifle Corps. There, C.O. Ermatinger moved, and J. M'Gillis seconded: "Resolved, 1: That this meeting considers it its duty to express its dissent from the opinion of His Excellency." The connection between colony and the mother country, and Englishmen's rights and privileges as British subjects, were indeed, they said, in danger from French Canadian activities.[33] Charles' grandfather Lawrence would have been proud of this defiance of the governor in defence of an Englishman's rights. Still, the British Rifle Corps came to naught.

Instead, Charles joined the Royal Montreal Cavalry. This volunteer unit had been formed during the War of 1812 and continued on in a small way afterwards. Members supplied their own horses, uniforms, and arms, and received no pay for their activities. These were mainly ceremonial, though occasionally the unit helped maintain law and order in Montreal. In the summer of 1837, as Patriote restlessness increased, the Royal Montreal Cavalry officially became a unit in the British Canadian forces. With this elevation to regular militia status, its men began receiving pay. Charles, a lieutenant in the unit, now had a paying job.

In early November, a group of Patriotes led by Pierre-Paul Demarais and Dr Joseph-François Davignon of St Jean fired a cannon at a detachment of British troops at St Athanase. They then scattered. Governor General

Gosford ordered the arrest of twenty-six leading Patriotes, including the two leaders in the cannon affair. On the night of 16 November, Charles and a sixteen-man cavalry unit formed an escort for a Constable Malo with orders to arrest the leaders.[34] The troop left Longueuil, on the south shore of the St Lawrence opposite Montreal, for St Jean, about forty kilometres away. They were armed only with pistols rather than with the troopers' normal carbines. Two companies of the 32nd Regiment stayed at Longueuil under orders to maintain communication with the cavalry.

The previous day a snowstorm had lashed the area. More bad weather and flooded roads slowed the advance, and Charles and his troop did not arrive at St Jean until a little before three o'clock in the morning. The village lay asleep. The troopers broke open the doors of the homes of the accused men and seized them in their beds. They placed the two captives in a wagon, handcuffed, tied to the side of the cart; and partially hidden under hay. Charles decided to return to Longueuil via Chambly, a route some twenty kilometres longer than the one they had arrived by. The troop stopped briefly at Chambly, where British troops were barracked, and moved the two prisoners into a covered wagon driven by Constable Malo.

Pro-Patriote writers later claimed that Charles chose the longer route through an intensely Patriote area so that sight of the shackled men would terrorize the local people. This seems doubtful. Much of the trip would have been in the darkness of a cold November morning, with little chance for people to see the chained prisoners, who were first hidden under hay, and then in a covered wagon (as if Charles, sensibly, did not want them to be seen). It seems more likely that travelling via Chambly offered a quicker, if longer, ride than the badly maintained road that had delayed the troop on its way to St Jean.

As Charles and his convoy approached Longueuil, a woman warned them that the Patriotes were massed ahead. Led by Bonaventure Viger, they had set up a roadblock about three kilometres from the town.[35] Lightly armed as his men were, Charles could have returned to Chambly for reinforcements. Overconfident, or disbelieving the woman, he continued on. Later the Loyalist paper, *Le Populaire*, would severely criticize this decision as rash.

Just what happened as the convoy approached the roadblock varies according to who wrote the account. A typical Patriote account claims that Viger cleverly hid about forty men behind hedges and in ditches. Viger jumped a fence and yelled orders to his imaginary battalions, convincing the cavalry that they were up against some 300 men. Only when the cavalry replied with shots did the Patriote leader order his own men to fire. In contrast, contemporary Loyalist versions have from 200 to 300 Patriotes lying in wait (Charles himself claimed 300). At eleven thirty in the morning, according to the *Gazette*, the cavalry reached the roadblock. Charles ordered a halt. The Patriotes fired. Only then, said the Loyalists, did Charles and his troop fire their revolvers before retreating.

Later an official government inquiry supplied more reliable information. Ten legible depositions by thirty-three Patriotes who took part in the ambush agree quite closely that the party numbered about 150 men. As the cavalry approached, Viger stood in front of his men and ordered a halt. The cavalry did halt for a moment, but then continued to advance. At that point, agreement ceases. Two depositions claim that the cavalry fired their pistols and then Viger ordered the counterfire. Three seem to imply the Patriotes fired first but make no mention of the cavalry firing at all. The other five depositions, including one signed by twenty men and another by six, say that the Patriotes opened fire, and then the cavalry responded with their pistols. Overall, the witnesses thus tend to confirm that the Patriotes did indeed fire first. Despite his rashness in not turning back to Chambly earlier, it seems hardly reasonable that Charles, with eighteen troopers armed only with revolvers, would have initiated an action against a large and quite well-protected body of men, about two-thirds of them armed with guns.

At any rate, they certainly exchanged shots. The affair was pretty much a rout for Charles and his men. Malo's horses reared up and overturned the wagon in the ditch, but the constable escaped. Charles, wounded in the face and shoulder with buckshot, fired his revolver at the ambushers. Then he and his cavalry, outnumbered and outgunned, were forced to quit the scene, while a wounded sergeant-major covered their escape. They scattered and returned to Longueuil by roundabout routes. Viger, now master of the terrain, freed Demarais and Davignon. Both sides suffered casualties. One account says that Viger took two balls, one grazing his leg, the other cutting off his little finger. Five troopers were wounded, plus Charles. Later, he had great praise for Sergeant-Major Sharpe, who had bravely covered the unit's retreat. In fierce fire, his conduct was "worthy of the character of a British soldier, and merits from you the strongest recommendation and the favourable consideration of His Majesty's govt."[36]

Next day's events bore out criticisms of the authorities that Charles' unit had been too small and too lightly armed to do the job. Four fully armed companies of the Royal Regiment under Colonel Wetherall, with two field pieces, crossed the St Lawrence. About twenty members of the Royal Montreal Cavalry, under the command of Captain David, accompanied the force. Charles, despite his wounds, rode with them. At the site of the ambush, the army found the overturned wagon and a dead horse.[37]

A charge against the cavalry unit of deliberate cruelty to the prisoners is difficult to assess. According to Davignon, they were shackled and tied to one another and to the sides of the cart. Despite the bitter cold, they were left kneeling in the cart outside the Hotel de Bunker at Chambly while the troopers allegedly bolstered their courage inside with liquor. Malo also allegedly threatened to shoot the prisoners if their friends attempted a rescue.

In the event, claimed Davignon, the troopers tried to do just that, riddling the canvas of the cart with balls before fleeing.

Without doubt, the two men were shackled and tied. But a few days earlier, they had headed a group of Patriotes and fired a cannon at British troops. So it is not very surprising that their captors treated them none too gently. The charge that the troopers tried to kill two bound and helpless men is more serious. If the canvas of the cart was, as alleged, riddled with holes, at least some of those holes may have come from friendly fire. With 150 excited men, unused to battle, firing muskets and shotguns at eighteen troopers who were returning their fire with revolvers, shots from both sides probably pierced the canvas. The prisoners could not have seen who fired the shots because they were lying face down on the cart's floor.[38]

The incident earned Charles mention in a romantic novel of the rebellion by Ernest Choquette. After the Longueuil incident, Choquette shows Patriotes Viger, Lambert, and others in a house, planning their next action. Someone says it would be very difficult to put fear into the English. At that, Viger jumps up and shouts furiously, "Put fear into the English! Damnation! Go and ask Ermatinger if he didn't flee on his great English paws."[39]

Whatever the truth of the various reports, the army judged that Charles had performed well enough to be promoted to captain.[40] To Governor General Lord Gosford, the Longueuil affair was something of a joke, "inferior," he apparently said, "to many a scuffle he himself had witnessed at an Irish fair."[41] Nevertheless, it was the opening shot in a more serious clash.

After this incident, the Royal Montreal Cavalry was stationed at St Hilaire, about forty kilometres east of Montreal. For the next few days, Loyalist and Patriote forces regrouped, occasionally exchanging shots. The weather was a miserable mix of rain and sleet, yielding icy roads. On the night of 20 November, Charles and Trooper John Lovell patrolled to the environs of St Charles, meeting no resistance. They did see a few insurgents in high spirits, shouting and singing, playing cards and smoking.[42]

After a small Patriote victory at St Denis on 25 November and a crushing defeat at St Charles two days later, rebel activity centered mainly on St Eustache in the Lake of Two Mountains area, west of Montreal. The British commander, Sir John Colborne, sent units of the Royal Montreal Cavalry, one commanded by Charles, to St Martin on Île Jésus. They were to reconnoitre prior to the arrival of the main force. Then on 13 December, two brigades of regulars and volunteers with artillery left Montreal for St Eustache, St Benoit, and surrounding areas. A detachment of the Royal Montreal Cavalry under Charles joined the second brigade. Charles' job was to protect a key bridge and to maintain communications with headquarters. The detachment played a role in the fighting, but no further reference to Charles himself has been found.[43]

St Eustache finished the rebellion for the moment. The Montreal Cavalry spent the next year patrolling the still restless countryside. Captain Walter Jones was senior captain, while Charles captained one of the two troops.[44] In November 1838 the rebellion broke out again but was easily put down. The army received orders to disarm the rebels and punish them for their treason. Certainly, the Patriotes had committed some barbarous acts. They captured then brutally murdered a young British officer, Lieutenant George Weir. And after a mock trial they executed Joseph Chartrand, a Loyalist and alleged spy. With their victory, however, the Loyalists on orders from above hurled a terrible vengeance at the Patriotes and their families by looting and burning their homes and businesses.

Charles and fellow officer Captain Sydney Bellingham received orders to destroy the house and store of a rebel. When they arrived they found the store full of goods, but only the wife and her baby in a cradle were at home. Reluctant to torch the premises, Charles returned and reported to General Macdonell. Macdonell told him, "Do your duty there!" Charles and Bellingham returned and did their duty: they burned the house and left mother and baby in the snow outside.[45] Whatever the Patriote provocation, this affair did no honour to the reluctant Charles, and even less to his enthusiastic British commander.

CHARLES AND GEORGE ERMATINGER'S FAMILY

Financial problems continued to plague Charles. His father's will had made him trustee for legacies to his uncle George from Frederick William, George's brother (£1,000), and from his aunt, Mrs Edward Gray (£1,000).[46] The interest was to go to George during his lifetime, the principal to his children on his death. In 1837 George wrote from the Sault asking for his annuity payment of $400. A year later, someone wrote on the back of George's letter, "Protested for non-payment, January 14, 1838."[47]

George died in 1841. Two years later an official of the American Fur Company in New York wrote to the firm's representative in American Sault Ste Marie that the suit of the "heirs of Mr. Ermatinger," presumably George, had finally been closed. The letter included a statement of account received from a firm of Montreal lawyers, plus the balance of $4,499.02 after expenses.[48] It seems likely that the American Ermatingers had successfully sued the Canadian family for the legacy protested for nonpayment in 1838.

Charles and his uncle George had had contact during the James Dickson affair, but the 1842 suit may have alienated the two families. Indeed, George and Charles Sr do not appear to have been close (see Appendix C). In 1968 Hugh MacMillan of the Ontario Department of Public Records interviewed Miss Annie Ermatinger, George's great-granddaughter, and Mrs Kathryn Ermatinger Hockenbrock, a cousin of Annie's, at Jim Falls, Wisconsin.[49] MacMillan asked Annie if she ever remembered hearing her father talk about the Canadian family. "No," said Annie, "I doubt I ever heard him say anything." To which Mrs Hockenbrock added, "He probably never saw any of them." The two branches of the family seem to have lost all contact.

THE POST-REBELLION YEARS

After the rebellion, in April 1839, the government disbanded many militia units, but the Royal Montreal Cavalry received orders to remain on service for at least another year.[50] In fact, it was not disbanded until 1850, and Charles continued to command the 1st Troop. The unit patrolled the frontier catching army deserters trying to reach the United States. Their intimate knowledge of the area made Charles and his troop quite successful. Charles, for instance, got credit for apprehending at least three deserters from the 85th Regiment of Troopers in 1842, two from the 46th Regiment in 1845, and one from the 77th Regiment in 1849. In the last case, Charles asked if the trooper in his command who had captured the deserter could get the usual reward of $20. His superior officer recommended that the full amount go to Charles. That would give "encouragement to righteous zeal in the apprehension of deserters."[51] It is not clear how any money was shared between Charles and the trooper.

The activities of the Royal Montreal Cavalry, however, were not limited to frontier patrols. They were also occasionally used to control riots and maintain order in Montreal. For example, elections for the Lower Canada Assembly were set for January 1848, and as always during elections the authorities feared trouble, especially from the canal workers at Lachine and Beauharnois, where labour conditions were terrible. On the 11th, the provincial cavalry stationed at La Prairie on the south shore received orders to cross the St Lawrence with the least possible delay, then to move on and guard polling booths in Montreal. Captains Walter Jones and Charles Ermatinger commanded the force. Flooded roads around La Prairie gave them no choice but to cross on the newly formed and unstable ice of the river. That meant building a road capable of taking the horses across almost five kilometres of "extraordinarily rough" ice. A Mr Trudeau, who operated the ferry when the river was not frozen, reluctantly undertook the hazardous affair. He assigned twenty men to search for a possible crossing place.

Next day at dawn about forty more men began building a road across ice that had closed barely twelve hours before. They worked from both sides of the river to meet in the middle. The traverse completed, at ten that morning Trudeau began to lead the crossing, helped by five or six sleds and twenty men. Other men were stationed along the route to assist any horses that broke through the ice. The seventy troopers were dismounted and leading their animals, each at least twenty metres behind the man in front. Even so, a horse in Charles' troop was lost through broken ice. For more than three cold and dangerous hours, they struggled to cross. Trudeau said he would never again try such a perilous and difficult undertaking. But on the morning of the election, 12 January, the cavalry, some of the men severely frostbitten, were at their posts at the polling stations.[52]

Ten years of catching deserters, however profitable, broken by only occasional forays into troubled Montreal, must have seemed pretty dull stuff for Charles. In 1849 he found the chance to rekindle the romance of his youth by returning to Sault Ste Marie.

Ojibwa Chief and Montreal Police Officer

In 1849, friction between Ojibwa of the Sault Ste Marie area and whites was causing the government concern. Charles saw a chance to use his influence as an Ojibwa to calm the situation. To understand his role, however, we must go back twenty years or more. In his trading days at Sault Ste Marie, Charles Sr had worked mainly on the south side of Lake Superior with the Sandy Lake and Fond du Lac Ojibwa. Among them of course were Katawabidai and his sons. Another band of Ojibwa headed by Chief Shingwaukonse lived at Garden River, close to Sault Ste Marie. Shingwaukonse became famous for his pressure on church and government to recognize Aboriginal land rights. Through intermarriage, he formed an alliance with another nearby chief, Nebenagoching, whose extended family included many of the Métis inhabitants of the Sault and surrounding areas. In time many of these Métis became de facto members of the Ojibwa band organizations.

Shingwaukonse saw the value of creating a stable and prosperous community of Ojibwa and Métis at the Sault. Charles Sr's retirement had commercially weakened the Sandy Lake Ojibwa in the Sault area, and Shingwaukonse decided to fill the vacuum. In 1842, he petitioned the governor general for the right of the local Ojibwa to take over the Ermatinger property in Sault Ste Marie. Since the general land question had never been settled between the Ojibwa and the Canadian government, the Ermatingers were legally little more than squatters. Shingwaukonse's petition apparently failed.[1]

Five years later the Ermatingers themselves submitted their own petition to the governor general's office on behalf of "Charlotte Kattawabidé" (reproduced in Appendix B). An accompanying letter warned the government that problems between the Ojibwa and several mining companies trying to locate near Lake Superior could result in loss of life.[2] The accuracy of this prediction suggests that the Ermatingers were maintaining links with their Ojibwa relatives. Janet Chute's biography of Chief Shingwaukonse says that the Ermatingers had their uncle Mang'osid support their claims.[3]

Charlotte's petition starts with the claim that she was the hereditary head chief of the Ojibwa.[4] Her ancestors, she maintains, had possessed the territory surrounding Lake Superior for hunting and fishing since time immemorial. According to an ancient custom, she, as the eldest child of Katawabidai, "the late hereditary head Chief of the Chippeway," had inherited his rights and privileges. She was sending the governor general a flag, given by the French government to her "great great ancestor" Brave Heart, then chief of the tribe. As the insignia of that chieftainship, he had handed it down to her grandfather, "Boy-Os-wa" (Bi-aus-wah); thence to her father, Katawabidai; and then to herself.

The petition then takes a patriotic turn. In the years Charlotte had lived in Lower Canada, and after the death of her father, Ojibwa on the south shore of Superior had received compensation for ceding their land to the United States. Neither she nor her children could share in this without forswearing allegiance to Britain and becoming Americans. As loyal subjects taught "to love and respect the flag of the Country under which they have been born and protected," they could not do so, though they "suffered great loss" by forfeiting all claim for compensation.

The Ermatingers were here referring to an 1826 treaty between the American government and Chippewa (Ojibwa) of the American Sault Ste Marie area. Article 4 said the "half breeds" of the area should be given permanent property and fixed residences. The Chippewa wished this because of the affection they bore to the Métis, and the interest they felt in their welfare. A schedule listed the Métis who would receive land grants, including "the children of George Ermatinger, being of Shawnee extraction, two sections collectively."[5] Thus the American children or grandchildren of Charles Sr's brother seem to have acquired Indian land through the treaty.

Until this point Charlotte's petition has based its land claims on the rights of Charlotte and her family. Now, the argument broadens. She has learned "with infinite regret and pain" that the provincial government was, without her consent, disposing of lands on the Canadian shore of the lake, "the proper inheritance of herself and her children." The provincial government had not, she pointed out, gained the consent of the Ojibwa people for the disposal of their Canadian lands. In similar cases since the treaty of William Penn in 1682,[6] the imperial government had invariably acquired such land "by regular and recognized principles of justice," specifically, through conventions and treaties. The civilized world had sympathized with the tribes forcibly removed from their possessions by the US government, even though that was done under the cover of treaty or convention.

This was probably a reference to a treaty signed on 28 March 1836 at Washington, DC, negotiated by Henry Schoolcraft on behalf of the United States with the chiefs and delegates of the American Ottawa and Chippewa.[7] Oddly, Charles Jr had himself been a witness at the signing, presumably invited by his Ojibwa relatives and friends, not by the US government.

This treaty had not worked out well for the Indians, because it forced all Chippewa to go to Sandy Lake for their annuities. They usually had to wait weeks there in highly unsanitary conditions, which lead to epidemics of measles and dysentery. Many died, many were unpaid, and others were removed to reservations in the West.[8] Andrew Blackbird, a Native historian, later wrote that the Ojibwa and Ottawa had signed under compulsion while the US government had reneged on $140,000 in payments.[9]

At this point, Charlotte appealed directly to the governor general and his "high and well merited reputation for justice." She wanted him to appoint a commissioner with no interest in the mining companies to investigate the claims of herself and others interested. Unlike earlier petitions from Charles Sr, this one based itself on the territorial rights of the Ojibwa from "time immemorial." The petition in effect asserted that Charlotte and her family, as Ojibwa, should share in the territorial rights of the tribe, and hence deserved compensation.

Whatever the legal status of the claim, the Ermatingers were publicly stating that they were Ojibwa with the rights of Ojibwa. More, they asserted that Charlotte, as the eldest child of a hereditary chief, was therefore herself a chief. This is very doubtful. The Ojibwa had no tradition of women as civil chiefs and none of the ancestral chiefs whom Charlotte named were women.

The Indian Department received the petition on 8 May 1847, and the government turned it down on 24 June. In the interim, on 30 May, Charles had received a letter from Samuel Atkinson of Sault Ste Marie (see Appendix B). Mr Ballenden, Hudson's Bay Company representative at the Sault, had approached Atkinson with a number of questions about the Ermatingers. Was Charlotte's father an Ojibwa chief? A chief of the whole nation? Did he "adhere" to the United States? Where were Charles and Charlotte married? Where were the older children born? Atkinson felt that Ballenden "was if anything adverse" to the Ermatingers' claim.[10]

Two years after the Ermatingers received the denial of this petition, they sent off another in the name of a very indignant Charlotte. She said she must "earnestly protest against the opinions and proceedings of your Excellency's late advisors which, in good faith," had led him to reject the petition. The information received by the Executive Council on Matters of State "was entirely of an ex parte nature." She had not been not notified of the discussion, nor given the chance to testify herself and counteract the evidence. She attached Atkinson's letter and claimed that Ballenden had inquired about her under instructions from Sir George Simpson of the Hudson's Bay Company. The company was "most hostile to the interest" of the Ermatingers, and was itself making claims to parts of the same territory. Yet, she claimed, it had been unfairly appointed arbiter of the petitioner's rights.

Even worse, some Ojibwa had apparently agreed to a treaty with a commission on land rights. Charlotte objected to any arrangements in which she and her children were not consenting parties. Proposed members of any government commission should have no interest in either the mining companies or the Hudson's Bay Company. Rather the commission should consist of an officer of the Indian Department with two others "not in any way associated with the question," and should be instructed to investigate the Ermatingers' claim. Charlotte also wanted the June 1847 decision reversed by the council. But on 11 August 1849, the council committee saw no reason to do so. Although both petitions failed, by arguing for Aboriginal rights, the family had supported Shingwaukonse in his fight for those rights. Later, Shingwaukonse would, in traditional Ojibwa fashion, return that support.

THE MINING COMPANIES AND THE OJIBWA

The British and the Indians had never settled the land question on the east and north shores of Lake Huron from Penetanguishene to Sault Ste Marie, nor along the north shore of Lake Superior to Batchawana Bay. With the discovery of minerals, mining companies began work and demanded the area be opened up. Local Ojibwa protested. In the summer of 1849, a group took over the buildings and property of the Quebec Mining Company at Mica Bay, Lake Superior, almost 100 kilometres from Sault Ste Marie. At a grand council, the Ojibwa decided to burn the buildings should company personnel with troops land at the bay.

Meanwhile, the government had sent a detachment of the Royal Canadian Rifle Brigade from Toronto to Sault Ste Marie via Penetanguishene. Captain A.P. Cooper had orders to take back the Mica Bay property. Rumours spread that Red River Ojibwa had agreed to send 2,000 men to help the locals in any fight. Cooper commissioned a steamship to carry the detachment to Mica Bay, but violent storms drove it back to Sault Ste Marie, where the brigade wintered.[11] By now, however, the protesters at Mica Bay had returned to their homes.

In addition to troops, the government sent Commissioner William B. Robinson to negotiate treaties with the Ojibwa.[12] Canadian Ojibwa certainly knew of American Ojibwa dissatisfaction with the Washington Treaty of 1836, and perhaps that poisoned the atmosphere at the Sault. Of the Canadian negotiations, Robinson wrote that interested parties had advised the Indians "to insist on such extravagant terms that I felt it quite impossible to grant them." Some individuals tried hard, he said, to create dissatisfaction among the Ojibwa.[13] The discussions drew newspaper reporters from across Canada and the United States.

CHARLES GOES TO SAULT STE MARIE

When the government sent Robinson to treat with the Ojibwa, it also commissioned Charles to be magistrate at Sault Ste Marie "should his services be required."[14] In November 1849 Lieutenant-General Rowan ordered him to the Sault. The storm and heavy ice that had driven Captain Cooper's vessel back to Sault Ste Marie also caused Charles great difficulty. The early freeze-up prevented him from travelling by steamer to Sault Ste Marie, but the stormy weather made it "both inconvenient and dangerous" to cross the lakes by canoe. Instead, he made a 500 kilometre journey around Lake Huron by canoe and on foot in terrible weather. He said the party, which included his brother James, endured "great hardship and misery." He did not exaggerate: at one point, the ice on Lake Huron destroyed two canoes in which they were travelling. The Robinson Commission later paid £2/–/– to "Papasainse, un Sauvage" for the canoes.[15]

At this time, Charles later explained in a petition to the governor general for a position in the Indian Department, difficulties between the Ojibwa and the whites were "imminently endangering the peace." (This echoed the warning in the letter accompanying Charlotte's 1847 petition.) He had been "selected on this expedition from his known influence with the tribe of Indians aforesaid, by his knowledge of their language, and by his immediate connexion with them as one of their chiefs." He had remained with Cooper's expedition till it was withdrawn after restoring order, and "after the conclusion of a most advantageous and favourable treaty for his Majesty's government with the Indians."[16]

Not long after he arrived in Sault Ste Marie, Robinson wrote in his diary that he had seen "Mr. Ermatinger" and arranged with him to go to Garden River the next day to see the chiefs. Two days later at Garden River he explained why he had come and fixed the time of the formal meeting to be held there: "Immediately after issue of the presents I took their agreement in writing to that effect. They all expressed themselves satisfied and promised in presence of Captain Ermatinger and others to offer no opposition to mining operations," relying on the matter being settled at the appointed time.[17] Robinson seemed to recognize that Charles had connections to, and some influence with, the Garden River Ojibwa.

The Robinson-Huron and Robinson-Superior Treaties were signed with "the principal men of the OJIBEWA INDIANS, inhabiting and claiming the Eastern and Northern Shores of Lake Huron, from Penetanguishine to Sault Ste Marie, and thence to Batchewanaung Bay, on the Northern Shore of Lake Superior; together with the Islands in the said Lakes, opposite to the Shores thereof, and inland to the Height of land which separates the Territory covered by the charter of the Honorable Hudson Bay Company from Canada; as well as all unconceded lands within the limits of Canada West to which they have any just claim." The Ojibwa ceded this huge area for £4,000 cash, plus £1,100 in annual payments. They received "full and free privilege" to hunt and fish on unoccupied Crown lands and they retained reserves that they could sell only to the Crown.[18]

Commissioner Robinson later wrote that the "half-breeds" of the area might seek to be recognized by the government in future payments. To forestall this, the commissioner had told them he came to treat with the chiefs. When the chiefs received compensation they could give as much or as little to the Métis as they pleased. This, he said, silenced the critics. He also advised non-Indian residents at Sault Ste Marie who were anxious to obtain title to their land to memorialize the government in the usual way. He recommended that the government deal liberally with those who could show a fair claim.[19]

Following Robinson's recommendation, the name C.O. Ermatinger headed a list of fifty-five inhabitants of Sault Ste Marie petitioning the government. All but five or six, said the petition, were "of mixed Indian blood and had been born upon the soil." They had all held and cultivated the land where they had resided for years. Many had inherited the land from their Indian mothers, or had bought it from Métis. But the land they lived on had been ceded by the recent treaty. If the properties came on the market in the usual way, the petitioners would lack the means to buy them and would be dispossessed. They prayed that they "would not be disturbed in their possessions ... or in any way molested" and that the lands would be confirmed to them by a free grant from the Crown.[20]

Four leading Ojibwa chiefs backed this petition. The chiefs said that the petitioners had settled and cultivated the land for upwards of forty years "by and with the consent of ourselves and peoples." With scarcely an exception, all had married Indian women and had families with them. They were "the children of the sisters and the daughters of your Memorialists, thus having an inheritance in the country equal to our own, and bound to it by as strong and heart felt ties as we ourselves." The chiefs also asked that 100 acres of land be granted freely to Métis scattered throughout the ceded territories. Included among the Sault residents listed by the chiefs for a free grant is Charles Jr, with four acres of land. Curiously, the three witnesses to the chiefs' petition were C.O. Ermatinger, his brother James Ermatinger, and Allan MacDonnell.[21]

The four chiefs also signed another petition specifically regarding the Ermatingers. They had asked Robinson to provide in the treaty itself "for those of their kindred who had claims upon them for past benefits and services." By this, they had "hoped to repay, in some measure, the benefits and services received by them at the hands of the late Charles Oakes Ermatinger and his wife, Charlotte Maun-nun-once Caw-daw-be-tai." Because Robinson had not done this, the petition asked that each of the Ermatinger children be granted a mining location of their choice in the ceded land. An accompanying document referred to the Ermatinger family and "their uniform kindness while they were living amongst us."[22]

The chiefs signing the petitions of 1850 were Shingwaukonse himself, Nebenagoching (Joseph Sayers), Piabetassung, and Kabaosa (John). The last two were Shingwaukonse's sons-in-law. None seem to be direct relatives of Charlotte, but the phrases "for those of their kindred" and "children of the sisters" demonstrate the closeness of the relationship.

Following the treaty, the commissioner of Crown land, John Rolph, recommended a grant of fifty acres of land to each Métis applicant at a nominal rate of one shilling per acre, provided applicants settled there within the next year.[23] Presumably for that reason Charles did not apply, since he was now living permanently in Montreal. In July 1852, he leased the old stone house to Mr and Mrs D. Pim, who began a hotel business. The following year he quit deeded the place to the Pims for $3,000.[24] Not only were the Ermatingers no longer resident in the house but they were not, after all, granted mining rights.

The chiefs' petitions, made no doubt at the behest of Charles, show he was no disinterested observer at the treaty negotiations; rather, he had three conflicting interests. As magistrate, he had a duty to support Robinson in keeping the peace. As a claimant for land in Sault Ste Marie and as one seeking mining rights, he had self-interest. And as one of the "children of the sisters" and an Ojibwa "chief," he had a moral obligation towards his relatives and friends. Yet we find him later pleading for personal compensation from the government for helping in "the conclusion of *a most advantageous and favourable treaty for his Majesty's government* with the Indians." The italicized phrase strikes a disturbing note: just where did his loyalties lie?

Charles was not alone in this conflict of interest. Métis had long participated in treaty making between Indians and government. In doing so, they were protecting their own interests, as were the federal government and the Indian representatives involved in the negotiations.[25] All the Ermatingers' many petitions aimed at securing their Sault Ste Marie land, including the petitions based on their claim to be Ojibwa. This did not prove insincerity. In Ojibwa culture the exchange of material gifts was itself part of the bonding process. The chiefs' request that land and mining rights be granted the Ermatingers in repayment of earlier "kindness" confirms their kinship with the Ojibwa.

Nor can Charles be faulted for supporting the treaties. In 1850 they were not, on their face, unjust. In particular, one clause promised the Ojibwa that the government would in the future increase the annuity if the lands proved sufficiently productive to do so "without Government loss." The annuities were increased in 1878, bringing the annual grant from 96 cents to $4 per head, or a total of $14,000.[26] That $14,000 was little enough considering the billions of dollars in minerals later extracted from the lands, however, and it was the only adjustment ever made. The Crown used the phrase "without Government loss" to avoid future increases.

According to the recent Royal Commission on Aboriginal Peoples, Robinson cannot be blamed for failing to predict either the scale of resource development in the area, or that the Ojibwa would lose their rights under the treaties due to the actions of both private interests and government. Despite the treaties' clause guaranteeing access to Crown lands, the Ojibwa were "denied even the same terms of access as non-Aboriginal people." For instance, one Ojibwa, after staking a gold mining claim, found his stakes pulled out and replaced by those of a white man. The authorities took no corrective action. Government officials took control even of Aboriginal lands, the commission found, with a stewardship that was "abysmal" and employment policies that were mostly failures. Government violations of treaty rights forced increasing numbers of Aboriginal people onto public assistance. Neither Robinson nor Charles Ermatinger could have foreseen that the treaties, seemingly fair in 1850, would largely fail to protect Ojibwa rights against encroachment by both government and private enterprise. But fail they did.[27]

THE END OF THE ROYAL MONTREAL CAVALRY

Lord Elgin dissolved the Royal Montreal Cavalry on 30 April 1850, perhaps as a punishment to English Montreal for the support of some Tories for the Annexation Manifesto.[28] In general, the unit had an excellent record among military men. In 1841, James Alexander, a visiting British officer, said that the cavalry unit guarding the Canadian frontier under the command of Captains Jones, Sweeney, and Ermatinger was "an admirable cavalry force, the men of good character, perfectly acquainted with their duties, and the horses excellent." They had done much to keep the frontier peaceful and to stop desertion, in his view. A number of other military men were equal in their praise.[29] Perhaps the finest tribute came long after Charles' death. Fenian marauders were raiding the Eastern Townships from the United States (see Chapter 11), and Canadian residents were unhappy with the protection the army provided. The Montreal *Gazette* reported an experienced officer as saying, "If the three troops of frontier cavalry commanded by Captains Jones, Sweeney and Ermatinger had been in existence during this raid, they could have done more, and in shorter time, to rid the frontier of the plunderers than any other force of twice their numbers."[30]

The disbanding of the cavalry meant that when Charles returned to Montreal from Sault Ste Marie about September 1850, he found himself without a job. He requested a position with the Indian Department or any other open civil service position. He was "qualified in every particular," and he cited his services to the government in the 1837-38 rebellions. He also requested an allowance for acting as magistrate with the expedition to Sault Ste Marie, similar to that allowed Captain Ironside of the Indian Department while he was acting in the same capacity.[31] But Charles received no extra compensation for his sojourn in Sault Ste Marie since he had been receiving military pay. He did not get land rights for the Stone House. He did not get mining rights around Lake Superior. His military career ended, and moreover, he did not get a job with the Indian or any other government department.

Eventually, however, the Montreal municipal authorities appointed him chief of the city police. As such, he worked closely with his brother William, recently returned from fighting in Spain. They had the unenviable task of helping maintain law and order in a Montreal marked by a series of riots.

THE GAVAZZI RIOT

In June 1853 a religious firebrand and ex-Catholic priest named Alessandro Gavazzi visited Quebec and then Montreal, preaching against the Roman Catholic Church in general and the pope in particular. A consequent riot in Quebec led the Montreal authorities to deploy troops in a building a short distance from the Zion Church, where Gavazzi was to speak. Fifty police officers were to be stationed at the church with Charles in command. This is the first record found showing Charles as police chief. He characteristically gave the officers a pep talk beforehand: "We are called upon to perform a duty, and in the performance of that duty we shall not know Catholic, Protestant, Jew or any other religion." He wished that the duty should be "well performed."[32]

By six in the evening, Charles had forty-six policemen lined up outside the church door. Two more waited on the north side of the church, and two on the south side. Forty-five minutes later Gavazzi started speaking to a full church, as a crowd of Catholics gathered outside. Then another group of Catholics, "screeching and howling," as Charles described it, came from the Hay Market on Commissioners' Square. They seemed intent on breaking into the church. One man shouted, "Turn him out! Turn him out!" meaning Gavazzi. Another man shouted, "Now's our time. There are few of them. We can beat them." Charles grabbed him by the collar, and paving stones began flying. Charles got "a dreadful thrashing with sticks and stones" as he and his men tried to keep the crowd away from the church. Soon he was cut and bleeding from the face. Dazed and separated from his men in the fighting, Charles found himself in Juror Street, unsure how he got there. With the crowd moving away from the church, he headed for Dr MacDonnell's office. He arrived, said the doctor, "very much exhausted," badly cut on the lip and eyebrow, and suffering from a painful blow to the chest.[33]

Meanwhile, in the streets a tragedy unfolded. Shots exchanged between Catholics and Protestants caused the mayor to read the Riot Act. Almost immediately, on whose orders is not known, the troops fired on the crowd. In a few seconds of firing, ten bystanders died and about fifty were wounded. Hearing the shots, Charles left the doctor's and returned to his men, but the riot was over. They patrolled the streets until the crowds disappeared.[34]

The end of this story was not a happy one for Charles (William's involvement is discussed in Chapter 10). In the municipal elections of 1854, the mayor, scarred by the Gavazzi riot, did not stand. Montreal elected a new chief magistrate, Wolfred Nelson. Though of British origin, Nelson had joined the rebels of 1837-38 and fought with them at St Denis in their only major victory. After the rebellion, former enemies often became political allies and even personal friends, but Nelson had no reason to love Charles after his service in the Royal Montreal Cavalry. Perhaps for that reason, the new municipal council replaced Charles as chief of police.[35] Once again, he was out of a job.

THE DEATH OF CHARLES

In 1856, two years after being fired as chief of police, Charles made his last hunting trip to Sault Ste Marie. The following year on 9 January he died, aged fifty-five, at the home of his brother William. He had been ill for many weeks, possibly from heart disease after the fatigue of his hunting expedition.[36] Charles had inherited the Longue Pointe farm and £500 from his father, but nothing is known of his financial position at his death. Without children, he apparently left nothing to his siblings; perhaps he had little to leave.

"Though long retired from active service," said the Montreal *Transcript* when describing Charles's funeral, "in remembrance of what he was, and what he had done when called upon to buckle on his armour, his comrades resolved to give him the last and highest testimonial of their regard, and bury him with military honours." All the Montreal volunteer militia units paraded. The 2nd Company of the Volunteer Militia Rifles acted as firing party. They presented arms when the coffin, swathed in the British ensign, was carried from William's house by volunteer artillery gunners and laid on a gun carriage drawn by four black horses. The Rifle Band, followed by the fifty-man firing party, preceded the coffin. After the principal mourners came the cavalry dismounted, the artillery, the rifles, the Water Police, and finally the Montreal Police. The Rifle Band played the *Dead March in Saul* as the procession moved along densely crowded streets, past the drawn window blinds of the houses. At the Old Burying Ground, the cavalry, artillery, and firing party formed inside the gate. An estimated 10,000 people paid their respects, and several were injured by the crush in the crowded cemetery, some seriously. After the service, three volleys were fired over the coffin. A hearse then carried it for burial.[37]

In the French-language press, neither *La Minerve* nor *L'Avenir* had anything to say about the death of Charles. Perhaps that is explained by a sentence in the *Gazette*'s description of the funeral: "It is generally known that the deceased commanded one of the companies of the Royal Montreal Cavalry, so well and favorably known during the rebellion of 1837-38." The *Transcript* obituary said, "By all our citizens he was well known and much respected. To his friends, he was greatly endeared. His quiet, unassuming manner; his loyalty and courage so conspicuously displayed during the rebellion, and so badly rewarded by the government of the day; his services to this city while he held the high and responsible office of Chief of our Police – all this will cause his loss to be regretted not by his friends only, but the public at large.

He had no enemies, and that is saying much for a man who has lived long in this city and age."[38]

CHARLES JR, A SUMMING UP

Charles Jr was a likeable if sentimental man, "quiet, unostentatious and unassuming," according to the *Transcript*.[39] Honest in giving credit to his sergeant at Longueuil, Charles proved his courage to the point of rashness when he advanced on the Patriotes, when he crossed the newly frozen St Lawrence with his troop, when he fought his way through terrible weather to Sault Ste Marie, and when he battled rioters during the Gavazzi affair. Then again, the abandoning of mother and child during the aftermath of the rebellion did him no credit, despite his reluctance.

From the age of twenty-six onwards, Charles spent most of his life in middle-class Montreal. His adherence to Tory principles of loyalty to the Crown and his career in the cavalry and the police, often pitted against the French Canadians and the Catholics, are both consistent with his paternal heritage. In contrast, many of his qualities and actions are consistent with his maternal background and its traditions: his ability to speak Ojibwa, his years in Sault Ste Marie, his link with the Liberator, his refusal to hide his Ojibwa background, indeed, his public claim to be an Ojibwa chief, his personal relationships with his Ojibwa relatives and friends extending long after the family's departure from the Sault, and his lack of interest in farming and bookkeeping contrasted with his love of hunting trips back home and his readiness to go to battle. Yet at a time when racism against Indians was widespread, Charles retained the admiration and affection of English Montreal.

Soldier, Clerk, and a Last Adventure

In 1831, Charles Sr found a position in Molson and Davies' Montreal counting house for James, his youngest son, then sixteen. The boy would go there immediately on leaving school, wrote Jemima to cousin Edward, which had given them all great pleasure. She added, with an elder sister's regard for a younger brother, "He continues to be a steady and good little boy. I sincerely hope he will do well."[1]

Two years later, when James was eighteen, his father sent him to stay with Edward in St Thomas and to work in Edward's bank. Charles wrote that he had been very anxious about the boy and dissatisfied with his prospects at Molson and Davies. He hoped James would not only be useful to Edward but would learn to make a comfortable living for himself. His two years' work in Montreal should have prepared him to learn the business of the Upper Province. James, said his father, was "delighted with the country."[2]

In September, soon after writing those words, Charles died, and James must have returned home to visit his family. On 14 October Charles Jr wrote to Edward that the ague had left his young brother until yesterday, when "his imprudence in getting wet" had brought it on again.[3] James returned to Upper Canada, but nothing is known of what he did for the next four years. Events during the Upper Canada rebellion in 1837, however, proved that the "steady and good little boy" had grown up to be, at the age of twenty-two, a steady and good young captain of a cavalry unit in battle.

JAMES JOINS THE CAVALRY

By November 1837, political dissatisfaction strengthened by food shortages in Upper Canada was provoking rebellion against the "Family Compact," a clique of Tory officials who ran the province. The opposition Radicals resented provincial land-granting policies and the favouritism shown towards the Church of England. With British troops withdrawn and sent to combat the Lower Canada rebellion, the Radicals declared independence. In early December, fighting occurred in and around Toronto, and rebels were gathering in Oakland and near Brantford, Upper Canada West. Loyalist forces soon beat down the rebellion, but its leaders, William Lyon Mackenzie and Charles Duncombe, escaped to the United States. Allied with Americans who wished to "liberate" Canada from British rule, they took control of Navy Island in the Niagara River and set up a Republic of Upper Canada. Loyalist forces then readied to oppose any further rebel invasion along the frontier.

James, following the family's Tory tradition, took up arms against the rebels. In late 1837 he helped raise a troop of horse, the St Thomas Volunteer Cavalry, and went to Toronto to get sabres.[4] At first he was paymaster for the troop but was gazetted captain on 1 June 1838. The unit at that time consisted of one captain, one lieutenant, one cornet, three sergeants, three corporals, and fifty-four privates.[5]

FIGHTING ISLAND

In February 1838, some 300 to 500 "piratical rebels" from Detroit, headed by "General" Donald McLeod, entered British territory and took Fighting Island in the Detroit River. They were well provided with arms, ammunition, and provisions, reported Colonel John Maitland, who was in overall command of the local British forces. He believed more rebels, with cannon, would soon arrive. Maitland ordered Colonel H.D. Townsend and some regular troops, with an escort of the St Thomas Volunteer Cavalry, commanded by James, to reconnoitre the rebels' position. Townsend reported they could see the enemy in great numbers on the island, and ordered Captain Glasgow of the Royal Artillery to open fire with his nine-pounder. The precision and rapidity of the fire, he said, "much discomposed" the enemy. Despite fears of walking on the ice, the troops crossed to the island. The rebels fled, leaving behind a gun (discharged once only), rifles, muskets, pistols, swords, powder, and shot. Among the officers whom Townsend thanked for their "zealous co-operation" was Captain Ermatinger of the Volunteer Cavalry. Maitland, in his report, called this "a trifling affair" but said it would "check the proceedings of the lawless banditti."[6]

PELEE ISLAND

Following the Fighting Island affair, the St Thomas Cavalry patrolled the Lake Erie shore east from Amherstburg and escorted prisoners to London.[7] Then more excitement flared when 400 rebels and Americans crossed the ice and captured Pelee Island. The island, about 85 square kilometres and covered with woods, lay about twenty-five kilometres off the Canadian shore. Events moved swiftly.[8]

On 1 March, American invaders fired on British officers on the mainland. On 2 March, because it was a severe winter, a test of the ice showed that an attack on the island using artillery was feasible. The British forces numbered about 400, or about the same as the rebels. In the early afternoon of a clear, bright, and cold winter's day, the force moved downriver from Amherstburg to the lake. At eleven that night they rested.

Two hours later, the weather was still clear and cold. The force began crossing the ice from Pigeon Bay to Pelee Island. The cavalry and artillery had their horses, the infantry were in sleighs. Many of James' cavalry lacked proper, or even any, arms. Trooper Samuel Williams, for example, had no gun but would later be given one left behind by the retreating enemy. Trooper Roswell Tomlinson was armed with a pike on the end of a three-metre pole.

At sunrise the attackers were within a kilometre of the island when the enemy spotted them. The rebels were well equipped, bayonets glittering in the light of the rising sun. Colonel Maitland split his force in two. With one detachment of troops and the artillery, he followed the enemy as they retreated south into the bush, the only direction offering a chance of escape to the American shore. Heavy snowdrifts hampered the British pursuit. The second party of two companies of British regulars in sleighs, along with the cavalry, headed down the ice and around the island to where the invasion force had first come ashore, planning to cut off the enemy's escape. The cavalry saw the rebels in retreat, stretched in a four-kilometre line across a frozen marsh. James dismounted his men and sent messages to Colonel Maitland for reinforcements. "The Captain examined our arms, and told us we would have to fight," wrote Trooper Williams later. "He said he hoped every man who was spared to go home would not be ashamed of having been there." They waited until James gave up hope of reinforcements. He remounted the troop and led it towards the detachment of British regulars.

The enemy, led by the veteran Colonel Bradley, re-formed. Halfway down the island they emerged from a cedar thicket, intent on escaping to the American shore. The British sleighs withdrew, leaving their troops strung out across the ice "like fence posts." The rebels approached at a quick march in a solid column, then they too spread out in a line. About 400 strong, they far outnumbered the ninety British regulars and the twenty-one members of the St Thomas Cavalry. Enemy firing began "with great precision" and "for about 15 minutes the bullets flew sharp and thick." The British major in command of the regulars said "he did not see a greater test at Waterloo," wrote Trooper Tomlinson. In the skirmish, a shot in the forehead instantly killed Colonel Bradley.

The St Thomas Cavalry caught none of the enemy's volley, but by now they were approaching the invaders' flank at a gallop. They heard the call, "There comes the cavalry. Fire on them." Bullets whistled around them. They halted and returned the fire. Williams saw a trooper named Thomas Parish on his knees. At first Williams thought Parish was reloading, but James lifted the man onto his horse and held him there until another trooper came up to help. "He's a dead man," said James.

Then Captain Brown led a charge with fixed bayonets in the face of still heavy fire. When the infantry were within about thirty metres of the enemy, the latter retreated in disorder, "running like wild turkeys every way." They left five killed, "staining the snow for a quarter of a mile width with blood," wrote Williams.

James was ordered to chase the fleeing enemy. Flourishing his sword he led the troop until his horse's foot broke through the ice. He ordered his men to wheel to the right and to the left. They did so, knowing thin ice lay straight ahead. The enemy, however, crossed directly on the ice and escaped, though it was thought that many fell through and perished. The cavalry then followed a trail and captured some of the rebel wounded being tended at a nearby house. James and his troop, including the horses, had had no food for twenty-four hours. They got none until they reached the mainland about nine o'clock that night. Maitland reported killing eleven rebels and wounding forty-five, with eleven taken prisoner. Twenty-eight of his own men were wounded and two were killed, including Trooper Parish of James' unit.[9]

DISBANDING THE CAVALRY

In July 1838, fifty members of the St Thomas Cavalry joined other units in guarding against a possible rebel invasion of London from the west.[10] Not many of the old troopers came along with James, but newcomers took their places. They mainly carried dispatches and did garrison work. Despite all the rumours, no further invasion came and the St Thomas troop was disbanded in April 1840.[11] James remained captain throughout.

The lieutenant governor congratulated the force, including the gallant body of volunteers and militia, for their "prompt and effectual manner" in expelling the rebels from Fighting Island. He wished to thank the officers, specifically including Captain James Ermatinger of the St Thomas Cavalry, for "their gallant conduct in this affair." He was especially gratified that cordial and mutual feelings existed between Her Majesty's soldiers and the militia men of the province.[12] Again, grandfather Lawrence would have approved.

Of James, Trooper Tomlinson wrote, "He was a fine and noble officer, and a Briton at that, and was well and beloved by all of his men. They would go any length for him when needed." Commenting on Tomlinson's reminiscences, Trooper Williams added, "I can confirm all that Mr Tomlinson has said recently in your columns as to the gallantry of the captain and of my comrades-in-arms."[13]

James evidently reciprocated the affection expressed by Tomlinson and Williams. When the fighting was over, he requested that military headquarters grant his men an extra month's pay. After the Pelee Island affair, he explained, they had not been given sufficient time to return to their homes under pay. Furthermore, when called out again in July 1838 the troopers had "incurred considerable expense" buying clothes, arms, and so forth. They thought they would be required for more than six days, but were suddenly dismissed.[14]

Despite the plea by James, no record shows that the men got additional compensation.

THE INTERVENING YEARS: MARRIAGE

No clear records have been found of James' career in the fifteen years following disbandment of his troop. In this period, James seems to have spent his time between Montreal and Simcoe, Upper Canada. On 4 January 1841, James married Mary Isabella Fraser. Mary, born in 1825 in Greenoch, Scotland, was living in Charlotteville, near Simcoe.[15] She was the youngest daughter of the Rev. James Fraser, Anglican rector in Woodhouse. James was twenty-six, and Mary sixteen or seventeen. Both his application for a licence to marry and his marriage notice describe him as a "Gentleman" of "the City of Montreal."[16]

A decade later, the 1852 census listed him as aged thirty-six, an Episcopalian, officially residing in Simcoe, Norfolk County, with his wife. But while most males are listed by occupation, James is again described as "Gentleman." An annotation by the census taker says that despite their official residence in Simcoe, James and his wife were in Lower Canada at the time of the census.[17] In 1849 he had taken that harsh trip with his brother Charles to Sault Ste Marie and witnessed the petition by the Ojibwa chiefs for Ermatinger land rights.[18] (Years later, Prime Minister Sir John A. Macdonald implied that James had helped pacify the Indians and "halfbreeds" in the 1849 treaty signing.[19]) Possibly James and Mary had stayed on with his family after the trip with Charles to the Sault.

COUNTY CLERK

In 1856, James and six other men petitioned for the position of clerk for the County of Norfolk, a job based at Simcoe. A jury recommended James, and on 29 October the County Council appointed him to the position. His pleasure in the appointment must have been mitigated when a councillor moved that the previous county clerk had been paid too much, and that the salary should be reduced to £75. The motion passed seven to four.[20]

The Norfolk County Council files show James opening council meetings after elections until the new warden could be sworn in, and keeping minutes of all meetings. He witnessed various petitions and other documents. His office was the depository for papers relating to county affairs ranging from finances to prison reports. He signed and issued licences "to carry and expose for sale Goods, Wares and Merchandise at all places" in the county, collecting the clerk's fee of $1.00 for doing so.[21] And he countersigned county bylaws including appropriations for improving county roads.[22] No personal letters or diaries exist to directly indicate satisfaction or otherwise with his job, but it was a far cry from hunting at Sault Ste Marie or chasing rebels on Fighting Island. Then came a chance to return to his past.

HIS LAST GREAT ADVENTURE

In 1869, the new federal government of Prime Minister Macdonald, anticipating the transfer of Rupert's Land and the North West Territories from Britain to Canada, appointed William McDougall lieutenant governor of the region. The Métis, under Louis Riel's leadership, protested the takeover. On 30 October when McDougall tried to cross the border from the United States to take up residence in Fort Garry, Métis insurgents turned him back.

Macdonald knew that to send troops out to pacify the troubled area, he needed to ensure that Indians and Métis around the Great Lakes would not oppose their passage. In November, the prime minister suggested to McDougall that Indian loyalty could be secured by sending emissaries trusted by the Indians. He would also send young James Ermatinger, whom he described as a "half-breed Chippewaian." James spoke the language, Macdonald wrote, and "was formerly employed in a similar work of pacification. You may find him of use also."[23] At this time, James was working in Rimouski as a valuator for the Intercolonial Railway being built between the Maritime provinces and Quebec. When and how he got that job, while apparently retaining his position at Simcoe, is not known.

On 2 December 1869 James was about to return to Simcoe to take up his regular duties when he received a summons to Ottawa for unspecified work "in connection with the Red River trouble." For the rest of December he was paid $5 a day for thirty days ($150), his expenses while in Ottawa, plus his fare from Ottawa to Simcoe. In Simcoe, James remained on standby for a possible call to go to the North West. In mid-February, James was informed that he would not be needed for work in the North West Territories "at least for some months." Although the Intercolonial still had a few weeks' work that had been left uncompleted when James had been summoned to Ottawa, James refused to resume it for such a short period. On 16 February, however, Joseph Howe, secretary of state for the provinces, wrote to James that his services connected to the North West were no longer required. The government proposed compensating him for his temporary detention at Simcoe by paying him $5 a day for the month of January, in addition to his December payment. "As the government did not, in fact, avail itself in any way of your services," and had paid his travel expenses from Ottawa to Simcoe, "you will, it is hoped, feel satisfied with the settlement of your claim." Clearly, Macdonald and his government had finished with James. James replied that he would accept the $5 per diem but regretted the Intercolonial Railway had not reinstated him.[24]

In the middle of all this, on 20 December 1869, he sent a telegram from Simcoe to Macdonald, a telegram that would not help him get work with the railway: "Beware, Sioux hereditary enemy of the Chippewas, Crees, Red River settlers and the Assinniboine [sic]. McDougall entering that country under Sioux auspices, places the Government against those they would conciliate. Complication arising of a disastrous nature, and such as I was afraid would occur, levying unauthorised war ought to be put a stop to at once. If success attends Mr. McDougall, in the first instance, the hostile feeling will remain." James' fears had some justification. Rumours abounded that McDougall was raising an Indian force, and that the Sioux were on the warpath. In the event, both rumours proved unfounded and it is very doubtful that Macdonald welcomed warnings from a county clerk about "levying unauthorised war." James got a cold, one-sentence reply from Joseph Howe: "My Dear Sir, Nobody here has any idea of employing the Sioux in the Red River country."[25] And that was that.

The Manitoba Act brought the Red River area into Confederation on 12 May 1870. Soon after, a military force under Colonel Garnet Wolseley started out from Upper Canada for Red River, arriving there in August. When passing through Sault Ste Marie, Wolseley stayed at the old stone house, by then a hotel.[26] James did not accompany him.

James continued to seek employment. On 30 June 1870, an assistant to Sir John A. Macdonald responded to a letter from him "on the subject of your position having been a valuator of lands on the Intercolonial Railway, which office you resigned."[27] The letter, to be referred to Macdonald as soon as he had recovered from an illness, did not say for what position James was applying. His letter to Macdonald has not been found.

At this time the government was considering a great new railway linking Canada to British Columbia. It ordered Sandford Fleming, the brilliant chief engineer of the Intercolonial Railway, to begin surveying for the proposed Transcontinental. Between 1871 and 1876 Fleming sent out numerous parties testing routes across the country in a series of increasingly sophisticated surveys involving hundreds of men.[28] The papers of Edward Ermatinger in the Canadian National Archives contain a handwritten document entitled "Report of J.E. of the Survey from Touchwood Hills [in what is now Saskatchewan] to Rat Creek Manitoba, via Fort Ellice, 1871-72." James' persistence had paid off with a job with the new railway. He conducted part of a preliminary survey of Division M, from Whitefish to the Red River near Fort Garry.[29]

James was in his mid-fifties in 1871 but must have been very fit. He and five companions, including a guide, left their camp in the Touchwood Hills on 25 November for a gruelling trip to Fort Garry. They started with four carts and twenty-two horses. Some of the animals were in such bad shape that James expected they would "retard us much." In the first half of their journey, the party walked southeast across the Touchwood and Little Touchwood Hills, around the eastern end of the Pheasant Hills, south to the Qu'Appelle River, then along the river to Fort Ellice at the junction of the Qu'Appelle and the Assiniboine, in Manitoba. In eight days of marching from dawn to dusk they traversed 260 kilometres, about 32 kilometres a day. Bitter cold, gales, and hard slogging through heavy snow made it miserable for the men; for the horses it was deadly. Much of the grassland they fed on was covered with a hard crust of snow that had thawed and then refrozen into ice; much of the grass itself had been burnt off the previous summer by widespread fires. Little remained for the horses to eat. James' account of three December days are an understated yet vivid illustration of the journey. The descriptions of geographic and other natural features are consistent with the definition of the preliminary surveys mentioned by Fleming.[30]

1 December Started at sunrise over the same undulating prairie, running into butes occasionally. Islands of poplar and willow became more frequent. About 9:00 o'clock a.m. it commenced to snow, a high wind blowing at the same time causing drifts with a hard crust, sufficiently hard to bear the weight of a man, but breaking with the weight of the horses and carts. Our progress was consequently slow. One of the [horses] having stopped from exhaustion, we again camped at an early hour, being anxious to reach Fort Ellis with the whole herd where it will be necessary to leave the weaker horses. We crossed the Broken Arm river which has a width of 31 feet at the ford and a depth of two feet, having steep banks of about 140 or 150 feet in depth, and having a valley about a quarter of a mile in width. It flows into the Qu'Appelle, its course at the ford and as far as we could see being South 40 deg East. It flows from Leach Lake. The crossing of this stream was attended with great difficulty on account of the snow having drifted into the trail. We camped about half a mile beyond its eastern bank where we found wooded islands of poplar and willow of small growth, and deep snow, the latter impeding our already jaded horses. Travelled 18.8 miles; the soil a gravelly clay loam. Very cold today.

2 December Started by sunrise over an undulating prairie. A cold wind from North West blowing and drifting the snow, the horses suffering much. Had to change the draft horses frequently today. One of the drove had to be left behind 3 miles from the encampment, being too weak to walk; am afraid a similar fate awaits others. Towards the afternoon, the prairie runs into butes of some height. The soil is a light sandy loam. The greater part of the plain passed today has been burnt. Camped near an island of poplars and willows with very little grass around it. Travelled 17.4 miles, the cold today severe.

3 December Started at sunrise. The night was intensely cold. The horses herded together and did not feed until towards morning. Sent for the horse left behind yesterday, but had to leave him again with two others before reaching the Valley of the Qu'Appelle. The plain crossed is about two miles in extent. The gale of wind blowing from the North West, with the intense cold, made it very severe for the horses and men, the latter suffering from frostbite. The draft horses were changed frequently and such was the severity of the march across this plain, when we got into the woods in the Valley of the Qu'Appelle, four more horses were left behind, making seven in all in this short distance. Arrived at Fort Ellice after dark, having experienced great difficulty in ascending the South bank of the Qu'Appelle owing to the depth of snow in the woods. Travelled 16.1 miles. Soil light and sandy.

At seven o'clock the next morning, James and his men quit the comfort of the fort and recrossed the Qu'Appelle to recover the horses left behind the day before: "Four had been frozen to death during the previous day and night and three were brought to the fort with some difficulty being scarcely able to walk."

The weather was so cold, they could hardly use their surveying instruments and, indeed, had to stop after measuring the levels of only the north side of the Qu'Appelle River. Convinced most of the horses would die on the next leg of the journey, James left some of them at Fort Ellice. He took only the five strongest, most likely to survive the journey to Fort Garry. He also exchanged three lean horses for two in good condition, and exchanged the carts for sleighs.

The party left Fort Ellice at 8 a.m. on 6 December. Again, "The fires have completely burnt up the grass. It is only here and there a small patch is left." But James was feeling more optimistic: "We may possibly get through with the horses if the weather keeps as mild as it is today." By 8 December, however, the cold was again severe and a gale kept the men up all night preventing their only tent from blowing away. For sixteen more days they struggled through snowdrifts, forded ice-cold rivers, and forced their way up steep riverbanks, all the time noting what little vegetation there was, the nature of the soil, the depth of the rivers, the height of their banks. And all the time, "the horses suffering much."

On 12 December the party met a stream that the guide took to be the Assiniboine, as they were walking cross-country. They followed it for almost five kilometres till it suddenly took a turn from the southeast to the southwest, and they realised it was the Souris River. They crossed the river and headed northeast, knowing they were greatly out of their course. The one lucky break came when their guide shot a deer "which proved a welcome change to our fare." They finally reached the Assiniboine on 14 December at a spot unknown to the guide.

Next day they began to walk upriver on a side trip, searching for the rapids and possibly to give the horses the rest they needed. At some point the guide recognized a feature of the land that located them about sixty-five kilometres below the rapids, too far to walk that day, so they returned to camp. There they found that a gale had blown down the tent, which could not be pitched again. They harnessed the horses and headed downstream, making almost thirteen kilometres before camping again in the shelter of some woods. On the 16th, the horses were again showing signs of exhaustion, and the next day they had to abandon one. Two days later they had to abandon "a bay with four white legs and a strip of white on the nose. The soil in the valley is a rich sandy loam."

On the 19th, the party picked up an Indian trail that had just carried many horses. They decided to follow it, but the deepest snowdrifts they had so far met covered the trail. At one point it took them two hours of hard work to get the sleighs to the top of the thirty-seven-metre riverbank. After another hour of slogging for the horses, "the poor starved animals fairly gave out; we had to camp on the lee side of the nearest clump of trees for shelter as the weather was intensely cold and stormy."

At that point, the guide started out on the Indian trail to get fresh horses. They guessed that the Indians could be no more than a dozen miles away, and unable to travel on such a day because of the children they would have with them. The guide returned about midnight with an Indian and two horses. Next day, the Indian leading, they travelled with most of their gear on a sleigh drawn by the two fresh horses while the other sleigh followed. They met the Indian party, who refused to carry their gear any further.

The party now had only two days of provisions. Leaving the guide in charge, James started for Rat Creek with two Indians as guides, beating a track through deep snow. The Indians left him when, about midnight, they struck the main trail from Fort Ellice. He walked until the moon went down at two-thirty and then camped. About an hour before sunrise, he started again on the main trail and arrived at the settlement at eight in the morning. A farmer, a Mr McKenzie, gave him every assistance. James, with two of McKenzie's sons, took three horses and provisions and walked the eighty kilometres back along a winding trail and through deep snow to where he had left his friends.

There, unfortunately, the account ends. Six years later, the new railway's chief engineer, Sandford Fleming, told a Senate committee that in 1871 he had sent an expedition to make a general examination of the country from Touchwood Hills to Fort Garry country. The team consisted of James Ermatinger, Frank Moberley, Mr Nicol, and Mr Horetzky. Fleming quoted the report at length to explain why he had rejected a proposal to take the line along a more southerly route than that finally chosen: "Mr. Ermatinger's examination from Touchwood Hills to Fort Ellice and Souris River, shewed that the bridging of all the streams in that direction would be very great, and there would be no advantage gained by carrying the railway along the general direction of the Assiniboine."[31] James had made his contribution to the building of the Canadian Pacific Railway, if only by ruling out one route.

Although James had returned to his quiet life in Simcoe and his comfortable job as clerk of the Norfolk County Council, he did not give up hope of a more exciting life in the country of his youth. In May 1873, after the survey trip, he asked Prime Minister Macdonald for a position as stipendiary magistrate in the North West. Macdonald could only promise that James' application would be placed on record; there were "numerous" such applications.[32] He never got the job.

MILITARY AND INDIAN IDENTITY
Throughout his life, James retained an interest in military affairs. When the St Thomas Cavalry disbanded, he asked that arms and accoutrements

be provided to the troops "to make them efficient, should their services be required again in defence of their country."[33] Years later he wrote to his cousin Edward, "I am afraid this Danish question is about embroiling the whole continent and no one can tell where it will end. We will be in a pretty 'fix' if England is drawn into it. In the meantime, our 'wise acres' at Quebec are busy in their usual squabbles – wasting valuable time in trying their useless question of who … is a scoundrel or not, instead of putting this country in some state of defence."[34]

On another occasion he wrote to the secretary of state for war in Ottawa to defend the notion that the government should retain plank roadways for military purposes. In the 1840s and 1850s roads consisting of wooden planks placed end to end began replacing corduroy roads in much of the country. The latter were simply logs laid across a trail, giving the rough texture of corduroy, and were a misery to travel on. Travellers were delighted with the smooth ride of the plank roads, while there was plenty of wood and sawmills to build them. Unfortunately, weather and traffic meant they lasted only two or three years, and other materials such as crushed stone and, slowly, macadam, soon replaced planks.[35] We do not have James' letter explaining the tactical advantages of plank roads, but the reply from the assistant to the secretary of war was not encouraging. It said simply, "Sir: I have to acknowledge the receipt of your letter of the 20th ultimo pointing out the advantages of plank roadways for military purposes, and in returning you my thanks for your communication, I beg leave to acquaint you that I have referred it for the consideration of the Secretary of State for War."[36]

In addition to his trip to Sault Ste Marie in 1849-50, and the recognition of his usefulness and of his Indian ancestry by Prime Minister Macdonald, James retained other links with his Native heritage. On 25 August 1874, he was among the guests when the governor general and his wife, Lord and Lady Dufferin, visited the Six Nations Indian Reserve at Brantford.[37] Moreover, the 1871 census listed his origin and occupation as "Canadian Indian, Clerk."[38] A manual of instruction to enumerators directs, "Origin is to be scrupulously entered, as given by the person questioned, in the manner shown in the specimen schedule, by the words English, Irish, Scotch, African, Indian, German, French, and so forth."[39] James may not actually have identified himself as Indian. Enumerators did not always follow instructions, and if James were not in town perhaps an unfriendly neighbour, in a prejudiced era, gave the information to the census taker. But this census enumeration took place in April 1871, after James' return from Ottawa and long before the Touchwood Hills episode, so it is likely that he was home at the time. The census entry does not mention any absence, as did the earlier 1852 census. But in the 1881 census, James listed himself as of Swiss origin.[40]

THE DEATH OF JAMES

James died at his residence in Simcoe on 8 December 1890, aged seventy-five years, after fifty years (less three weeks) of marriage. He was buried in Oakwood Cemetery. The *Norfolk Reformer* noted that he was a son of Charles Oakes Ermatinger and "Charlotte Kattawabide, chief in her own right of the Ojibeways." Mary died at Hamilton on 27 March 1902, aged seventy-seven years, and was buried in the same plot as her husband.[41] They left no children.

James' funeral would surely have pleased him. Like his brother Charles, he was given military honours, the 39th Battalion supplying the band and firing party. "A large concourse of citizens [were] present in carriages and on foot," according to the *Reformer*. They included all members of the County Council, which was in session when he died. The pallbearers included his St Thomas cousin, Judge C.O.Z. Ermatinger (son of Edward) and the judge's son, Frank. Later, the council drafted a resolution of condolences to James' widow, and granted her $200.[42]

JAMES, A SUMMING UP

James is the simplest of the three brothers to interpret. He began as "a steady and good little boy" and somehow retained the best of those characteristics into manhood. His speech to his men on Pelee Island illustrates that simplicity. "He hoped every man who was spared to go home would not be ashamed of having been there," and then he showed his own courage on the battlefield. His letter warning Macdonald of the Sioux, and his military advocacy of plank roads, also show his naïveté.

James, however, displayed the same dichotomy as his older brothers. He lived most of his life in the middle-class milieu of a town in Upper Canada where he was highly thought of, especially by his fellow troopers. But as soon as he had the chance he broke at least temporarily with that life to go off fighting the rebels on Pelee Island, or adventuring with Charles on their trip to Sault Ste Marie in 1849, or working with the Intercolonial in Rimouski, or making the hazardous western survey of 1871. With no real battles to fight, he still worried and wrote letters about military matters. He was identified as half-Ojibwa by the prime minister and identified himself at least on occasion as an Indian, as did his obituary. Finally, in later life he tried to go back to the Upper Country of his youth as a stipendiary magistrate. Many men in post-Confederation Canada sought an adventurous life in the new North West, but it is doubtful that many were aged fifty-five with a wife and a comfortable job in Upper Canada. And only an aging man with powerful motives would actually live out the dreams of his youthful adventures on a venture as hard and dangerous as James' winter survey trip, and then apply for an equally adventurous job in the new North West. In short, his constant search for an adventurous life reminiscent of that of his youth suggests that he was no more enamoured of a sedentary career than were his brothers, though perhaps a little more realistic in finally accepting its necessity.

Dandy Turned Hero

In a letter to his brother, Frank Ermatinger described Charles Sr's son William as a dandy: in fact, "the completest lump of dandeism that was ever formed, by a long and narrow cut coat, tensed stays, starched collar and ruffles, high heeled Boots, etc. etc. and that too at his father's house above. This does not exactly agree with the accounts I have heard of our uncle's penurious disposition."[1] Five years later, at the age of twenty-one, young William was still dressing in style. His clothes bill over an eleven-month period in 1830-31 totalled £35/19/9. Of this, £25 had been paid with the balance on account. The clothes bought were a superfine olive cloth frock coat, double breasted, with silk facings, silk velvet collar, and velvet lapels; a superfine black cloth frock coat, double breasted and the skirts faced with silk; a superfine black cloth coat; two pairs of superfine double milled trousers; two beaver hats; five pairs of kid gloves; two pairs of silk braces, one light blue; one muslin bow stock; one black silk handkerchief; some best black silk lapels; one silk neck stiffener; half a yard of silk; and repairs to a blue cloth coat with new silk facings.[2]

William was not the only brother to like fine clothes. An 1820 bill paid by Frederick notes, "For son Charles. Superfine Blue Cloth Coat £6/5/–; pair of Superfine Doub. Milled Blue Cassie, £3/–/–; a Toilanette vest, £1/3/4. – For son George. A superfine olive cloth frock surtout, faced with silk & olive silk velvet collar."[3] Such bills for the Ermatinger brothers were quite common. This "dandyism" is consistent with the Ojibwa belief that fine dress and ornamentation were a sign of prosperity, and prosperity a sign of spiritual blessing.

William's clothing suited his lifestyle. His sister Jemima Cameron wrote that his family saw him as something of a social butterfly. In 1831 she wrote her cousin Edward, "I see his name in the papers for the fox hunt as usual, and [he] performs with the amateur players."[4] He stayed at T. Rasco's in Montreal from 18 November 1830 to 28 April 1831. Aside from his room charge, his bill shows mainly breakfasts with occasional other meals, and on several occasions dinners in a private room for two or three. He and his friends drank sherry, port wine, Madeira, punch, whisky, brandy and, sometimes, lemonade. The bill also included charges for oranges, sugar almonds, and pastries, and makes reference to a fox hunting club.[5]

In 1829, aged nineteen, William had started his career in the legal office of Samuel Gale of Montreal, his father's lawyer. Three years later, his father wrote to cousin Edward, "William you will find much changed for the better, and is very attentive to his office and is improved much since last year; and employs his time fully."[6]

In 1832 a tragic incident occurred in the west ward during a Montreal election. The supporters of one candidate advanced on the poll shouting, screaming, and shaking their fists, clubs, and umbrellas at the constables guarding the polling booths. A witness testified at the investigation, "I remarked at the same time to Mr. W. Ermatinger, who was standing with me, that I was sure Mr. Tracy's party intended to attack the constables."[7] As the situation worsened, the mayor read the Riot Act and handed authority to the military.[8] The commanding officer of the 15th Regiment saw danger to innocent bystanders and to his own troops, and gave the order to fire. Three civilians died and many others were wounded. The colonel and captain of the unit were arrested for murder though they had acted quite legally; that is, they had followed the strict military rules laid down for quelling riots. The officers were later released with no charges laid. Seventeen years later, as he himself struggled with riots, William would have cause to remember that night.

The next year, William became a lieutenant in the Royal Montreal Cavalry, and the uniform must have appealed to him. He bought the cavalry's shako (a peaked cylindrical military hat), a blue cloth uniform jacket, a pair of gauntlet gloves, a cavalry girdle, a pair of regulation grey hunter's cloth trousers with broad scarlet cloth stripes down the side seams, a pair of rich silk shoulder scales, a black beaver hat, a silk handkerchief, a specially made blue silk racing jacket and trimmings, and white cord breeches.[9] The Royal Montreal Cavalry was the same unit his brother Charles later joined prior to the Lower Canada rebellion of 1837. William himself, however, was not present for the rebellion, because he was in Spain fighting a much bloodier war.

THE CARLIST WARS

In 1833 King Fernando VII of Spain died. His infant daughter, Isabel II, took the throne with her mother, Maria Christina de Bourbon, as regent. Fernando's brother Don Carlos, along with a group of conservatives and clerics, contested the succession. Popular support for Don Carlos came mainly from the nationalist Basques in the north. The Christinos, named after Isabel's mother, represented the more liberal groups in Spain. In October the northern provinces proclaimed Don Carlos king and the country fell into civil war.

In Britain, the Whig government of Lord Palmerston supported the Christinos, and in April 1834 Britain signed an alliance with France, Spain, and Portugal to keep Isabel as queen. Britain supplied arms and ammunition, and a small naval force. Then in May 1835, Palmerston's government gave the Spanish permission to recruit in Britain. The force that emerged became the British Auxiliary Legion under Radical MP and retired British officer Colonel George De Lacy Evans (1787-1870). During his service in the War of 1812, Evans had led the troops that burned down the Washington Capitol after the Americans had destroyed Toronto.[10]

The 9,600 men of the legion were a rough lot, many of them physically unfit. The Tories disliked the whole project, and the Duke of Wellington virtually forbade serving officers to volunteer. So Evans sought 400 officers wherever he could find them – personal army friends, officers on leave from the East India Company, British mercenaries serving in the armed forces of Greece, Colombia, and Portugal, and militia officers in the colonies including Canada and Australia. He also gave commissions to more than forty sergeants. Lack of official standing in Britain and a largely hostile British public forced the legion to go to Spain for its training.[11]

The early days of the British Legion were disastrous. Forced marches, illness (especially typhus), and the rigours of winter killed off many. Once even their bread was allegedly impregnated with white lead, straw, and bones, including human ones. The Spanish authorities garrotted the poisoner, a Carlist baker, after twice publicly flogging him. Even within the legion, some sadistic officers made life miserable for the men. Alexander Somerville's *History of the British Legion* contains an illustration of flogging, with a description of another flogging ordered by an unnamed colonel in the 1st Lancers, the unit William would join.[12] Despite sickness among his men, Evans took the legion into several battles. By July, with pay heavily in arrears, drunkenness and mutiny were spreading through the force.[13] This was the British Legion that William joined.

WILLIAM JOINS THE LEGION

Sometime in 1835, word of legion recruitment had reached Canada, and William decided to enlist. No doubt General Evans was happy to have militiamen with some training, but Ermatinger military connections in Britain may also have helped William's career. His uncle, the late Lawrence Edward, had been assistant commissariat general and probably had friends still serving in the British forces. Such connections may be the reason that, at one point, William became aide-de-camp to General Jockmus, quartermaster general of the British Legion. The legion included two cavalry regiments: the 1st Reina Isabel Regiment of Lancers and the 2nd Regiment of the Queen's Own Irish Lancers. Army lists show that on 19 May 1836, William received his commission as a cornet attached to the 1st

Reina Isabel Regiment, commanded by Lieutenant-Colonel Wakefield.[14]

When William took up his posting, he must have wondered what sort of outfit he had joined. In August and September 1836, just prior to or soon after William's arrival (the exact date is unknown), several battalions of the legion were near to, or did in fact, mutiny, among them William's 1st Lancers. The army weeded out the mutineers and put the ringleaders under guard on British warships. The troops then got some back pay. With that, one regiment went on a drunken orgy. Evans and his officers did not fully restore order to a much diminished legion until September.

The force remained unpopular in Britain, especially with the Tories. An editorial from a British paper reprinted in the Montreal *Gazette* in 1836 shows that the widespread British dislike of the war had spread to Canada. "The 'never ending just beginning' war in Spain" was as inconclusive as ever. An English officer wrote that all was dull as dishwater. He believed his countrymen who had volunteered in this quarrel were misguided, and some had deserted in disgust. By September the *Gazette* was saying that the sooner General Evans left Spain, the better for everyone. The paper added that the condition of the force "becomes every day more and more deplorable."[15] In short, William was fighting in an unpopular and dirty war.

The first clue to William's activities comes in the early morning of 22 August 1836. In a field near San Sebastian, two officers of the British Legion stand back to back, each holding a pistol. They wait for the command to step the required paces, turn and fire. This is a debt of honour: Colonel R.C. De La Saussaye of the quartermaster general's office has charged the 4th Fusiliers with misconduct, and Major John Richardson of the 4th Fusiliers has countered that the colonel had shown cowardice in battle. "Lieutenant [sic] Ermatinger, of the Lancers, and attached to the Quartermaster General's Department, acted for Colonel La Saussaye," wrote Richardson years later. When the order comes, the duellers try to turn and fire. They find that ankle-deep sand makes it almost impossible to do so with any accuracy, and they try several times with no success. Then, apparently, William persuades La Saussaye to accept Richardson's apology that is not quite an apology, which stops the farce. Later, Richardson finds out that his own second and William had conspired in choosing the sandy location to minimize danger to their principals. Possibly they also fiddled with a first set of pistols so they would not fire.[16]

WILLIAM IN ACTION

Mention of William in more serious action came in March 1837. The legion had suffered another terrible winter with little military activity. Heavy snowstorms had given way to biting frosts, then more snowstorms. The men were ill fed, badly clothed, and seldom paid. In March, the high command decided to attack the enemy massed in front of the legion's entrenchments at San Sebastian and around Hernani. After an early success, the Christinos failed to take the Carlist centre on a rocky hill. The overall attack was disastrous, with nearly 1,000 Christinos killed or wounded.

A fellow officer, Captain R. Henderson, described the affair and its prelude. An hour before daylight on 12 March, heavy Carlist artillery opened fire on the Christino centre in the Loyola valley. A Carlist brigade savagely attacked an artillery battery. Spanish troops and British legionnaires began retreating before Carlist bayonets, leaving the guns in enemy hands. The situation was critical. Then William galloped into the fray. He halted the retreating men, rallied them, and led them back to the guns at the *pas de charge*. The struggle was desperate, but under counterattack the panicking Carlists retreated to their former positions. William and his men recaptured all the guns.[17] For his gallantry in action, on 23 March "W.H. Etaminger [sic]" was promoted to lieutenant and transferred to the 2nd Regiment, The Queen's Own Irish Lancers.[18]

Heavy fighting involved the legion almost incessantly for the next few days. Then, at one in the afternoon on the 15th, in snow and rain, Evans launched a 9,000-man attack on the strongly entrenched Carlist force of 14,000 men. The opposition fought savagely, and William's 1st Lancers on the right flank had great difficulty crossing the rough terrain. A barrage of Congreve rockets forced the Carlists to spike their guns and withdraw. By six in the evening, the legion was in command of the ridge. Next day, legion artillery began softening up the town of Hernani for its final capture, which seemed assured. But with a brilliant manoeuvre and some fast marching, the Carlist commander, Don Sebastián, counterattacked and forced Evans to give up his gains.

Military historian Sir James Marshall-Cornwall writes that this battle was the most serious engagement the legion had taken part in since its arrival in Spain.[19] The British press and the legion's critics in England scarified Evans and his men, calling the battle a national disgrace. But Evans told his troops, "The soldier is never so formidable as when he is called on to vindicate his honour. Let us then once more march on to the combat and show that we are worthy soldiers of liberty."[20] Two months later the Christinos finally took Hernani.

By mid-June 1837, the two-year term that most legionnaires had signed on for came to an end. The legion disbanded, and Evans and most of his men returned to England. During those two years, about 2,500 legionnaires had been killed or wounded in battle, and many more died from disease.[21]

THE SECOND AND THIRD LEGIONS

Some 1,700 officers and men stayed to form the New British Auxiliary Legion under the command of Colonel Maurice O'Connell.[22] About 190 volunteers from both Lancer regiments, including William, formed a single regiment, the 1st Lancers. In September, skirmishes near Andouin killed or wounded some 200 men and eleven officers of the legion. The Carlists allegedly butchered some who had surrendered.

The only sure signs of William in Europe during this period are three bills totalling £135 that turned up in Canada for his brother Charles to pay.[23] William's dandyism must have been satisfied by the typical officer's uniform of the lancers. Spanish and regimental symbols fronted the tall, flat-topped lance cap, while a skull on two crossbones bore the words "O Gloria." The lower part of the cap carried a band of gold lace with two thin red lines and a pattern of oak leaves and acorns marking the men's English origin. The jacket was red with green or white facings, with the oak leaf and acorn pattern appearing again on the gold embroidery of the collar. The gilt buttons were embossed with a crown on crossed lances.[24]

The Spanish government failed to pay the legion, and officers had to buy food for the men with their own funds. Colonel O'Connell could not get the conditions he wanted from the Spanish government and disbanded the force, condemning the "culpable neglect, or wilful malevolence" of the Spanish government's agents.[25] Despite this, William stayed on. In May 1838, the Montreal *Gazette* carried a story from Britain: according to news from San Sebastian dated 27 March, remnants of the British Auxiliary Legion had been incorporated in a "brigade" that mustered about 400 strong, including officers. The list of officers of the Reina Isabella Lancers under Colonel Wakefield included Lieutenant W. Ermatinger. The *Gazette* did not mention that William was Canadian.[26]

Records of this small – on the large scale, almost insignificant – rump force of British cavalry are difficult to find. According to George MacMunn, a historian of the legion, the small unit became a *corps d'élite* of artillery and cavalry in the Spanish army, and served with distinction till the end of the war.[27] In January 1840, General Evans wrote that some 350 artillery and lancers "continued in Spain, commanded by Col. De Lassaussai; and have conducted themselves in a very distinguished manner on various subsequent occasions, even up to the present time."[28]

Records of William himself have been impossible to find. Yet he did emerge as a lieutenant-colonel with a decoration and must have been involved in many of the Reina Isabella Lancers' subsequent engagements. One such occurred on the left bank of the Ebro River near Logroño on 3 December 1838. A battalion of infantry and five squadrons of cavalry, including the British lancers, were sweeping the area to seek out and destroy the enemy. They could see a strong Carlist force of eight battalions and seven squadrons of cavalry on the hills above their right flank, but the enemy delayed attack until the afternoon. Then five of the seven squadrons descended on the loyalist rearguard consisting of one company of the Spanish battalion and twenty British lancers. The rearguard held off the attackers until the commanding general, Don Diego Leon, ordered a counterattack. Two Christino squadrons failed to attack, while a third did so with great bravery but was soon close to defeat by a much larger force. At that critical moment, Colonel La Saussaye brought up his cavalry, who charged with such spirit that they broke the Carlists. The enemy fled in great disorder, leaving behind 180 dead on the field, and thirty men and eighty horses captured. Later, General Leon issued a general order handsomely thanking the colonel and his lancers.[29]

Next day, at Carascal, when Carlist cavalry attacked a convoy, a protecting Christino squadron fled, leaving a small British unit from the lancers. They pretended to withdraw, then attacked and almost destroyed the Carlist units. After the massacre of their comrades at a previous encounter, the lancers took no prisoners. Later that month, a Christino cavalry force, including William's lancers, charged Carlist cavalry. With only one shot fired, they routed the enemy. The last record yet found of the British squadron came in June 1839 in the Battle of Allo, when two Spanish units and the British lancers were attacked on the flank while they were destroying Carlist crops. The British and one of the Spanish squadrons routed the enemy.[30]

The Vergara Convention of 31 August 1839 effectively ended the war except in the east, where General Cabrera kept on fighting. His "final battle" came after the besieged city of Morella fell to the Christinos in June 1840. Cabrera began to make a last stand at Berga. As the first Christino shells fell on Berga, on 6 July 1840, the Carlists retreated across the border into France.[31] With victory for the queen's forces, William could finally come home, a decorated lieutenant-colonel.

THE LEGION'S RECORD
The contemporary press and some historians have castigated the British Auxiliary Legion for inefficiency, cowardice, and worse. Certainly, it was seldom better than half-strength. Too many of its officers were both unskilled and brutal, and many of its men were capable of both desertion and barbaric treatment of civilians. But some historians, and many ex-members of the legion, disagree with the widespread condemnation. Historian George MacMunn maintains that, had Lord Palmerston and not the Spanish financed it, "this brilliantly appointed force would have achieved great success and kudos instead of the misery and often undeserved abuse that it received." Another historian, Drummond E. Burgess, writes that although of course the legionnaires acted for money, political ambition, and career advancement rather than just an abstract love of liberty, "nevertheless, they went, and fought, and suffered." While it is easy to dismiss idealism as an unconscious justification of lower motives, he points out, if idealism had not been present, the British Legion would not have been present either.[32]

Many years later, at William's death, the *Evening Telegraph* wrote that William left Canada about 1835, without being admitted to the bar, to join the

British Legion in Spain. There he earned the reputation of "a dashing cavalry officer. He was engaged in several actions, and was once wounded in the face." For his services, according to the *Telegraph*, he received several decorations from Queen Isabella, and returned to Canada only at the close of the Spanish civil war in 1839.[33] The family historian, Judge C.O.Z. Ermatinger, claimed that William was "knighted on the field of battle for conspicuous gallantry." Quebec historian Pierre-Georges Roy writes that William was aide-de-camp successively to Sir Duncan McDougall and "General Sochmus" (Jockmus), and that he won the rank of lieutenant-colonel in the service of Spain for his bravery at the decisive battle that placed the queen on the throne. Soon after, according to C.O.Z. Ermatinger, William received the thanks of General Espartero and was made Chevalier de Saint-Ferdinand.[34]

These sources give no documentation for their claims. The *Telegraph's* reference to a wound in William's face is false: the writer may have been confused by the facial wound suffered by William's brother Charles at Longueuil. Nor is it clear just what battle finally placed the queen on the throne. In 1846, however, Archibald McDonald, a Hudson's Bay Company employee, told Edward Ermatinger that while in Montreal he had met "your gallant cousin the Knight of the Golden Fleece," suggesting contemporary knowledge of William's decoration.[35] In all, the evidence shows William acquitted himself honourably and with courage in a long and savage war.

For both Charles and James, it might be argued that their participation in battles against rebel forces in Canada was a product of their Tory heritage. No such argument can explain William's decision to fight in a terrible overseas war that was not even a British war, and which the British Tories, including the Duke of Wellington, bitterly opposed. His choice surely stemmed from a sense of adventure, and a desire to distinguish himself in battle, entirely consistent with Bigsby's description of the Ermatinger and Johnston boys in their Sault Ste Marie youth.

Suppressing Riots in Montreal

It is not known exactly when Lieutenant-Colonel William Ermatinger returned to Montreal, but it was probably in 1841. He did not rejoin the Royal Montreal Cavalry, though a number of ex-officers of the British Auxiliary Legion had been given military positions in Canada, including a former legion captain appointed adjutant of militia.[1] Instead, William joined the Montreal police force in January 1842, and for the next decade, as commissioner of police or equivalent office, he fought the riots that plagued Montreal. In 1846 William was admitted to the bar, but he never practised.[2] His legal training, his experiences in Spain, and his skill in handling tricky and potentially violent situations while causing the minimum enmity contributed to a highly successful police career. Early on in that career, as justice of the peace, he faced the first of many crises he would encounter (Figure 7).

By the 1840s, some 3,800 labourers were using picks and shovels to dig the Beauharnois and Lachine canals near Montreal. During three months in the winter of 1842-43, contractors cut pay by nearly one-third, with the pay given partly in credit. This forced workers to buy inferior products at excessive prices in company stores. They also had to pay high rents for premises that had been promised rent free.[3] Low wages and high rents brought near starvation. Hostility between Irish and French, and between Cork and Connaught Irish, at first deflected anger away from the contractors. In spring 1843, violence between the Irish groups flared, with at least two men wounded by gunfire. In late February, troops stopped the combatants from getting at company explosives, but when fighting continued, local magistrates asked for reinforcements. That's when William got his orders.[4]

From Montreal, he was told, he must travel by sleigh as quickly as possible to the Lachine canal, accompanied by troops of the 71st Regiment. If the rioting construction workers there did not cease their violence and disperse within an hour, he should read the Riot Act. If the violence continued, he was to request the military to fire upon them with blank cartridge. If even this did not stop them, then he must ask their commander that the troops load

Figure 7
Lieutenant-Colonel William Ermatinger

and fire with ball. Consequently, at two thirty on the bitterly cold afternoon of 3 March 1843, William and the troops set out from Montreal. At the canal, William faced the mob, the troops behind him ready to load and fire. He prepared to read the Riot Act. The rioters broke and fled.[5]

Later in March, with labour trouble brewing at the Beauharnois canal,

Provincial Secretary Dominick Daly instructed William to organize a police force but to place it under the command of the local magistrate at St Timothy, Monsieur Laviolette.[6] William's typically vague orders were to maintain "a general surveillance" over the force's activities.[7] The government also sent troops to the town. By now the Irish groups were combining against the contractors. On 1 June, a month-long strike began at Beauharnois and Lachine. On 12 June, faced with a large menacing crowd outside the Hotel Grant, Laviolette read the Riot Act. He then ordered the troops to fire. One man died immediately, and six more died of wounds.[8]

William was not a patient man. "You are always in a d___d hurry," a colleague once wrote, "and never give me any news."[9] William showed that impatience three days later. A man named Martin Acton, a ringleader of the riot, was lounging around near the Hotel Grant along with about thirty workers. William calmly walked up and, without a warrant, arrested Acton. He took the man to Montreal and sentenced him to six months as a vagabond.[10] Later, magistrate Laviolette arrested six more men, also without warrants. Challenged on the legality of his arrests, Laviolette justified himself on the grounds that he had seen William make his arrest on a simple oral order.[11] An official enquiry into the St Timothy affair concluded that although the arrests were allegedly made under the Police Act, since the Police Act – covering the Island of Montreal and the adjacent parishes of Laprairie, Longeuil, Boucherville, and Île Perrot – did not extend to St Timothy all seven arrests were "flagrant abuses" of the law.[12]

THE MONTREAL POLICE

The City of Montreal had been incorporated in 1840. It had power to make bylaws with fines of up to £5 or imprisonment up to thirty days, and to create a police force financed by tolls and property assessments. The city appointed the members of the force, but the provincial government appointed the commissioner of police. The commissioner informed city council how much money the force needed to operate, up to a maximum of £5,000 annually, and he issued warrants to cover the operating costs.[13] He did not control the force itself.

A committee of the city council immediately appointed fifty-seven constables along with a chief of police and three subordinate officers. The force was a careful mix of French Catholics, Irish Catholics, and English Protestants.[14] On 1 February 1842, William got the job of commissioner, a title that changed the next year to inspector and superintendent of police.[15] Over the years, he often held the office of justice of the peace concurrently.

The administrative split between the government-appointed inspector superintendent and the council-appointed chief of police caused great difficulties. An 1855 commission of enquiry into the police said that appointment of the force by the council meant lack of constant employment for the men, lack of rules and regulations, lack of discipline, and lack of any means for enforcing it. The commission recommended a government-appointed force, independent of the city council and under the authority of the commissioner of police.[16] It did not materialize. Moreover, for long periods from 1842 to 1853, the single position of inspector and superintendent of police was held jointly by William with other men.[17] Just how they shared their responsibilities, and what conflicts occurred between them, is unknown.

With these bureaucratic difficulties hampering him, William had to bridge the many fissures that split Montreal citizens. Social tensions often led to violence: francophones versus anglophones, Catholics versus Protestants, Cork Irish versus Connaught Irish. Politically, the old Tories (determined to maintain the rights of Englishmen even if it meant annexation to America) opposed the Reformers of Upper and Lower Canada (equally determined to bring responsible government to the province). Later the radical Grits and Rouges opposed the Tories to produce the political instability of the 1860s. When William was in Spain, friend and enemy had been clearly defined, and morality clearly determined. Now he had to maintain peace in a divided Montreal where little was so clear.

ELECTION RIOTS

In April 1844, canal workers at Lachine and Beauharnois were once again on strike. During the city elections, some 600 strikers marched into Montreal and began disrupting candidates' meetings with sticks, stones, and fists. Some Tory voters were stripped nearly naked and beaten up, with at least one man killed. At one meeting, Lewis T. Drummond (the canallers' man) and William Molson (the Tory) were speaking. A fight broke out. The returning officer drew his sword and jumped off the stage. William Ermatinger and the two candidates followed him, arm in arm. With Drummond waving a white muslin handkerchief, they managed to clear a space between the factions and restore order.

At this time voting was by open ballot. On the first voting day at the Viger Market polling booth 400 "ferocious looking fellows" outnumbered the Molson voters. In a mêlée, "Everyone who looked like a gentleman" was assaulted and his clothes slashed, according to the Montreal *Gazette*. Two companies of the 43rd Regiment arrived and with them, William Ermatinger. As justice of the peace, William read the Riot Act. Though he and Chief of Police Alexander Comeau went from poll to poll trying to impose order, rioters forced virtually all the polls to close early. When they opened next day, violence continued with canallers dominating the scene. William's conduct was determined and resolute, reported the *Gazette;* had he and Chief Comeau been properly backed, many of the difficulties would not have occurred.[18]

Montreal elections were similarly violent in March 1846, when William was again supervising the polling booths. He later told a select committee of the House that in the streets he met "an immense number of persons" armed with sticks and axe handles. The five policemen at the St James poll proved totally inadequate to preserve the peace, so a troop of the 93rd Highlanders arrived. With the new chief of police, Thomas Wyley, and his officers, William disarmed the mob. They confiscated sixty to seventy axe handles, bludgeons, and other weapons including two or three "life preservers" – "an instrument loaded at each end with a couple of ounces of lead and consisting of whalebone tied together with twine." At another polling station a shower of stones greeted William, "but I cannot say by what party they were thrown." In the presence of troops, he again disarmed many of the mob and arrested seventeen men. William was convinced that similar disturbances would occur at future elections and wanted walls at the polls to separate the supporters of one candidate from those of the other. "I think decidedly, the vote by ballot [presumably secret ballot] ought to be resorted to in these elections, as the only means of preserving peace in a mixed population like that of this city," he told the committee.[19]

WILLIAM MARRIES
Between riots, on 14 July 1845, William married Caroline-Elisa Juchereau Duchesnay at the bride's family manor in St Ours. She was twenty-six years old, and he was thirty-four.[20] Caroline's family were prominent in Lower Canada. During the War of 1812, her father and uncle had fought with the Voltigeurs in the famous battle at the Châteauguay River. There, by tricks and false signals, a greatly outnumbered French Canadian militia unit sent 4,000 invading Americans back across the border. Lieutenant-Colonel William Ermatinger, son of an Ojibwa woman, decorated hero of a Spanish war, was therefore joining a distinguished Loyalist Quebec family that had played a key role in Canadian history.

WILLIAM AND YOUNG LAWRENCE
In 1846, when William's cousin Frank Ermatinger was in Britain, Frank's Indian-Canadian son Lawrence turned up in Montreal. William discovered him, dressed in tatters, wandering the streets. He clothed the boy in his own cast-off uniform and found him lodgings at two and a half dollars a week until he could decide what to do with him. An old family friend, Archibald McDonald, talked to Lawrence. "He does not like work," McDonald wrote later. Lawrence said he had been robbed of everything, "bible, prayer book & all; in short he is a miserable wretch." William asked his brother Charles, then in the Royal Montreal Cavalry, if he could do anything for the boy. Charles declined on the grounds that he could not give the impression of favouritism. McDonald's advice to William was to cut off Lawrence's beer and board him

somewhere cheaper until his father came back, when he should be "bundled off to Oregon."[21] Eventually "the miserable wretch" drifted back to western Canada and disappeared from his family and from history.

SON OF AN OJIBWA CHIEF

Although William had left Sault Ste Marie with his father in 1828, a link with his Ojibwa past came in 1847 when he drafted Charlotte's petition (described in Chapter 7). In the covering letter he wrote, "I have the honor to transmit the accompanying memorial of Charlotte Kattawabide, hereditary head chief of the Indian tribe called Ojibway Saulteaux, and also a copy of the power of attorney in my favour for the consideration of his Excellency the Governor General." A second document requested power of attorney from Charlotte Kattawabidé for William: she wished that all her rights, privileges, interests, and claims or demands as chief of the Ojibwa territories be assigned to William.[22]

Charles, as the eldest son and his father's principal heir, had generally spearheaded the family's claims for the Sault Ste Marie property as well as for the contested lands in the American Sault and on Drummond Island. In this case William acted for the family, presumably in his capacity as a lawyer. His association with the petition, and the statement that he was the son of an Ojibwa chief, with the implication that he himself was an Ojibwa, is especially significant. He was a prominent and sometimes controversial figure in Montreal politics during various strikes and riots, but his Ojibwa background apparently had no adverse effect on his career in a city where racism was endemic.

THE REBELLION LOSSES RIOTS

Drowsy members of the Legislative Assembly were debating the Lower Canada Judicature Bill in the evening of Wednesday, 25 April 1849 when a volley of stones crashed through windows all around the building. The Montreal *Pilot* reported that the flying rocks and shattered glass sent the members scrambling for the safety of the corridors. The mob invaded the building, wrecked the chamber, and beat the protesting sergeant-at-arms, grabbing his mace, symbol of legislative authority. Someone set fire to a storeroom. Very quickly the fire consumed the building, its legislative acts and records, and its valuable library.[23]

This incident stemmed from the general election in early 1848. Governor General Lord Elgin asked the Reformers, who gained a majority in the legislature, to form the new government, in effect establishing responsible government in Canada. The anglophone Tories of Montreal hated the idea since it entailed the end of their political dominance. When the new government introduced a bill compensating some of the 1837-38 rebels for property damage, the worst riots in Montreal's long history of rioting broke out. Given their paternal traditions, the sympathies of Charles and William must have lain in large measure with the Tories.

Earlier on the afternoon of 25 April, a mob had thrown rocks and eggs at the carriage of Lord Elgin as he left the Parliament building. Some time between five thirty and six, the government ordered William, as inspector and superintendent of police, to find the ringleaders. This he could not do, he said, because eyewitnesses would not name them. They were unwilling "to be dragged into public notoriety as a mark for the popular ill will."[24]

At about eight fifteen that night Inspector General Francis Hincks warned William of people massing in the Champs de Mars. He wanted troops called out. William replied that if he went to the commanding officer, General Gore, with only suspicions, he would be laughed at.[25] However, he instructed Police Chief Wyley to get his men to the Parliament building. That took thirty minutes. Meanwhile, at eight thirty, William consulted with Prime Minister Louis-Hippolyte LaFontaine at the House.[26] The prime minister asked him to requisition the troops. Here lay a problem. In the riot William had witnessed in 1832, the troops had fired on the crowd and killed three men. Two officers were arrested. Although they never came to trial, from then on the commanding officer of the British troops would take military action only on written request from the civilian authorities. So William had to track down the mayor for his signature on the requisition. Only then could he present it to General Gore, who agreed to send out his men. But as he ushered William to the door of his home at nine fifteen, they saw flames from Parliament House.[27] William and the troops arrived too late to help.

During the night, affidavits were sworn against five prominent anglophone Montrealers who had allegedly helped set the fire. Police arrested the men next morning. William, as justice of the peace, examined them in the courthouse and refused them bail. He insisted that he did so acting as an independent magistrate. Untrue! shouted the *Pilot,* a Tory newspaper: William was acting under the orders of the "malignant and revengeful" LaFontaine. The suspects' committal for further examination, said the paper, would unjustly keep the accused in prison for several days longer. Some 2,000 men cheered the accused men as a heavy troop escort took them to jail.[28]

Next day, Colonel Bartholomew Conrad Augustus Gugy, a member of the Legislature, read to the House a letter from the accused. The letter alleged that William had broken his promise to allow them bail, he was guilty of trickery and deceit, and the whole process was illegal. Gugy added that he himself was "perfectly disgusted" with the way William and the government had proceeded.[29] The *Gazette* reported that on the next day William finally concluded his examination of the men and released them on bail. Four days later Colonel Gugy read a second letter to the House, almost a letter of apology from the accused, "intended to exonerate Col. Ermatinger from the charge of duplicity."[30]

William, however, had other problems. The day after the fire, in the early evening, a crowd of 500 to 1,000 had milled around in front of Government House "hooting and jeering." At eight it began to disperse, but at eight thirty someone told William the mob was attacking the Quebec Hotel in St Paul Street, where several Reform members were staying. General Gore agreed to send more troops, but when they, accompanied by William, arrived at the hotel the crowd had again disappeared. At Government House William learned that the rioters had moved on to Inspector General Hincks' house on Beaver Street. He rushed back to St Paul Street to get the troops but found that they had returned to barracks. Word arrived that Hincks' windows were being smashed, so yet again William went to requisition troops from Gore. By the time they arrived at Hincks' place, the crowd had gone on to LaFontaine's and set the stables on fire. On to LaFontaine's went William, but once again he was too late. Only a few curious bystanders remained, watching the dying flames in the stables. The rioters had smashed dishes and furniture and destroyed the library. For William it was a frustrating night. As he wrote later in a report, without prior notice of where the mobs would strike next, neither the town's small police force nor the army itself could have prevented them from attacking and burning buildings.[31]

Throughout the following days, the mob and the British troops maintained a quite friendly relationship. At one point, however, William feared that the worst crisis so far was approaching since mobs of 2,000 to 3,000 were bent upon mischief. "The slightest collision with the troops," he wrote later, "must have produced the most dreadful results." Finally some gentlemen harangued them until they finally dispersed.[32]

On the 28th, LaFontaine told William that he was giving responsibility for the future peace of the city to John Young. "In relieving me of this onerous duty, the government could not have made a happier selection," William wrote. He also claimed that some incorrect statements had been made in the legislature among heavy criticism from the opposition that the government had been too slow in protecting the Parliament building. Underlying this complaint was frustration at the legalities hampering his efforts to get out the soldiers. Also, Inspector General Hincks had claimed that he approached William at Têtu's Hotel and asked him to call out the police at seven, with the implication that William should have moved faster than he had done. Not so, William replied; he had not met Hincks till eight fifteen, and he enclosed a letter to prove it. He also offered the confirming evidence of another "highly credible person," not named in his report.[33] By thus taking on a powerful cabinet minister, William showed that his courage was not confined to the battlefield.

William concluded his report with some dignity: "It has been to me a source of infinite satisfaction that up to this period, no life had been taken on either side, the more so as up to this time the responsibility for the preservation of the peace of the city had been entrusted to me." He then returned to his more normal police and magisterial duties.[34] At the end of April, the governor general appointed Captain Wetherall to head the civil force of the city of Montreal. (It appears that the appointment of John Young came to naught, since no further reference to him in this position has been found.) But a few weeks later, he appointed William King McCord and William Ermatinger to be associated with Wetherall as special magistrates for the city of Montreal. It seems that they could not do without William's services.[35]

Tension persisted through the summer. On 15 August, nine men charged with burning down Parliament were arrested. Some 100 troops and a half-battery of artillery guarded the courthouse and foiled an attempt to rescue the accused.[36] By nine thirty a large mob had collected on Notre Dame Street. The magistrates (Wetherall, McCord, and William) called out the cavalry. William was present when the troops, with bayonets, cleared a barricade near Orr's Hotel. At some point the three magistrates were in the hotel with the mob outside. Wetherall persisted in going alone onto the street. McCord later reminded William, "In about 2 minutes [he] came back saying, 'I have just escaped with my life.'" At that, McCord and William both laughed. "This was owing to his [Wetherall's] unpopularity after [illegible]'s arrest. We all then went out, but not with troops as the Gentlemen had dispersed."[37]

William was apparently not present later when ministers of the government, sheltering inside LaFontaine's house, fired at the attacking mob. One of the seven or eight defenders killed a man. Troops then guarded the house all night and easily controlled the crowd. Finally, the hot summer came to its end, and the worst was over.[38]

Seven officials, including William, applied for extra remuneration for their work during the 117 days of riots and tension over the summer. A government committee happily recommended additional pay to four magistrates and two constables, with thanks. The committee also granted the £100 claimed by William, but very reluctantly and with harsh, insulting words: "The duties performed by this gentleman ... strictly belonged to the situation which he holds." The members therefore had "some difficulty" recommending any extra allowance. William was a public servant who received an annual salary for performing his duties not just when they were "comparatively light, but for doing so at all times, and in all circumstances, through the year." He had to take his chances about the amount of work. The report went to Inspector General Hincks, whose versions of the events of 25 April William had publicly challenged.[39] Nevertheless, William continued in his job.

This episode amounted to a major break in the paternal tradition of the Ermatingers. In the 1770s Lawrence had several times actively petitioned the Crown against the actions of the governors in promoting institutions inherited from New France. In 1836 Charles Jr had spearheaded a verbal attack on the governor general for a similar reason. But William as justice of the peace had imprisoned Tories and protected Reformers. All this because the governor general had decided – the Tories claimed – to sacrifice their rights. Charles was also committed to the governor general's cause, but only tangentially as a lieutenant in the Royal Montreal Cavalry, which was standing by if called for. Wherever the Ermatinger sympathies lay, their offices made it impossible for them to disobey orders. It may be significant, however, that William was unable to identify any of the Tory rioters on 25 April.

WILLIAM AND THE WATER POLICE

In 1849 interests hurt by the opening of the St Lawrence canals began to obstruct vessels from the west while they were unloading in Montreal. John Young, now chairman of the Montreal Harbour Commission, persuaded the government to establish a special body to police the harbour.[49] An 1851 act established the River Police as an extension of the Montreal Police Force. The governor-in-council would appoint the man to head the unit, and also decided the number of men and their rates of pay. Tolls, rates, and wharfage dues not used by the Harbour Commission for other purposes financed the force.[41]

William was made head of the harbour force and for the first time directly controlled the policemen he was responsible for. This post was in addition to his duties as police inspector and superintendent. During the ice-free season, the force aided and protected shipping in the harbour by preventing desertions, picking up floating timber, tracing stolen boats, and generally maintaining order. In December 1853, the Water Police had one chief constable under William, two constables, and thirteen sub-constables, though the numbers varied from time to time.[42]

A letter William received from his friend William McCord at this time perhaps says something of the Water Police. After talking business, McCord finished, "I hope the next policeman you send me in muffty *will be better dressed!!!*"[43] William's dandyism did not extend to his men.

THE GAVAZZI RIOT

As mentioned in Chapter 7, Alessandro Gavazzi, an ex-priest turned violently anti-Catholic, was due in Montreal by ship in the early morning of 9 June 1853. William with a detachment of his Water Police waited on the wharf for Gavazzi's arrival. Already in Quebec City the man's vituperative attacks on the Church had caused a Catholic riot. The government had warned William to be on watch for the preacher's arrival in Montreal in case of a repeat. The expected Protestant mob did not appear, so Gavazzi disembarked peacefully and made his way into town.[44] But the tragedy was to come.

William spent a tense day.[45] First he consulted with Montreal's Mayor Wilson and with Lieutenant-Colonel George Hogarth, officer commanding the 26th Regiment, a British unit newly arrived in Montreal.[46] Then the mayor and William led 100 soldiers to a building a discreet distance from the Zion Church, where Gavazzi was to speak. By six in the evening Charles Ermatinger, now chief of police, had his men in position outside the church.[47] William stood nearby with seventeen or eighteen Water Police plus some special constables. Although he had the authority to swear in more special constables, his extensive experience in Montreal elections had shown that special constables, usually partisan, made for more trouble than they prevented.[48] Neither William nor Charles were armed.[49] He had never armed himself on previous occasions and did not think it necessary then, William said later. He had gone to preserve the peace, not to fight. He thought that the only weapon needed was "my commission as Justice of the Peace in my pocket."[50] In that he was wrong.

At six forty-five Gavazzi started speaking to a church full of Protestants with a crowd of Catholics gathered outside. By seven, said William, applause from inside began to "agitate" the crowd. More angry Catholics arrived. William tried to calm the crowd, but every burst of applause inside the church heightened the tension outside. Paving stones began flying. William saw men pulling his brother by the coat, but then the mob assailed William himself. Fists and sticks struck him painfully on the shoulders and breast. His commission as justice of the peace not sufficient after all, he borrowed a staff from one of his constables. Flailing about him, he defended himself while trying to control the rioters. During the action he lost sight of Charles.[51]

Some eyewitnesses said the two brothers and their men forced the mob away from the church. Others said that the mob routed the police and then moved away of its own accord. Later, rumours spread that either Charles or William had fired a gun, and that William had told the people in the church to come out and defend themselves. Both brothers firmly denied both charges, and the evidence of others backed them up.[52]

Protestants emerged from the church "firing off their muskets in different directions," said an eyewitness. The Protestant party claimed they were simply returning Catholic fire. At any rate James Welsh, standing outside, received a ball through the chest. He later died.[53] The next day, police found fowling pieces, pistols, clubs, and a double-barrelled shotgun in the church basement.[54]

The crowd drifted towards Hay Market, and William tried to disperse them. Separated from his own men, he searched for Charles' force but in the mêlée could not find them. Still fighting with his borrowed baton, he drove off several rioters who were throwing paving stones at him. One stone cut his head, leaving him dazed. An Irishman helped him, saying, "Lord, Colonel, are you hurt? I am sure it was never intended for you." He supported William to the rear of a building.[55]

According to William, he met Mayor Wilson and begged him to call up the troops.[56] According to the mayor, William, bleeding from his forehead and waving a stick, came up to him shouting, "The troops! the troops!" and admitted the police had been worsted.[57] The mayor rushed to Colonel Hogarth "in a great state of excitement," said the colonel later, "ordering us to turn out immediately as the police were getting murdered. We did so." The colonel deployed his troops near the church in two divisions, back to back. By eight, said Hogarth, things were "tolerably quiet." He met William there, wounded in the head and bleeding badly.[58] As the appearance of the troops had stopped the fighting, William felt he could safely go nearby to Dr MacDonnell's for treatment. He arrived with his left eye bleeding and his face covered in blood, and found the doctor binding Charles' wounds.[59]

MacDonnell briefly examined William, but stopped to treat a man brought in with gunshot wounds. William decided the cut to his head was "of no great consequence," and went back on the street. Some time after eight, a "rush of people" arrived in the area. Some among the newcomers fired shots at the troops. Shots also came from the Zion Church corner. William estimated that the crowd now totalled about 800, including a good number of boys and some women. Many of the crowd were trying to get between the two lines of troops, apparently for protection.[60]

The next step in the tragedy was never clarified. Certainly the agitated and confused mayor, himself a Catholic, read the Riot Act. He did so without first informing any of the officers, though by reading the act, he legally handed authority over to Colonel Hogarth.[61] The mayor had no right to order the troops to fire; only Colonel Hogarth as commander could now do that. Hogarth firmly rejected the charge that he had given any order to fire.[62] The mayor equally firmly rejected the charge that he had ordered the troops to fire.[63] Maybe the mayor called, "Fire in the Queen's name!"[64] Maybe one of the officers gave the order "Ready! Present! Fire!"[65] Or maybe a mischief-making Irishman with a straw hat under his arm and his hand at his mouth was responsible. Each proposition was put forward and the first two denied by their principals (the alleged Irishman was never found).[66]

Whatever the catalyst, both divisions began firing at the crowd. When William saw the shooting, he desperately tried to find the mayor. He finally saw him about halfway between the two companies. "Great God, what is all this about?" William yelled. He got no answer. A number of men surrounded the mayor. They asked so many questions that the mayor "hardly knew what to do," said William.[67] Colonel Hogarth ordered the bugler to sound the cease fire, which at first could not be heard. The mayor was shouting, "Stop! stop! enough! enough!"[68] Although the firing lasted only a few seconds, the results were disastrous.

The first casualty to arrive at Dr MacDonnell's surgery, when William and Charles were there, had been Peter Gillespie, with a wound in his right temple. He was insensible and foaming at the mouth, and he died at three twenty the next morning. Then casualties came flooding in: a boy about eight years old with a wounded knee, a man with a shattered left hand, a young lad shot through the left lung, and several dead bodies. From those few seconds of firing, ten bystanders finally died and about fifty were wounded.[69]

On 11 July, the coroner charged the jury appointed to investigate the affair. Nine jurors, all with British-sounding names (such as Mulholland, Ladd, Townsend, Anderson) and presumably Protestants, blamed the Catholic mayor. Ten jurors with French or Irish names (such as Belle, Beaudry, LaFlamme, Conway, Doherty), presumably Catholics, blamed a person unknown for the order to fire. They found the mayor had been justified in reading the Riot Act since there was indeed a riot.[70]

During the inquest, the Montreal *Transcript* carried an item from the *Pilot* reporting that the government had appointed a commission of inquiry into the Gavazzi affair, made up of "A.M. Delisle, C. [sic] Ermatinger and H. Driscoll." The *Pilot* approved, but the *Transcript* was scathing, saying various regular tribunals existed for this purpose, including military courts martial. The *Transcript* had supported William when his honour was unjustly assailed, "But it does seem strange, that Colonel Ermatinger, as Commissioner, should [sit] in judgment on Colonel Ermatinger, the Chief Magistrate of Police."[71] In the event neither Charles nor William sat on any such commission.

One curious thing about all these riots is that neither brother could ever identify their assailants on the night of the burning of the Parliament building, during the 1846 election riot, or during the Gavazzi riot. Yet William had spent years in Montreal and was acquainted officially and socially with many of its leading citizens, as well as many of the lesser citizens who had passed through his magistrate's court. This tact may perhaps account for his longevity as head policeman and as justice of the peace in a city bitterly divided by language, religion, and politics.

Murder, Militia, and Military Intelligence

In November 1853, following the Gavazzi tragedy, letters patent revoked William's appointment as magistrate.[1] But soon, reappointed magistrate once again and still head of the Water Police, he was involved in a nasty murder case involving religious bitterness that nearly brought down the government.

THE CORRIGAN MURDER
The date: 17 October 1855. The place: the annual agricultural fair at St Sylvestre, a village south of Quebec. In pleasant weather farmers, labourers, prosperous landowners, military officers, and magistrates watched the cattle and sheep judging.[2] But under this placid surface, violence was building. At about noon someone accused sheep judge Robert Corrigan of unfair judging. He was a strong man, said to be good natured but always ready for a fight. About thirty angry men milled around him. Some struck him viciously with sticks; others kicked him. He fell, got up, fell again under more blows. Someone helped him, bruised and bleeding, off the field. Three days later he died.

Two days after that, Magistrate Laurent Paquet issued a warrant for the arrest of seven men, all Roman Catholics, on a murder charge. The deceased, a Protestant, had often expressed anti-Catholic sentiments. A £100 reward was offered for information leading to an arrest, while residents were warned that sheltering the accused could get them punished as accessories. The government sent William and the Water Police to help find the fugitives.

Among the public, mutual accusations of abuse and violence were hurled between Catholics and Protestants. The Protestants were especially furious at the government for not catching the alleged murderers. The Church of England minister at St Sylvestre, Rev. King, stood at the centre of their protests. Among many inflammatory statements, King twice alleged that a group of Catholics intended to steal, mutilate, and burn Corrigan's body, a charge rejected even by Protestant justice of the peace John Hume as a false rumour. Later, stipendiary magistrates Ralph Johnstone and William Ermatinger declared King a prime troublemaker.

Catholics were equally adamant that Protestants were committing outrages. Magistrate Paquet claimed that on 22 December, King's son with an army corporal and some police under William abruptly entered his house. The soldier demanded "in a thundering voice" whether Paquet had rum for sale. Told no, he grabbed Paquet's seventeen-year-old daughter, put his arm around her waist, and tried to kiss her. William allegedly did nothing to restrain him.

For two months the fugitives hid in heavily wooded country, aided by those sympathizing with or fearing them. On 21 December, William commanded a force of thirty men of the Water Police armed with carbines, plus the Quebec police, plus two British army companies. The searchers, led by untrustworthy guides, spent four days scouring the wilderness for an eighty-kilometre radius around St Sylvestre, and searching the houses of alleged sympathizers in the town. Realizing further pursuit was useless, on Christmas Eve William decided to return by train with his force to Quebec. Near Craig Road Station he felt a jolt as in "a violent earthquake." The train stopped abruptly. The car was resting on the upturned tender at a forty-five degree angle, ready to roll down the embankment. All the men climbed free without injury. William had to stop soldiers from bayoneting a man seen turning the switch that had derailed the train, and the police arrested the saboteur.

Later, Dunbar Ross, solicitor general for Canada East, called the search for the alleged murderers "a complete success."[3] True, they had made no arrests, but the "demonstration of force," he claimed, had restored confidence in the law and in the authorities. In fact, the opposite happened. Protestants were further enraged at the government for not catching the accused.

Then on 18 January 1856, Ermatinger telegraphed Provincial Secretary (Canada East) George-Étienne Cartier. Seven accused had surrendered "at discretion" in St Sylvestre. The subsequent, often farcical trial by what appears to have been a predominantly Catholic jury ended in acquittal for all seven. The verdict aroused a furor in Protestant Lower Canada and in Upper Canada that nearly brought down the Liberal-Conservative government in which John A. Macdonald was the rising star.

ADMINISTERING JUSTICE

Over the course of his career, William's work as policeman and justice of the peace was varied. In 1847 André Benjamin Papineau, himself a magistrate, had allegedly opposed a provincial education bill. This highly unpopular bill imposed taxes on all households whether or not they had children at school. Papineau had said at the door of his church that he would pay his school tax assessment only "with snowballs," in effect telling citizens to refuse to pay the tax. William heard the evidence against Papineau, who admitted making provocative statements. But he had done so, he insisted, as a private citizen, not as a magistrate. William dodged the issue. He thought that the government should decide whether a magistrate, with all his "weight and influence," had the right to express himself as a private citizen even though that might lead the county and parish to disobey the law. Papineau later paid his tax.[4]

On another occasion, William was ordered to investigate Rev. Abbott, rector of Grenville, charged by a lady with an attempted criminal assault in the vestry of his church. The reverend gentleman was defrocked and deprived of his living.[5]

On the night of 27 August 1848, the immigrant schooner *Ann* from Ireland collided with the barque *Hampton* in the Gulf of St Lawrence. In evidence presented to William, one passenger on the *Ann*, Hugh Brereton, swore that he and others were below deck when they heard the cook and second mate hammering down the hatch, imprisoning them. Brereton forced his way through an opening by the side of the hatch and let the trapped people up on deck. Meanwhile, the crew and other passengers had escaped to the *Hampton*, anchored eight kilometres away. Another brig arrived and took the abandoned passengers aboard. Later, the chief agent at Montreal said the *Ann*'s master had made no attempt to regain the *Ann*. By not reaching port he had avoided paying £160 head money on the immigrants. Insurers said the unnamed owner had been under suspicion before. Everyone deplored the inhumanity of the act, but nothing could be done to punish owner or captain.[6]

Not all of William's work as a justice of the peace concerned the larger issues of riots, murder, and insurance fraud. During six years on the bench, 1849 to 1854, he heard some 10,500 cases, or an average of 1,750 annually. The most common charge was vagrancy (43 percent of the cases, with half of those charged being women), followed by assault and battery (19 percent). There were seven murders, plus other charges including horse theft, keeping disorderly houses, maiming, assaulting a customs officer, using light weights, and ship desertion.[7]

Once William was on the other side of an inquiry. When a run on the Montreal Provident and Savings Bank caused its failure in 1851, a commission accused management of "flagrant violations." Large unpaid loans, many of them to the managers themselves or their friends, had cost the bank up to £3,000. The books showed that William had borrowed two sums, one of £113/3/6 (for which judgment was obtained with interest and costs), the other of £314/11/8. The commissioner said he was not aware that the bank held any security for the first amount. For the second, the bank held a co-signature on property William had bought, but nothing more substantial. The report shows that he paid off his debts.[8]

WILLIAM AND THE MILITIA
In 1856, William left the Water Police for an appointment as inspecting field officer of volunteers under the Militia Act.[9] On his departure, his men in

the police affectionately gave him a silver tray, now in the Ermatinger old stone house in Sault Ste Marie. The inscription reads, "This tray, with a tea and coffee sett [sic], is presented to Lieut. Col. William Ermatinger, by the Officers and Men of the Montreal Water Police, as a token of regard for his kindness to the Corps. while under his Command, March 20, 1856."

After the years of warfare in Spain and of policing Montreal during the riots, William must have found administrative work in his new militia job, covering all of Canada East, irksome. Letters from the commanders of various units concerned their states of readiness, uniforms, equipment, pay lists, requests for the permitted ten days' drilling, requests for practice ammunition and ball, requests for inspection, and so on and on and on. Inadequate equipment was a common problem. An artillery officer wrote very reasonably, if ungrammatically, "It strikes me that there must be some mistake in sending Infantry Drill Books [when] Books of instruction on artillery is what I most require." A lieutenant-colonel asked for "250 greatcoats and knapsacks and 250 stand of arms and accoutrements," praying that the belts be white to go with the red uniforms and that the arms be rifles not muskets. He wrote, "you are aware how almost impossible it is to keep men drilling with a condemned weapon," that is, a musket. Captain Thomas Burns also wanted arms and uniforms. He reported that he had "fitted up a handsome armory" as good as any other in the city, and all at the expense of the company.[10]

Requests that William use his influence to get the writer an appointment were common. In 1862 Charles Nelson, captain in the No. 2 Rifles, St Hyacinthe, wrote, "My Dear Colonel, I write you a few words as an old friend of my father's." Nelson, possibly a son of George Nelson, Charles Sr's friend of Lake Winnipeg days, wanted to know how he should seek the job of adjutant to the local militia. He said he had started the militia in St Hyacinthe. William did not record any action.[11]

Lack of attendance at parades was worrisome. One year, William inspected forty-two units in Lower Canada. Together they had ninety-two officers and 1,412 men, but many were absentees. He wrote that the men wrongly thought they had to attend parades only during the annual ten days of exercise.[12] Nor was the militia well equipped. In an unsigned letter, undoubtedly written by William to his superior officer, he described the results of his inspections of several companies. One cavalry troop had horses but no uniforms. In another troop, only eight of twenty-five horses were passably good, the rest inferior. In a rifle company, the men had uniforms but lacked greatcoats (a common complaint), as well as blankets and haversacks, while their rifles were without slings. In yet another unit, the seventy-one members were armed with old cavalry sabres, "heavy and of an inferior description." William hoped they would soon be exchanged for more efficient weapons. He concluded that lack of equipment for the cavalry would make it difficult to maintain the required number of troopers.[13] These continual complaints and requests for equipment were symptoms of a problem that would eventually erupt during the Fenian crisis of 1866, long after William had left the militia.[14]

The work had its social side. In July 1859, Captain George Hunt in command of the Sorel militia asked William for an inspection. At the same time, he said, William could "take a crack at the snipe." If he could put up with common fare and a hard bed for the weekend, then "I will drive you down to the islands in time to be among the first to astonish the unsuspecting birds." William did not immediately accept. After several invitations, Hunt pointed out that once the navigation season opened, many of his men would not be available for inspection. This argument was successful. In March, Hunt wrote, "I hope you got safe home without smashing sleigh or drowning horse, [other] than that occasioned by your rash attempt at forcing a passage through six miles of *Têtes de* [S??C??abbots.] The review has raised your humble servant six inches in the eyes of the Sorellers."[15] William had not forgotten his hunting days at Sault Ste Marie, and his rashness on horseback had obviously impressed the locals.

THE AMERICAN CIVIL WAR

With the start of the US Civil War in April 1861, William may have seen his chance to escape routine and return to real battle. At that time an American, Harrison Stephens, was director of the Bank of Montreal. When President Lincoln called for 75,000 volunteers to fight in the Union Army, Stephens wrote to the US secretary of war offering to raise a regiment of 1,000 men, and arm and equip them ready for service at a cost of about $30,000. He suggested that "Col. E.R. [sic] Ermatinger, a very brave British officer" heading the Quebec militia, be colonel of the regiment. The secretary of war declined the generous offer "in the most cordial and most grateful terms."[16] It is very unlikely that Stephens would have made this offer without William's knowledge and agreement. William was now about fifty years of age.

In late 1861, the United States and Britain nearly went to war when a Union warship took two Southern diplomats off the British ship *Trent*. Britain replied by sending 14,000 troops to Halifax, prepared for war, but the crisis faded when the diplomats were returned in December. The exuberant George Hunt of Sorel was no doubt referring to this situation in his February 1862 letter to William. He had been drilling away "hammer and tongs" every night for the previous eight weeks, he said, terrible uphill work. If he were not such a "bigoted teetotaller" it would cost him a bottle of porter every night to wet his throat after drill. "I was in hopes for a while we were going to give up playing at soldiers for the real thing, but them infernal, sneaking Yankees having curled their tail between their legs, have disappointed us all," he concluded.[17]

In May 1862 the Liberal-Conservative government that had appointed

William to his militia post was defeated. The new Liberal government, faced with problems arising from the Civil War in the United States, brought down another Militia Act. As a result, William lost his job.[18]

By March 1864 the Liberal-Conservatives, with John A. Macdonald the dominant member, were back in power and soon reappointed William as justice of the peace. At that time, American bounty hunters were kidnapping Canadians and forcing them to serve in the Union Army. In September, William was hired to visit the frontier districts of St Francis, Bedford, and Iberville to stop the kidnapping and to bring the guilty to court.[19] Then the plot changed. In October, a Southern force based in Quebec raided St Albans, Vermont, set fires, robbed banks, and killed one man. On 21 October, the Montreal *Transcript* announced that William, "our efficient magistrate," was to give all possible assistance to the US authorities in arresting the Southerners when they fled back to Quebec, and to go himself to the spot, without waiting for a warrant.[20] Within two days, William and his police had captured fourteen of the Confederates.[21] Unfortunately, a local magistrate released them on a technicality. After the furious North threatened harsh retaliatory action, the government suspended the magistrate, and William temporarily got his job.[22]

Rumours of further Southern raids from Canada persisted. In December, Governor General Monck informed the US secretary of state, William H. Seward, that the Canadian government had taken measures to prevent further hostile acts. He had permanently stationed on the frontier a strong force of police and volunteer militia called the Government Constabulary for Frontier Service.[23] The Montreal *Transcript* announced the appointment of William as head of the frontier police: "Colonel Ermatinger is precisely the style of man to see that the patrol shall be effective." The paper reported that his force would be more than sufficient to cover the countryside effectively. The *Transcript* later added that William and a similar magistrate for Upper Canada would take special steps against any breaches of the law bearing on international relations. The paper supported the government's actions on the frontier. Like many Canadian newspapers, however, the *Transcript* was not much concerned with preventing Confederates from raiding American towns. Instead, the paper turned its wrath against the "numerous northern kidnappers and bounty brokers" who had for too long had carried on "their infamous business" in Canada. These, said the *Transcript*, were the proper targets for William and his police.[24]

William had an early success. A Southerner named Crawford, probably one of the St Albans raiders, was planning to break out of the Sherbrooke jail, where he was being held for extradition. Friends in Canada intended to use a "cutting machine" to sever an iron grating for his escape. Meanwhile friends in the United States were drilling to seize a train and take him to safety. William found the cutting machine and foiled the scheme.[25]

In June 1865, with the end of the Civil War, an order-in-council proclaimed that because "the deplorable troubles" in the United States had ceased, and "thorough tranquility" now existed on the frontier, the active volunteer militia on the frontier would be withdrawn. The frontier police force under William would be reduced immediately to the smallest number of officers and men needed to perform the service. To this end, William and his opposite number in Upper Canada, Gilbert McMicken, were each told to select no more than five of their most competent people to act as detectives. Even these might be discharged at a month's notice.[26] But the government turned out to be very wrong in its prediction of frontier peace.

THE FENIAN TROUBLES

In Ireland, organizations were preparing to launch a civil war to free the country from the British. Simultaneously, American Irish had formed a Fenian organization to support the rebels. One faction hoped to divert British troops from Ireland by launching an invasion of Canada. In the Civil War atmosphere, thick with hostility and suspicion against Britain, the Fenians had assembled a war chest of $500,000, with about 10,000 Civil War veterans organized into military clubs. John A. Macdonald and his government feared that Fenian raids into Canada might trigger a major war. Macdonald again looked to William, along with William McMicken, a former politician and at this time an excise officer. On 16 and 17 December 1864, they were ordered to set up security networks along the US border with Lower Canada (William) and Upper Canada (McMicken). William was to use his Water Police for this operation, McMicken had to hire his men as constables. McMicken's instructions, as stated in what was called Special Order no. 1, said the force must seek "any plot, conspiracy or organisation whereby peace would be endangered, the Queen's Majesty insulted, or her proclamation of neutrality infringed."[27]

The Water Police in this period varied in size from time to time, but during the five months from January to May 1865, it numbered forty-four men at a cost of $10,319.35. Travel expenses suggest its level of activity. Between October 1864 and April 1866, three sergeants and twenty constables claimed expenses for some fifty journeys to towns along the frontier. They travelled by sleigh, wagon, and train, often with prisoners. In 1867, they rented sleighs eleven times and carriages on twenty-seven occasions. That year, William himself rented sleighs on five occasions and carriages on seven occasions.[28] Still, they were kept on a tight financial rein. On 11 January 1866, an Ottawa official disallowed the $6 per diem expenses claimed by one of William's men, reducing it to $4 since he had no responsibility for others.[29]

William's detectives, strung along the border, collected information and rumours from agents and informants in both countries. He had to sift out what was useful and pass it along to either or both Macdonald and Cartier. Typical were the reports of Michael Burns, a constable in the Water Police. Burns visited various New York border towns during November 1865. Everywhere he found a hatred of England along with popular support for Fenian activity. At an Ogdensburg tavern he saw a large number of recently cast rifle balls and took a handful to forward to William. Other saloons had firearms and US Army equipment. On the train he met a Mr J.A. Judson, who had received a commission as brigadier-general from the Fenians after he gave $3,000 to their cause. At Malone, pressed by a Fenian agent, Burns said he would consider joining the society. Membership would cost a dollar initially and half a dollar a month afterwards, while he should also invest twenty dollars in Irish bonds. At Trout River the former editor of an Ottawa newspaper was successfully stirring up pro-Fenian feelings. Chateaugay Four Corners had an active Fenian organization but at Moore's Junction he found only some low fellows in a tavern wishing perdition on England. At Hattsburgh an Englishman, now a Fenian captain, hoped he would soon march against Canada, which he hated. In Champlain, a tavern keeper told Burns that his French Canadian friends in Sorel had plenty of drilled men and "an abundance of arms and ammunition and by G-d said he, we can walk into Canada as we all prefer the American government."[30]

In January 1866, Cartier gave William a supposedly less strenuous assignment as joint clerk of Crown and peace.[31] It seems to have made little difference to the weight of his responsibilities, and he continued using the Water Police. In early February, Burns was again on the trail of Fenians. But William felt that the agent's travelling and questioning had made the Fenians suspicious, putting his life in danger. So he decided to withdraw Burns and send in another man.[32]

William had problems with other of his men. In February, the sheriff of St Jean wrote that several suspicious characters, thought to be Fenians, had come through Montreal on the noon train that day. None of William's police had met the train at St Jean. Moreover, the train's conductor had recognized a member of the police force, "perfectly drunk," on the train when it left St Albans. The sheriff thought it his duty to warn William of this lapse, which, he said, he could fully prove.[33]

By March rumours were floating along the border that Fenians were massing for an invasion over the New Brunswick border. One of Macdonald's spies in Toronto telegraphed the attorney general of Canada West that local Fenians, led by Michael Murphy, head of the Toronto Fenian Centre, were travelling by train through Montreal to join the invaders. Macdonald could not arrest the men on suspicion only, so he instructed William to meet the train at Montreal and shadow the suspects. Unfortunately, three senior members of the cabinet had ordered the men's arrest when the train stopped at Cornwall. To Macdonald's embarrassment, the mayor of Cornwall called out the militia and in a spectacular but illegal fashion took all nine Fenians into custody.[34]

When the case came to trial, a detective from Toronto claimed that he recognized some of the accused. He had seen them attending a seditious speech by Murphy in Toronto on 17 March. Unfortunately, said the Hamilton *Evening Times*, the detective's "visual organs proved exceedingly defective." When asked to point out the three men he recognized, he got all three wrong. One of William's Water Police said that ten or twelve days earlier he had seen fifty or sixty men, supposedly Fenians, on the steamer *New York* allegedly bound for Eastport, Maine. He had also seen a box of arms. Again unfortunately, he was unable to connect the men with the arms. "Colonel Ermatinger is still here," the *Evening Times* said, "and appears confident of being able to convict the prisoners, or some of them at least, of high treason. He seems to have a keen corps of detectives busily engaged in working up the case and, being a most indefatigable officer, he will, doubtless, leave no stone unturned to bring guilt home to the prisoners."[35]

After a month of unsuccessful efforts by William and others to find incriminating evidence, the affair was turning into a comic opera. Finally, the government happily learned that Murphy and four others had dug a tunnel under the stone wall of the Cornwall jail, crept through it, walked past a sentry box with the sentry standing inside because of a thunderstorm, found a boat that somebody happened to have left on the bank, and escaped across the St Lawrence to the United States. Soon after, the authorities quietly released the remaining three suspects.[36]

The Fenians twice defeated militia forces: in New Brunswick in April, and on the Niagara frontier in June. On 7 June about 1,000 crossed into Quebec at Missisquoi Bay and occupied Pigeon Hill, plundering St Armand and Frelighsburg. They retreated across the border after twenty-four hours. William reported that the following day one of his men had got to within two and a half kilometres of the Fenian camp at Franklin Centre before guards turned him back. The camp held about 2,000 "soldiers" and was flying the British flag taken at Frelighsburg.[37]

During this raid, Canadians arrested Joseph Kelly, an American reporter for the *New York Tribune* who was with the Fenians. The US consul general, John F. Potter, protested to Governor General Monck that Kelly was not a Fenian but simply covering the news. He demanded Kelly's release. Monck replied that since Kelly had been found in the company of an armed force acting with hostile intent towards Canada, "he can scarcely have a right to complain if *prima facie* he was adjudged to belong to them." Meanwhile, Monck had ordered Colonel Ermatinger to investigate. Potter then protested even more strongly. He saw the whole affair as a "violation of his [Kelly's] rights as an American citizen, and as manifesting a contemptuous disregard of the demand made for Kelly by the Government of the United States." If Canada did not free Kelly, Potter would close the consulate for all but American citizens in Canada. Monck replied giving William's response: "Kelly's case will be investigated carefully, at once," William wrote. "The evidence touching him appears to be conflicting. It does not seem improbable that he was acting in a double capacity." In the end, however, William recommended Kelly's release. Kelly then boasted that Potter, backed by the might of the United States, had secured that release. The Montreal *Gazette* replied that William, backed by the attorney general, had himself decided to free Kelly, quite unaware that "the formidable Mr. Potter had taken any special interest in Mr. Kelly's case." This lack of awareness seems unlikely.[38]

In December 1866, the remaining prisoners taken at Missisquoi Bay were ordered to stand trial at Sweetsburg (Cowansville) in the Eastern Townships. An army unit of about 130 men, plus thirty members of the frontier (Water) police under William's command, escorted the accused to Sweetsburg and guarded them during the trial.[39] Sweetsburg was quite near the frontier, and Fenians on the American side threatened a rescue attempt. Seven army posts ringed the town with an in-lying picket of twenty-five men guarding the jail. In intensely cold weather, the jail square had to be kept clear of snow. The men were not allowed to remove even their accoutrements, and some of the posts, though very exposed, lacked sentry boxes.[40]

In February 1868, the Fenians were again making threats at St Albans, Vermont. William instructed his detectives on the frontier to be on the alert and to give him daily reports. He told Macdonald that the warnings by Fenian "General" Spears of operations against Canada were merely to keep money flowing into the Fenian treasury. The general would hardly risk his "legions" in the frozen north: "That game has been tried and played out on a much larger scale by a greater genius than himself in the person of the first Napoleon in the Russian campaign." Given the narrow roads in the area, a Fenian column would have to spread out into the countryside, which they could not do without snowshoes.[41]

In March the British consul in Boston sent an alleged Fenian diary to Macdonald claiming that Fenians were caching arms along the border. Macdonald asked William to investigate and return the diary "with all speed" while keeping the inquiry as secret as possible. William ordered his agent at Malone to ask his friends about the rumours. This was the best and only method for discovering the truth, he said, without creating suspicion and probably endangering the life of anyone sent there. Two weeks later, William's agents reported they could find no basis to the diary's claim that the Fenians had had arms delivered to Hemmingford in Lower Canada, though a Fenian organization was certainly active there. William bluntly told Macdonald, "From the foregoing, it will be seen that in most instances, the information given to the Imperial Authorities in the States, though based on some truth, is usually exaggerated and the information given is usually known and reported on by us weeks before."[42] He was unhappy to see his turf invaded by British bureaucrats, and was not afraid to tell Macdonald so.

By May the news was more disturbing. An agent reported that twenty "suspicious looking Irishmen" from Montreal had passed through St Armand heading for the United States. Other Canadian Irishmen were going to neighbouring states, possibly to train for an invasion. "Now is the time to prepare for their reception," wrote William, who had instructed his men to be doubly vigilant. He planned to send one over the border to get advance information of any move. The same agent said the Fenians were active around Boston and New York. He warned that a Captain Smith [presumably of the Canadian militia] kept his arms in the drill shed, "not a very good place for it as it is only one mile or so from the line."[43]

Even though "General" O'Neill then arrived at St Albans, William changed his mind again, deciding O'Neill would not attack until the middle of the month, if at all. His scepticism only increased when rumours of arms movement and of invasion preparations flowed in. He sent the information to Macdonald to be on the safe side but believed there would be no invasion.[44] In that he was quite right. O'Neill did not "invade" Canada ("raid" would be a better word) for another two years. By that time, William would be dead.

On 29 June 1868, William travelled by steamboat to Ottawa by order of Attorney General Cartier, and returned on 2 July. His travel expenses were included under the Water Police. This is the last known record of his official activities.[45]

Of his performance during this period, the *Evening Telegraph* said of William, "By his courtesy and good nature he managed to keep up the most friendly relations with the American authorities, and by his vigilance he kept the government fully informed of each Fenian movement."[46] A later historian, Robin Winks, writes, "Monck's quick action in every case that was presented to him in the winter of 1864-65, combined with evidence of considerable activity – even if it were undefined or misunderstood activity – on the part of McMicken and Ermatinger, undoubtedly did much to mollify the North."[47]

WILLIAM'S DEATH

After William's death, a friend named R. Campbell wrote of him, "He did not spare himself during the Fenian scare, and the sad affair at Cornwall did for him, he was never well afterwards. I used to laugh at him when he talked of being finished, but he was right. He never rallied, but dragged in a wretched existence till death put an end to his pain."[48] Maybe this ill health resulted from some physical cause. The rigours of William's frontier work during the Fenian troubles, and especially the hardships of inspecting the guard posts during the bitter cold of the Sweetsburg trials, had battered his constitution. Probably his decline was triggered by depression caused by the ridicule surrounding the comic-opera affair at Cornwall and his role in it, a ridicule painful for a proud man. A severe cold followed by constant bronchitis led to a long and painful illness. On 22 January 1869, William died aged fifty-eight.[49]

The *Evening Telegraph* wrote, "Unfortunately, the exposure and night work which he had to undergo laid him open to the attacks of the lurking enemy in his constitution. Scarcely recovered from a severe cold caught on the frontier, he was obliged to start for Cornwall. On his return he was attacked by bronchitis which he was never able entirely to shake off." The paper continued, "a large number of prominent citizens" attended the funeral in Christ Church Cathedral. He was buried in the Mount Royal Cemetery.[50]

The Montreal *News* announced William's death with regret. He had occupied important posts, said the paper, where his fine judgment, his skills, and his delicacy were much appreciated; his friendly manner and his cultured spirit made many friends who would long regret his loss.[51] The variety among his pallbearers testified to the *News'* testimonial. They were the Hon. A.A. Dorion, a respected Liberal and former cabinet member; Judge William Badgley of the Court of Queen's Bench and a Tory of the old school; the Hon. Louis-Antoine Dessaules, a controversial anti-clerical Liberal; Walter Shanly, a prominent Montreal engineer and Conservative; Theodore Hart, an influential Jewish businessman and philanthropist; and a military man, Captain De Montenach.[52]

The *Montreal Herald* said of William, "His handsome figure, noble and good humoured face, and pleasant manner had endeared him to a very large circle of friends." In his youth as a cavalry officer in Spain, he was "in appearance the very beau ideal of a *sabreur*." For many years he had been "a public functionary, and while in a position which renders a man open to attack, he had been singularly free from censure." Even the "necessary discharge of unpleasant duties" had made him no personal enemies.[53]

The French press had little to say about the death. *Le Nouveau Monde* carried a six-line paragraph headed "Nouvelles Diverse." It simply said that the English press was reporting the death of Lieutenant-Colonel William Ermatinger, who had been the chief of Montreal's police force and a justice of the peace. *La Minerve* was almost as brief but more gracious: "We sorrowfully announce the death of Lieutenant-Colonel Ermatinger, Justice of the Peace." The report continued, erroneously in part but generously, "Since his arrival in this country, which dates from 1837, he has filled several posts with confidence and to general satisfaction. He was of great use to the government during the Fenian movements. His death will be sincerely regretted."[54]

WILLIAM, A SUMMING UP

William was the most complex of the Ermatinger brothers. A dandy, and a man who loved adventure, he was impatient (whether with legal "niceties" such as warrants or with obstacles in the path of a hunt), courageous both physically (in Spanish battles and Montreal riots) and morally (when he challenged Hincks and admonished Macdonald). He had the intelligence and tact to make his way successfully through the booby traps of mid-nineteenth-century Montreal politics. And like his brothers, he was much admired by the English-speaking population of his hometown, his defence of the Reform government in 1849 forgiven and forgotten by the Tories.

Like his brother Charles, William was socially active and well integrated in Montreal society. He became a member of the exclusive Shakespeare Dramatic and Literary Club when it was founded in 1843 and in 1844 was a steward in the Montreal Turf Club.[55] He was also honorary steward for the St Maurice Turf Club. In 1863 he was a member of the Council of Montreal's Grand Rifle Match under the patronage of Governor General Monck and in 1866 was at the Montreal railway station with other dignitaries to greet the governor general on his official visit to the city.[56]

Unlike Charles and James, William probably never returned to Sault Ste Marie following his father's retirement. Given his activities in Montreal after returning from Spain, he could hardly have had the time. But he appeared neither ashamed of, nor anxious to hide, his Ojibwa ancestry. On the contrary, he named his second son after the boy's grandfather, Charles Henry Catawabiddy. And he made one other known connection with his Ojibwa heritage when he sought his mother's power of attorney, declaring himself to be the son of Charlotte, an Ojibwa chief. Rejection of a legal career for the adventures of war, riots, and espionage are quite consistent with his Ojibwa cultural background. Despite the status he achieved in Montreal, however, he died a broken man, both in spirit (as discussed by Campbell) and financially (as discussed in the following chapter).

"The Girls Have Turned out to Be Fine Women"

For all the heroics of the three Ermatinger brothers, the end of their family line arrived quietly and sadly in the early twentieth century. Two of the sisters and a wife would die married and apparently well off, but childless. One sister would die early and her son disappear in Britain. Another would die in poverty, begging money from an old friend, and her children would be absorbed into the Canadian population. Another wife, after fighting a losing battle with Sir John Macdonald to get jobs for her sons but successfully entreating him for thirty dollars, would watch her sons die or drift to the United States, all without issue.

JEMIMA AND HER FAMILY

Jemima, daughter of Charles and Charlotte, in 1829 married Thomas Cochrane Cameron, a lieutenant in the 70th Regiment of Foot. Before marriage they signed a prenuptial agreement similar to that of her aunt Anna Maria. It gave Jemima the enjoyment and management of her property, while she renounced all dower rights to her husband's.[1] Jemima's property was substantial. A favourite of her uncle Frederick, Jemima had stayed with him while attending school in Montreal. His will left her £1,000 at her majority or at marriage, and the interest on £3,000 during her lifetime, the capital going on her death to whomever she chose. Both legacies were at her disposal "for her sole use and benefit," as was his farm at Côte Ste Marie with all its buildings and their contents.[2] Given that inheritance, her father left her only £500. He explained in his will, "My equal parental affection would have induced me to bequeath as much [to her] as to the other of my children," but bequests by her uncle Frederick had made that unnecessary.[3]

The Camerons spent time in Kingston, where Jemima's letters mentioned balls and parties. In 1831 the military transferred them to York, and she soon became pregnant. Her father's sister from Montreal, also named Jemima, stayed with her niece during the bad pregnancy. The baby was stillborn at seven months.[4] Jemima later had a son she named after her uncle, Frederick William.

While Jemima was in Kingston and York, her father managed her Montreal affairs for her, including the lease of her farm in the early 1830s. Someone else bought the house on the farm, paying annual interest on a £2,500 mortgage. Charles sent his daughter careful records of farm finances, mentioning events of importance. For instance, in 1830 the barn on her farm Côte Ste Marie burned down but the insurance he had taken out covered its rebuilding.[5]

Though Charles had ensured that Jemima retain control of her money, he was not reluctant to give her advice. In 1830, when she was in Kingston, he wrote, "I am afraid, [the financial report] will not be as satisfactory as you could have wished or anticipated. However, we are all born to meet with disappointments in this world." The accounts showed her in the red, but he hoped for improvement next year. Her current account with Charles also showed her to be his debtor. He admonished her kindly: "This I presume you must have known without my reminding you, but in commencing housekeeping, a great deal is required more than one at present anticipates, which accounts for the amount drawn." By next December, he said, she would have most of the half-year's farm revenue "which with economy may serve you a long time."[6]

In the same letter, her father showed unease on another front. Lieutenant Cameron wished to purchase a commission. This would require at least £1,300, with £1,200 to be taken from Jemima's property. She should not spend that much, he wrote, unless she could refund the capital out of revenue. Her revenue came principally from the mortgage on the farmhouse, but any misfortune to the new owner's business would stop her interest until the house was resold: "This I merely mention to you as a matter of caution, and recommend economy and thereby be prepared for every event." The following year, Charles again offered cautions about the best way to finance the purchase of Cameron's commission.[7]

Tensions soon appeared between Charles and his son-in-law. Charles wrote directly to Cameron in March 1832 saying he had made arrangements for a letter of credit for the commission. He was perfectly ignorant in military matters so he could not advise Cameron, but "I sincerely hope and trust what you have determined on will ultimately turn out to your material advantage." A month later Cameron wrote that Jemima wanted to make her will but was worried that she could not leave her property to whomever she wished – presumably Cameron meant himself. Charles replied that the prenuptial agreement in no way restricted where she could leave her estate, but merely protected her during her lifetime. The same day, Charles wrote reassuring Jemima: "The advice Mr. Cameron received at York in this respect is not correct." He then sent her money received from the sale of some of his own property in York.[8]

Cameron bought his commission, presumably with Jemima's money, since later documents refer to him as Captain Cameron. But Jemima had little time to enjoy her husband's promotion. In 1838 she was back in Montreal, where she died aged just thirty. Following her death, Captain Cameron apparently moved back to Britain with the baby.[9]

Jane

Amid the Ermatinger accounts and business papers, a notebook entitled "Washing Book" has the name "Jane Ermatinger" repeated several times on the cover. Along with various scribbles, the notebook contains a list of clothing and a recipe for "plain bread pudding." Two charming sketches show a curly-headed young male with a devil's tail, probably a mischievous sister's image of her oldest brother, Charles Jr.[10]

Jane inherited from her father a farm alongside her sister Anna Maria's in the parish of Montreal. Jane's was smaller and "not the equal" of Anne's, so Charles left her an extra £400. The possessions on both farms were to be taken together, then divided equally between the two daughters.[11] Jane married James Roderick McDonald, a merchant. They moved to Hamburg, Germany, where they lived until her death in 1875. She returned to Canada for at least one visit in around 1863.[12] In 1872, the McDonalds advertised the sale of a farm on Montreal Island, described as "one of the finest on the island … very fertile and convenient to the city markets."[13] In her later years, Jane sent a small stipend to her sister Frances. At her death in 1875, Jane's body was returned to Montreal for burial. She had no children and left her estate to her husband or, if he died before her, to her surviving siblings, Frances, Anne, and James.[14] It seems likely that the siblings outlived the husband.

Anna Maria (Anne)

After her father died, Anna Maria lived for a while with the Perry family. Charles bequeathed her, as mentioned above, a farm in the parish of Montreal. In 1841, a Miss Ermatinger (probably Anne) was elected to the Committee of Management of the Protestant Orphan Asylum.[15] She married Carl Becherer of Montreal at an unknown date but died childless in 1889.[16]

Frances

Frank Ermatinger once wrote to his brother that Charles Sr's daughter Frances "will be a fine chance for some young buck out at Grass."[17] John Bigsby paid her a more gracious tribute as a fairy shepherdess (see Chapter 5). Thomas L. McKenney, another admirer of Frances, wrote of meeting Charles Ermatinger's "very accomplished and polished daughter. I was introduced to her at Dr Pitcher's, and was afterwards shown some drawings made by her by Mrs Doctor F_____. She was educated, and by the best masters, at Montreal."[18]

At least one admirer wished to marry the beautiful Frances while she was still at Sault Ste Marie. The local agent for the Hudson's Bay Company wrote that a Dr Hoskins had left the area but, according to rumour, would be back in the spring to be married "to the amiable Miss Fanny." The doctor was said to be a fine young fellow and certainly deserving "of a handsome and good wife, as Miss E. would make." Apparently the doctor hoped Charles would invite him back to Sault Ste Marie, but the marriage never happened.[19]

In 1830 in Montreal's Christ Church, Frances married Francis Perry, who had been assistant to her uncle Frederick William, sheriff of Montreal. Sister Jemima wrote of her, "Now for Mrs Perry. She gave her hand to the amiable sub-sheriff last 15 September. She has got a neat little establishment in St Louis st."[20]

A year after her marriage, Frances had a daughter, Frances Ann Perry. Charles Jr described her as "the smallest little thing I have ever seen with fine blue eyes, auburn hair and a complexion not surpassed by any of her age and as gentle as innocence itself." The next year, however, Charles Sr told Edward of "the distressing illness of our granddaughter during the period of upwards of a month under our own eyes and personal attention." He wrote that it had pleased the Almighty to take her from them and from her much distressed mother and father.[21]

Frances went on to have three more children, continuing with the family names of Charles, Jemima, and Frances Ann. After her husband died, Frances married James H. McVey, a customs officer in a small village called Mansonville in eastern Quebec, a port of entry from the United States. They had at least one son, James William Frederick McVey (1846-75).[22] For a time, McVey Sr was stationed at Georgeville, Quebec, on Lake Memphremagog. The family lived on Channel Street. This beautiful lake is near the home of the legendary Princess Minnehaha. According to one story, Frances (described as "an Indian woman of some of the tribes near Montreal") told the locals that she had once been a close friend of Minnehaha. The princess, she said, was very beautiful and an expert with her birchbark canoe on the "sparkling waters of the lake." Her boast of this fictional relationship shows that she did not hide her Native background. In 1851 in Montreal, Frances exhibited an Indian dress that she had made herself. The illustrated catalogue described it as "entirely wrought by hand in imitation of porcupine work; it is all of purely Indian design and pattern ... the costume of the chief's daughter of the Ojibway nation."[23]

As a young woman, Frances had been well off. Her uncle Frederick had left her the interest on £1,000, the capital to go to her children on her death.[24] Her father had left her a farm that Frederick had left to him, though she (along with Jemima) did not share in their father's residual estate.[25] Somewhere along the line, Bigsby's shepherdess lost her second husband, her beauty, and her wealth. Many years later, Annie Ermatinger, the daughter of cousin Edward, wrote to her brother, "Mrs. Perry was a rich young widow when I was in Montreal as a child, and I saw her later on as Mrs McVey, an old woman in almost indigent circumstances. She had a grown up son, a McVey with her, a useless fellow."[26]

In 1874, Frances had written to Edward,

My dear Cousin Edward: No doubt you will be very much surprised to receive a letter from me at this late date, and I can assure you it is not a very pleasant subject that forces me to write to you now. I am now and have been for years in extremely bad circumstances but at the present time I am so completely without resources that I am compelled to solicit aid from someone. I have, I know, no claim upon you further than our relationship and former friendship, but if you could spare me something, no matter how little, it would relieve me from actual distress. My sister Jane [living in Germany] gives me a small allowance, but I cannot touch that untill [sic] it is due and they are so far away I would not be able to get relief from them for immediate necessities. This winter has been a very hard one for me, and at my age trouble comes doubly hard but the great consolation I have is that I won't trouble anyone much longer. Trusting that you will forgive me for the liberty I have taken in troubling you on such matters, and with kind wishes for yourself and family, I remain, yours affectionately, Frances McVey.[27]

Her youngest son, James McVey, that "useless fellow," was still alive when Frances wrote this letter, though he died the following year. At least one of her older three children by Frank Perry was also alive at this time. Charles Ermatinger Perry (born 17 March 1839) became a collector of customs at Sherbrooke in 1871 and held the position until at least 1875.[28] Beyond that, nothing is known of her children.

Among Edward Ermatinger's papers an undated scrap (possibly 1874) refers to some unknown piece of property: "James sold me his interests for $800," wrote Edward, "and his share of the money sent to [illegible], calculated on the number of acres he has as compared with [illegible]. The house and garden are reserved to the two sisters [presumably Anne and Frances] so long as they or either of them may wish to occupy the same. I am to pay to each of the sisters [$17.50?] each anniversary for life, and pasturing for one cow between them. [Illegible] is to give them in provisions $40 per annum."[29] This was possibly land from an inheritance from sister Jane. Even in the 1800s, that was not much to live on, and from her earlier letter to Edward, Frances had little else. The fairy shepherdess lived ten more years in poverty before dying on 15 October 1884. She was buried in the Mount Royal Cemetery.[30]

Of the sisters, Frances is the only one for whom we have some evidence of the influence of her Ojibwa background. Bigsby had found her at ease among "her Indian friends and the whitefish" of Sault Ste Marie. She apparently told her neighbours at Georgeville of her Indian background while claiming the friendship of the fictional Minnehaha. And she exhibited the dress, made by herself, of an Ojibwa chief's daughter at a Montreal Exhibition in 1851.

CAROLINE-ELISA AND HER CHILDREN

At William's death in 1869, his widow had five sons and a daughter to bring up, aged twenty-three down to eleven. They were William Roch Daly (1846-70), Charles Henry Catawabiddy (1848-?), Edward Juchereau (1851-91), Edmund Monk Tancred (1855-?), Wilhelmina (1857-1905), and Hildebrand (1858-92).[31]

The Ermatinger family had generally been Anglican, but Caroline-Elisa was Catholic. William and Caroline's marriage took place in the bride's home without appearing in the list of marriages for the Parish of St Ours, and they were buried in separate cemeteries. This suggests that neither took the other's faith. The children were probably brought up as Catholics. Son Edward was listed on the Post Office staff as a Roman Catholic but married in the Unitarian church, and daughter Wilhelmina married a professor at the Catholic Commercial Academy.[32]

William, like his brother James, had inherited £1,500 from his father, plus a share in the residual estate, but no property.[33] During his years in high-ranking positions in the Montreal police and in the militia, he never managed to save money. Soon after his death Caroline petitioned the government "for relief." When her husband died, she wrote, she and her six children were "entirely destitute." Only the oldest child had reached majority, and his health was so precarious he could not help support the family. William had worked for the government, she pointed out, since 1842. From 1865 almost until his death his confidential duties as a stipendiary magistrate on the frontier had required "great prudence, activity and vigilance." Caroline hoped that members of the government would remember William's "devoted fidelity and zeal" in defeating the Fenian marauders, especially since his arduous exertions and exposure, particularly during winter nights, had greatly accelerated if not caused his fatal disease. Caroline asked that, on account of her destitution and her husband's faithful service, she be granted a pension or some other support. Senator Duchesnay submitted the petition. A supporting letter from an R. Campbell to Sir John A. Macdonald said that Caroline had been left "without one copper" to support her family. The oldest boy (William Roch Daly) would never be able to do anything for himself. The second (Charles Henry Catawabiddy) had a place in the Post Office, but the others were too young to support themselves. Macdonald knew better than anyone except Sir George Cartier what William's services had been, wrote Campbell. William had not spared himself during the Fenian troubles despite ill-health.[34]

In June, Caroline followed up her petition with a letter to Macdonald: "You were a friend of my poor husband and though personally I am unknown to you, may I not trust to that friendship when I plead for his orphan children who are left utterly penniless!" But in July, Macdonald regretted that the government had no legal grounds to grant a gratuity. "As your sons grow up," he added, "they might perhaps be employed in the public service, should you desire it."[35]

Had William stayed in the militia, his family might have fared better. In 1866 the adjutant general of militia recommended that the volunteer militia receive annuities and pensions equivalent to those awarded the widows of British officers who were killed in action, died from the effects of wounds, or died "by sickness contracted in the field." An order-in-council confirmed this.[36] Three months later, an annual pension of $110 was paid to the widow of a militiaman who had died from a "disease contracted on service," along with $27 for each of his three children. A similar "widow's" pension was paid to the mother of another militiaman who had similarly died. In two other cases, lump sums were paid to the fathers of militiamen who had died from diseases contracted while on service.[37] Though William may have died because of illness contracted while in the service, that service was not in the militia.

Over the next twenty years, Macdonald probably regretted mentioning the possibility of the Ermatinger sons being employed in the public service. Perhaps he had forgotten that in March 1869 he had received a letter from Edward Juchereau. William's third son requested a position in the postal service as an ocean mail clerk on a trans-Atlantic steamer. Macdonald replied that he would speak to the postmaster general, Sir Alexander Campbell, but that Edward should get testimonials from Sir George Cartier and other Montreal members of Parliament.[38]

After the pension was refused, Caroline pressed Edward's application in another letter. Macdonald replied that he had immediately sent Edward's application to the postmaster general but there were so many before him he could not promise immediate employment. Perhaps he felt some unease of conscience. Two days later he wrote again, enclosing a private note from the postmaster general: "Please read and return it," Macdonald wrote. "You will see I have done all I could in the matter. I shall keep your son in view." A series of letters to Macdonald from Caroline, Edward, and Samuel C. Monk, senior puisne judge of the Quebec Court of Queen's Bench (a relative of Caroline's) all urged Edward's appointment.[39] Macdonald forwarded the Monk letter to Campbell and wrote across the top, "Can you employ young Ermatinger?"[40] In 1872 an E. Ermatinger, presumably Edward, was listed as a third-class postal clerk in Montreal.[41]

Edward was an athlete, winning gold medals in track events with the Montreal Rackets Club and the Montreal Football Club.[42] He married Mary Josephine Alger, daughter of Cyrus Alger of Boston, Massachusetts, on 8 October 1874. They apparently had no children. Edward died in April 1891.[43]

Caroline had other sons to fight for. In 1878, Charles Henry Catawabiddy applied for a post with the North West Mounted Police. The minister of justice, Toussaint A.R. Laflamme, took up the cause in a series of letters to R.W. Scott, secretary of state and responsible for the force. The judge said that Charles' father had been a police magistrate and Charles was connected with "all the best families of the province of Quebec." The next letter mentioned that Charles "speaks English, French and German and, as I told you, he belongs to one of the best families in Quebec." By 4 May, the minister showed some desperation: "Mrs. Ermatinger writes me almost every week to ascertain whether there is any chance for her son in the North West Police. I have written to you strongly about him. Please let me know what the chances are." On 7 May, the minister's next letter came down to a curt, "My dear sir, Can you let me know if young Ermatinger is appointed to the Mounted Police Corps."[44]

Finally, Scott took action. The police engaged Charles Henry at Fort Walsh on 17 June 1878. He was aged twenty-nine, six foot one, 200 pounds (195 centimetres, 90 kilograms), and had black eyes. His previous occupation was as a mail contractor. But he served only one term of three years as constable No. 127 with C Division before discharge at Fort Walsh on 18 July 1881. His discharge form says he "served as Constable, Corporal and Constable" and was discharged "in consequence of expiration of term of service." The seeming promotion followed by demotion is explained by the entry "Conduct during service: Indifferent."[45] Charles Henry clearly did not have his father's ability. One source says Charles Henry died in 1891, another that he was alive in 1909. His whereabouts were then unknown, though he lived for a time in the United States, apparently a bachelor.[46]

In 1887 the youngest son, Hildebrand, was also working in the post office. That year he wrote to Macdonald asking him to support his application for a promotion. Hildebrand's words were not likely to warm Macdonald to his cause, however: his mother had been "refused the help by your government. At the same time you wrote her that as her sons grew up they would be employed in the public service" (a stronger statement than that in Macdonald's letter). Thanks to his local MP, Hildebrand was employed in the post office "at the *enormous* salary of $440 per annum and cannot live and help my mother as I am a married man." Macdonald referred him back to the postmaster general. Hildebrand thanked Macdonald "for his kind letter," and no more was heard of the matter.[47] Hildebrand had married Fanny Bruneau at Sorel St Pierre on 31 May 1881.[48] In 1892, the *Evening Telegraph* announced the death of a promising young post office clerk. He was P.T.H. Ermatinger, "a son of the late Lieut. Col. Ermatinger, a well known officer in Her Majesty's service in Canada years ago." He had been in the post office for some twelve years and "anxious to get along in the world had been able to complete his medical studies in this city."[49] Hildebrand and Fanny left no children.

Edmund Monk Tancred was something of an athlete, like his elder brother Edward. In 1872 his first place in the young boy's quarter-mile at the Montreal

Racquet Club won him $5.[50] In 1880, aged twenty-five, he was a janitor at the El Paso Club, Colorado.[51] He remained a bachelor living in the United States. Of the other members of the family, William Roch Daly, William's sickly oldest son, was apparently never able to work and died in Montreal aged just twenty-four. William's only daughter, Wilhelmina, married P.E. Smyth, a lawyer and professor at the Catholic Commercial Academy of Montreal. She died in 1905, leaving no children.[52]

In the long, sad list of Ermatinger petitions and letters for aid, the saddest and most humiliating came on 29 April 1889. Caroline, then seventy years old, once again wrote to Macdonald, even at the risk of being thought a great nuisance. Despite his promise to help place her sons in the public service, three of them had "had to exile themselves" for lack of government employment, "although quite fit for it." A fourth son, Hildebrand, was employed in the post office at a "petty salary, hardly sufficient to support himself." She then got down to the real reason for her letter:

> I come now to you, my dear Sir John, to ask a great favour and one which costs me more than I can tell, but I feel sure that your great and generous heart will not refuse the appeal of a widow placed in a most pitiful position. I will not tire you by long explanations. I know that you have no time to waste. Will you please lend me $30. I have a note of $150 to meet, and if you will kindly lend me that amount, it will be taking a great load off of my sore broken heart ... I cannot say how utterly I feel the humiliating position I am placed in.

Thirteen days later, she wrote again to the prime minister: "Many thanks for your great kindness in sending me $30. I shall never forget it and in return shall offer up my earnest prayers for the continuation of your health and prosperity."[53]

So ended the relationship between the family of Charles and Charlotte Ermatinger and the government of Canada. That relationship had begun with Charles Sr's service in the War of 1812, continued through the rebellions, the Great Lakes Ojibwa treaties, the Montreal riots, and the Fenian raids. Sixty-seven years after it had started, it ended with a letter to the prime minister from the widow of a distinguished Canadian soldier and police officer, begging for $30. Caroline-Elisa survived William by twenty-one years. She died at the St Ours manor on 7 October 1890 and was buried in the church of St Ours.[54]

THE END OF THE ERMATINGER-KATAWABIDAI LINE

Of the seven children of Charles Oakes and Charlotte Ermatinger who lived to adulthood, Charles Jr never married. James, Jane, and Anne (Anna Maria) married but had no children. Of William's six children, three never married and three married but had no issue. Jemima's only surviving child

Figure 8
The Old Stone House today

was taken to Britain by his father. Frances had four children, one of whom died unmarried, and virtually nothing is known of the others. In summary, Charles and Charlotte had eighteen descendants who probably reached maturity: seven children and eleven grandchildren. Of these, eleven had no children, and three had at least one child each. It is not known whether four grandchildren had children, as they were absorbed into the general population. That is, a known 61 percent of the descendants had no children, and if we exclude the four whose fecundity is unknown, eleven of fourteen, or 79 percent, had no children. The number of childless family members seems to go beyond what pure chance could account for. There seems no genetic reason for the anomaly. Charles Sr's parents, Lawrence and Jemima Ermatinger, had eight children; Charlotte's father, Katawabidai, and wife or wives had at least five children; Charles and Charlotte themselves had twelve children; and son William had six. Infertility did not seem to be a common hereditary problem. Whatever the reason, a few years into the twentieth century the Charles Oakes Ermatinger line had died out or, in the case of his daughters' children, disappeared into the general population. A comparison would be interesting of the survival rates and fecundity of other bicultural children who went to the Canada and Britain for their education.

After the Ermatingers gave up their Sault Ste Marie claims, the ancient isolation of the village and the Upper Country gave way to the modern communications systems of the new rural but already urbanizing Canada. In 1829, the first Welland Canal bypassed Niagara Falls and, with the St Lawrence canals, made the old canoe routes via the Sault unnecessary: in summer, vessels could sail the Great Lakes to the head of Lake Huron, almost to Sault Ste Marie. In 1863, the Hudson's Bay Company abandoned its post in the town; the fur trade there was virtually dead. By 1887, even the transport problem of winter ice was solved with the opening of a Canadian Pacific Railway branch line from Sudbury.

Meanwhile, the old stone house in the Sault saw many transformations: courthouse and jail, church, tavern, post office, tea room, dance hall, and apartment building. In 1932, the US Army brought back the flag Americans had torn from the staff in 1814. In 1959, the public successfully protested plans to pull the down the stone house for a parking lot. Finally, in 1964, the City of Sault Ste Marie bought and restored this elegant mansion as a tourist centre and museum (Figure 8). Among the early nineteenth-century furnishings are table linens with the initials "F.W.," once used by Frederick William (Charles Sr's brother); a sword said to have belonged to James, presumably the one he flourished during the action on Pelee Island; and the inscribed silver tray presented to William by the officers and men of the Montreal Water Police.[55]

Many fur traders and company officials of the eighteenth and nineteenth centuries, including the Ermatingers, have left us accounts, day books, letters, journals, and other documents. None, however, has left a physical memorial quite so impressive, or so evocative of the past, as the old stone house built by Charles Oakes on the north bank of the St Marys River. Some 170 years after the Ermatingers abandoned their claims, and a century after the Charles Oakes Ermatinger male line died out, the restored house still stands at 831 Queen Street East, Sault Ste Marie, Ontario.

A Lost Past, a Future Unattained

Biography has been challenged as a legitimate tool for the historian. As Carl Berger put it, "Historians in general no longer [regard] the art of narrative biography as a model for their work ... Academic scholars have increasingly occupied themselves with anonymous social patterns, with groups and classes rather than with individuals ... [Most historians writing lives are] uncomfortable with the psychologists' truth that people are driven by forces of which they are unaware, or that patterns of behaviour are shaped by buried childhood experiences."[1] The biographer must therefore face the problem of relating inner states such as influences, motives, and intentions to the observable behaviour and words of the subject. For the Ermatingers, the question is why all three brothers abandoned comfortable if quiet careers in farming, the law, or clerking and enthusiastically went off to battle in Spain and the Canadas, then pursued either hazardous military and police careers in riotous Montreal, or in the case of James, sought escape from clerking in the more adventurous West. Notably, they did this into their late middle ages.

The simplest explanation is no explanation at all: the tautology that they led adventurous lives because of an innate love of adventure. Certainly, this was not just a *youthful* sense of adventure. All three brothers were still taking on dangerous new projects in their mid-fifties. Rather, these were the actions of men acting under some motivation more powerful than simple nostalgia for their youth. If only one brother had exhibited this trait, there might well be no discoverable answer for its origin. Its emergence in all three brothers prompts a search for a common influence. The obvious motivation lies in their upbringing in the "wild man's land." The careers of the Ermatinger sons are certainly consistent with the hunter and warrior values of their Ojibwa relatives and the Métis friends of their youth. But does that prove that such values motivated the Ermatingers?

With the experimentation of the physical sciences and statistical tests of the social sciences denied him, the best a biographer can look for is not absolute proof but intuitive probability judgments. Such judgments may be made on the basis of a priori theory: what Karsten R. Steuber calls "folk-psychological and 'rationalizing action' explanation."[2] Without being sociologists, faced with such a problem historians might well look at role modelling and peer influences to explain adult behaviour. Living in the "wild man's land," the Ojibwa-speaking Ermatinger sons daily encountered such warrior-type role models and peer influences in their Ojibwa cousins and "mixed blood" neighbours. They played with them as children, socialized with them in their homes and no doubt in the great Native festivals at the Sault, and as young men Charles and William hunted and traded with them on the traplines, in hunting parties, or at trading posts. Only extraordinary youths would not be influenced by their friends and relatives.

George Nelson and John Bigsby supply strong confirming evidence here. Nelson wrote of the Ermatingers, "The boys I am told are wild fellows." According to Bigsby, "The young men of this neighbourhood were brave fellows, who could steer the canoe and point the rifle, and would ask nothing better than a roving war commission at the head of their Indian friends to kill and be killed at ten shillings a-day for all time."[3] Bigsby may have exaggerated and Nelson's evidence may be hearsay, but they strongly suggest that Charles and his brothers carried into their adult lives Ojibwa hunting and warrior values learned in their youth. That is, the Ermatinger sons sought status in a white society using Ojibwa values learned in their most formative years, namely, the value of heroism, especially heroism in battle, and of hunting skills, although both values were filtered through their later urban, middle-class education and experience. I call this the "Ojibwa thesis."

This thesis is based on the same intuitive probability judgments that we use when making decisions in our daily lives. These decisions range from assessing whether a poker opponent is bluffing to deciding in a jury trial whether an accused is guilty of first-degree murder, second-degree murder, or manslaughter. Such decisions require judging a subject's internal state at the time of his external action. Much simplified, murder is first degree only when it is an intentional act both planned and deliberate. In second-degree murder the homicide must still be intentional but the intention to kill in effect arises after the act began. Murder may be reduced to manslaughter when the act follows great provocation leading to uncontrollable passion. It seems strange that a juror must rule on a living man's future by inferring his internal states from his words and actions, while a historian cannot rule on a dead man's past using the same sorts of evidence.

David Carr in *History and Theory: Studies in the Philosophy of History* writes, "The situation in which a historian confronts a historical agent is just a special version of the ordinary situation in which we confront another person. Some of us are better than others at taking the other person's point of view into account, of putting ourselves in the other's place, and this is no doubt as true of historians as it is of the rest of us."[4]

In this approach to the behaviour of the Ermatinger sons, the intuitive probability that the historian assigns to the Ojibwa thesis may depend in some measure on personal experience. In the case of hunting, those brought up in a hunting culture would give a nod of understanding when reading Bigsby's description of the Ermatinger and Johnston youth of the Sault as "brave fellows, who could steer the canoe and point the rifle." In these anti-hunting days we might in adulthood either continue with or react against such hunting values and the role models that helped create them, but we would still be strongly affected by them. By extension the same reasoning applies to socialization in a warrior culture, albeit modified by values acquired later. As Bigsby said, the young Johnstons and Ermatingers "would ask nothing better than a roving war commission at the head of their Indian friends to kill and be killed at ten shillings a-day for all time."

A fourth brother at first glance seems to be a counterexample. George, who died in 1822 at the age of sixteen, probably intended to be an Anglican priest, far removed from the warrior hero role of his three brothers. Ojibwa society, however, attributed high status to one group other than the warrior-hunter, and that was the Midewiwin society, of which George's uncle Mang'osid was a powerful practitioner. Midewiwin membership and Anglican priesthood do not of course play precisely analogous roles in their respective societies, but both conferred high social status. In seeking the priesthood, the teenage George followed an Ojibwa custom for achieving status in white society, just as his brothers would later seek it in a different way.

The Ojibwa thesis gains increased probability from the fact that the Ermatingers consciously saw themselves as, in some sense, Ojibwa. They stated their Ojibwa heritage explicitly in the petitions they presented to the government: Charles' petition for a job with the Indian Department, and William's petition on behalf of the whole family, for land rights at the Sault. They also acknowledged it when Charles flirted with the Liberator expedition to establish a Native kingdom in California, when James described himself as a Canadian Indian in the 1871 census, and when William named a son after his Ojibwa grandfather. All the children proudly proclaimed their heritage by burying their mother under her Ojibwa name, Kattawabide, rather than Ermatinger.

They were also seen by others to be, at least in part, Native, if not always seen as Ojibwa. The four Ojibwa chiefs explicitly recognized this relationship by acknowledging them as "the children of the sisters" and as "kindred." The Ermatingers' uncle Mang'osid implicitly recognized the same claim by supporting their bid for land at the Sault. On the Canadian side, Sir John A. Macdonald described James as "a half breed Chippewaian." James' *Norfolk Reformer* obituary named his mother "Charlotte Kattawabide, an Ojibwa chief in her own right." W.B. Robinson used Charles' connections to meet with the Garden River Ojibwa chiefs. And the Ermatingers' Native heritage was well known in Montreal.

About the daughters we know too little to generalize. Bigsby wrote of Frances, "My shepherdess was quite at home among the Indians and the whitefish."[5] It seems that she learned Ojibwa domestic crafts from her mother. And in later years in Quebec, she let her Indian background be known when telling of her "friendship" with Minnehaha.

It is true that the Ermatinger claims to their Ojibwa heritage were associated with land and mining rights, and in Western eyes could be considered as self-serving. But in Ojibwa culture gift giving was an essential element in social bonding. The chiefs said they were providing for "those of their kindred," specifically the Ermatingers, who had claims upon them for past benefits and services. As children of their sisters, the Ermatingers were participating with the chiefs in the ancient Ojibwa cultural rite of gift giving.

In what sense, however, could the Ermatingers claim to be Ojibwa when they lived almost all their adult lives in urban Canadian society, and generally conformed with its social and legal customs? Here Harriet Gorham's concept of a sliding identity becomes important. As people of dual descent, the Great Lakes Métis did not usually follow, say, the Red River custom of melding their two cultural backgrounds into a new, third culture. Rather they understood and could take on and discard many of the characteristics of each culture as they moved from one to another. The Ermatingers could join Montreal's elite and hunt with the hounds across the fields at Long Point or "take a crack at the snipe" with William's militia colleague in Sorel; they could also join their Ojibwa friends and hunt with their canoes and guns in the lakes and forests of Indian country. Given their peculiar knowledge of both societies, they could, as Gorham found with the Great Lakes Métis, mitigate conflict between the two. Charles claimed to have done just that during the Robinson Treaty negotiations.

It is perhaps curious that though the Ermatinger family claimed an Ojibwa identity, not one member chose an Ojibwa spouse. The reasons for choosing a life partner are of course many, complex, and often contradictory. However, Gorham says of the Great Lakes Métis that they had "a general preference … to marry outside their own 'group,' and to re-establish contact with the Indian bands and White traders *with whom they did business*."[6] For their adult lives, the Ermatingers mainly "did business" with whites, who they married.

But can such an ambiguous identity survive without serious internal conflict? A number of writers have pointed out that bicultural children of fur trade fathers usually faced psychological problems when living in a white, urban society. Jennifer Brown finds that men born in the Upper Country but educated in Montreal lived with a bicultural tension that tended to political activism, even rebellion. She cites Cuthbert Grant Jr, son of a North West

Company official who took part in Dickson's Army of Liberation, and Louis Riel, both of whom received their schooling in Montreal.[7] The Ermatingers were exceptional in that their father did not pressure them to suppress their Indianness, as did so many fur trade fathers. They were exceptional again because they apparently faced no overt racism in Montreal and Simcoe. Still, the suspicion remains that, for them, certain bicultural tensions did exist. Conflicting loyalties must have posed a problem for Charles and James at the 1850 Lake Superior treaty negotiations. And when James protested the possible use of the Sioux for "levying unauthorised war" in the North West, he must have known his views would not be popular in Ottawa.[8]

Nevertheless, however sincere the Ermatingers were in claiming their Ojibwa identity, their expression of it and their behaviour exhibited a certain romanticism. Ojibwa culture did not appoint women as civic chiefs; that function passed down from father to son. So Charles could not have been a chief, as he claimed, nor Charlotte a chief as William claimed, nor William therefore the son of a chief. Frances was certainly not a friend of the fictional Minnehaha. The battle experiences of the sons have a similar romantic quality. The rash and badly armed Charles at Longueuil, wounded in the face and shoulder, fires his revolver at his ambushers before he is forced to quit the field. James, amid flying bullets on Pelee Island, lifts his dead comrade onto his horse. William, in a distant Spanish valley, halts his retreating men, rallies them, and leads them at the *pas de charge* to recapture their artillery. Charles flirts with General Dickson while James seeks a return to the Upper Country of his childhood and William is proposed as a colonel in the US Civil War. This is the stuff of heroism in the best romantic fashion.

Unfortunately, that heroism could not be maintained. When he quit the battlefield, Charles stayed in the peacetime cavalry, then joined William in the police, the closest he could get to battlefield conditions. Fired from his police job, he died soon after one last hunting trip to Sault Ste Marie at the quite early age of fifty-five. After his Spanish exploits, William also sought a substitute for battle, first in the police, then in the militia, and then in counterespionage against the Fenians. Finally, he dragged out a "wretched" end and died depressed and impoverished. James, in later life a county clerk issuing permits for retail outlets, could do nothing more martial than write letters on military tactics to the secretary of state for war, deplore the military unpreparedness of the nation, and unsuccessfully seek a return to his youth as a North West magistrate. Without the excitement of battle, or at least of high adventure in the "wild man's land," all three seem lost.

The twentieth century brought the end of the Charles Oakes Ermatinger line. On the male side, the last known surviving grandson died, and any descendants through the daughters disappeared. That leaves the haunting question: could social or psychological stress arising from their Ojibwa cultural heritage expressing itself in a Canadian society have contributed to the family's decline, even reaching down to William's children? Unfortunately, as suggested by Jennifer Brown, there is little comprehensive and detailed analysis of the fates of other Indian-Canadian children sent to the cities, and still less about the progeny of these children and their fates, with whom the Ermatingers could be compared. More such studies over generations could lead to a richer understanding of the class to which they belong.

The sentimental but touching letter by bachelor Charles Jr about the "sweet unattainable woman" provides a clue to the psychology of the Ermatinger children. "Why distract one with images never to be realized," wrote Charles. "Such a being seldom exists or only in the wild vision of the romantic and poet."[9] It requires no great psychoanalytic jump to see Charles' sweet unattainable woman, along with Frances' "friend" Minnehaha, as symbolizing both memories of an Upper Country Ojibwa past that had escaped the Ermatinger children, and dreams of a white, urban future that could never quite replace what they had lost. In their lifelong pursuit of heroism, whether in war or in riots, or even at a desk writing letters about military strategy, perhaps all three sons were romantically motivated by the spirit of an old Ojibwa song:

> I fall – but my body shall lie
> A name for the gallant to tell;
> The Gods shall repeat it on high,
> And young men grow brave at the sound.[10]

Appendix A: Extract from John Bigsby's Journal, 1850

We had scarcely seen a human being for ten days, when all at once we came in sight of two villages, British and American, on their respective sides of the river, and several canoes passing to and fro, or fishing.

The river itself (seventeen miles long by half a mile to a mile and a quarter wide) is deep, silent, broad: massive woods overhang its banks. Directly before us, at the distance of two miles, are the boiling rapids, called the St Mary's Falls.

On the British, or left side of the river, an accidental conflagration was raging in the woods. The horizon was considerably darkened by smoke; and every now and then a gleam of fire, faint in the distance, reached us, newly fed by some resinous trees. [There follows a description of the fire.]

The surveying party of the Boundary Commission, with whom I was now travelling, passed rapidly through St Mary's into Lake Superior. This journal ought to be continuous with their movements; but I beg the reader's permission to delay for a little our excursion into Lake Superior, in order to assemble in one chapter all our proceedings in, and remarks upon, Lake Huron. We shall be glad enough to join our friends.

At the time of this visit St Mary's was a very modest settlement. I imagine it remains so.

The Canadian village is, or was, a straggling line of fifteen log-huts on marshy ground, with, at its lower end, the comfortable dwelling of Mr Ermatinger, whose daughter's acquaintance I had unexpectedly made on the western branch of the Ottawa.

The North-west Company of fur-traders have an important post near the head of this village, close to the rapids, on the broad tongue of lowland full of little water courses, which is the British portage. This post consists of a good resident's house, large storehouses, stables, labourers' dwellings, garden, fields, and a jetty for their schooner. The cattle were in remarkably good condition.

The American village is but small; it has, however, two or three houses of a better class, and is on higher ground, with a few Indian wigwams interspersed.

The Americans have a stout barrack here, called Fort Brady, and two companies of infantry.

Mr Johnston, a much respected Indian trader, lives here most hospitably in a house whose neatness is in striking contrast with the careless dilapidation reigning around.

A few potatoes and some Indian corn are raised on either side of the river, and there is a little pasture land.

Mr Ermatinger built a windmill, in a vain attempt to induce the people to grow wheat. It is said that the cold mists and draughts from Lake Superior check the growth of corn.

St Mary's is healthy. I did not hear of ague there. Our party enjoyed excellent health in Lake Huron.

But in point of agricultural improvements there is both room and opportunity, by the drainage of swamps and shallow lakes. It is now in these countries as it was in the early times of Britain. A great part of England was then taken up by unwholesome marshes and woods, so that the lower levels were but little inhabited. Many of the towns, villages, and Druidical remains, were on the hill tops. Now our valleys are healthy, warm and productive. We therefore inhabit them.

The white and red inhabitants of St Mary's live chiefly on white fish caught in hand nets at the foot of the rapids, and they, as before said, are salted in very large quantities.

The rapids rush tumultuously in a white mass of eddying, billowy, foamy surge, through a strait only half the usual breadth, and half a mile long, bordered on both sides by almost inaccessible swamps and dense woods, where the lowness of the banks has permitted a number of petty channels to form. Looking up from the middle of the river the scene is full of life, and stir, and strong contrasts. We see dark woods and dazzling waters, often crowded with Indian canoes. One reef, or ledge, very visible from the shore, is supposed to cause a drop of six feet. An American surveyor had calculated their total descent to be twenty-two feet ten inches. The underlying rock is horizontal sandstone, mottled red and brown, belonging to the Silurian Age. Father Hennessin (edit. 1696, p. 64) describes St Mary's Falls exactly as they are now.

In 1824, I remained three weeks a guest at the North-west Company's post, enjoying the great kindness of Mr Sivewright, the superintendent, an old officer in the fur trade, familiar with the most remote regions of the north-west, and very communicative.

Every place has its own peculiarities, I suppose. Here it was the correct thing to live almost solely upon white fish morning, noon and night. Rich and delicately flavoured as this food was at first, in the end I loathed it, and for ten years afterwards could not see fish on the dinner table without a shudder. White fish here varies from three to six pounds in weight. In Athabasca Lake they run to twenty pounds.

I was much pleased by my visits to Messrs. Ermatinger and Johnston. The former was every inch a trader, public-spirited, skilful, sanguine, and indefatigable. Save two rooms, his whole dwelling was a warehouse. My shepherdess was quite at home among the Indians and the white fish. Her *boudoir* was full of little tokens of Atlantic City education. She seemed mosquito-proof, and did the honours of her home with kindness and grace.

Mr Johnston was a merchant, with the generous and social qualities of the old Irish gentleman. He had been plundered and burnt out by the Americans in the war of 1814, in one of the many unchristian ravages which both parties committed on the unoffending citizens on the frontiers. Up to the time of my visit (ten years afterwards), Mr Johnston had received no compensation from his own government although his loss was very heavy, and his claims respectfully urged in the appointed manner.

I was surprised at the value and extent of this gentleman's library; a thousand well-bound and well-selected volumes, French and English, evidently much in use, in winter especially; and not gathered together in these days of cheap literature.

Mr Johnston was an Irishman of good family, and died in 1828.

He was so kind as to invite some of his few neighbours to meet me at a good dinner, and produced a bottle of crusted port of an especial vintage – a sort of good thing of which I was utterly unworthy.

Mr Johnston had married the daughter of a powerful Indian chief, residing on the south shore of Lake Superior, which, of course, brought him the friendship and trade of all his tribe. She was a portly, bustling, happy-looking creature, and had imbibed all her husband's notions; and she united to the open-handedness of the Indian the method and notableness of the English woman.

They had several children, the eldest at that time a gay half-pay lieutenant of a Canadian corps. His eldest daughter has since married Mr Schoolcraft, formerly an Indian agent, but now at Washington at the head of the Indian department; a gentleman in every way worthy of his advancement, and to whom I am considerably indebted both for information and attentions. She then strongly reminded me of Walter Scott's Jeanie Deans by her quiet, modest ways, by her sweet round-oval features, expressive of the thankful and meek devotedness so universal in Indian women. The style, manners, and conversational topics, both here and at Mr Ermatinger's, were remarkable, and quite distinct from those of the cities we had left behind us.

I shall not be so ungallant as to describe the dress of the ladies. No lady likes to be described in a fashion ten years old, although no obsoleteness in dress can hide goodness and intelligence.

I could not help inwardly smiling at the garb of our male company in their vast collars *"a la régent,"* and waists so high that the coats were all skirts. Their pantaloons were slit up outside, and adorned with a profusion of bullet-headed brass buttons; while, in imitation of the Mexican *rancheros* and the English dragoons in Spain, these good people, who never crossed a horse, made the inner parts of this nameless garment almost wholly of leather.

I envied the masses of long black hair which rested upon the shoulders of my friends. They had enough hair to make perukes for twenty duchesses.

The unsettled postures, dark hue, and wandering black eye of the Indian, were well marked in some of the guests, and the perfect gypsy face. Their English was good, and without the disagreeable nasality of the American.

It is true that we ate fast and in silence, but this being over we were very merry, in spite of an abundance of mosquitoes. Each took up his own easy position, uncourtly but not uncourteous, and talk became plentiful. We wasted no words upon civilised man. We dilated about the prospects of the fishery, of the wild-rice harvest, the furs of the last winter's hunt, the rumoured incursions of the Sioux and other Indians upon the quieter tribes, the massacre of the whites at Red River, then recent, while I obtained from one or another descriptions of the adjacent regions.

All this made me feel that I was near the wild man's land; and I was confirmed in the idea by one day meeting in the village a handsome white woman, who wore a broad silver plate on her head on account of having been scalped.

The young men of this neighbourhood were brave fellows, who could steer the canoe and point the rifle, and would ask nothing better than a roving war commission at the head of their Indian friends to kill and be killed at ten shillings a-day for all time.

Their principal occupation in winter was to follow the Indians to their hunting grounds to the south and west of Lake Superior, for the purpose of taking their furs almost as soon as ready, to ensure repayment of the usual autumnal advances made to the Indians.

In summer my friends performed the functions of country gentlemen. They farmed, fished, and sported.

The great defect in colonial life is the lower civilisation which characterises it; where the inferior appetites, the animal instincts, prevail, and are exclusively gratified; where a man's thoughts seldom go further than himself, his shop, farm, bottle, horse, and rifle.

In the country parts of Canada few young men get above the class of "gents.," and the elders seldom rise higher in their notions than the second-rate retired tradesmen at home. There are here and there some few loftier minds, driven into hiding places by misfortune; but they only mark, and so thicken, the general gloom. There is not enough of the fine gold of English society to make a public impression. In England the female gentry, in their respective rural neighbourhoods, do a large amount of good, as living examples of wisdom, generosity, and gentleness.

I advise only the uneasy classes of Great Britain to live in Canada; the easy classes, however, I strenuously advise to visit it.

I did not find my time heavy at St Mary's. Opportunities of leaving are rare, and must be made; so my friends contracted with two very young Indians to take my old travelling companion, Mr Tabeau (on a second missionary tour), and myself to Collier's harbour, on Drummond Island, in Lake Huron, forty-five miles from St Mary's. It was 1100 miles from Quebec, and the most westerly British post.

Appendix B: Petitions of Charlotte Katawabidai

CHARLOTTE'S 1847 PETITION

Memorial No. 211. Charlotte Kattawabidé, widow of the late C.O. Ermatinger, Esq.

Council Secretary's Office, Indian Department, 8 May, 1847.

[Salutations omitted.]

The memorial of Charlotte Kattawabidé, widow of the late Charles Oakes Ermatinger Esquire in his lifetime of Elmwood in the Parish of Long Point, and late of the Sault de St Mary, Lake Superior.

That your Memorialist is the hereditary head Chief of the tribe of Indians called Ojibway Chippeway or Saulteaux, part of the once Great Tribe of Adirondacks known and styled by the French Algonquin in their earliest records.

That your Memorialist was the Eldest Child of her immediate ancestor Kattawabidé Lebrocheu, the late hereditary head Chief of the Chippeway [illegible] who departed this life in the year 1828 at Fond du Lac, the western extremity of Lake Superior.

That as such Eldest Child of the deceased Chieftain according to the ancient custom of the tribe she succeeded to and inherited the rights and privileges of the Chieftainship.

That the Ancestors of the Memorialist have from time immemorial [been?] in possession of Lake Superior and the surrounding Territory as hunting and fishing grounds.

That your Memorialist has the honor to transmit a flag, given by the French government, to her great great ancestor [Muckodé?] (Brave Heart), as the recognised hereditary Head Chief of the Tribe then actually in possession of the lake, and by whom it was transmitted to his successors, consecutively [Boy-Os-wa? Bi-aus-wah] LeBrocheu, Grandfather to Memorialist, & Kattawabidé LeBrocheu the Younger, her late father thro' whom it has descended to Memorialist in direct line as the insignia of Chieftainship.

That your Memorialist has been absent from her tribe for some years, having since resided in Lower Canada with her late husband Charles O. Ermatinger esquire.

That during such absence and subsequent to the death of her late father, the tribe have entered into a Treaty with the United States by which they have ceded to that government the South Shore of the Lake, as far as LaPointe.

That from having adopted and borne allegiance to the flag of her late husband's Country, she and her children (viz. Charles Oakes Ermatinger, Frances Ermatinger, William Ermatinger, James Ermatinger, Anna Maria Ermatinger and Jane Ermatinger) could not become parties to this treaty without foreswearing their allegiance and becoming subjects of the United States.

That your Memorialist and family have from this fact suffered great loss and have forfeited all claim to any compensation for any part of the Territory under the jurisdiction of the United States.

That your Memorialist has always been a loyal and faithful subject of Her Britannic Majesty and has, from their earliest infancy, taught her children to love and respect the flag of the Country under which they have been born and protected.

That your Memorialist trusts that they have not forfeited the protection of Her Majesty's government from any causes to her unknown.

That your Memorialist has learned with infinite regret and pain that the lands on the North Shore of the Lake, the proper inheritance of herself and children, have been and are now being disposed of by the Provincial Government without any [illegible] from her or from any person duly authorized by her, or by the Tribe, which is and has been in possession for centuries, or without having as in similar cases first entered into a treaty by which any portion, part or parcel of the said Territory could have been duly acquired by the said Government.

That the Imperial Government has invariably treated with and acquired from the Aborigines, lands or territory by regular and recognized principles of justice, by forming regular conventions and treaties, by which one party became bound to the other for Certain Considerations to Acquire, and the other to alienate certain territories or lands. And this from the earliest English settlements on record on this continent, which practice has been strictly followed up from the celebrated Treaty of William Penn in 1682 down to the present day.

That your Memorialist is aware that great sympathy has been manifested by the whole civilized world for the several tribes which have been from time to time forcibly removed from their original possessions by the Government of the United States in their several [spoiliations?], tho' invariably acting under the cover of Treaty or Convention, by which they gave to the Aborigines a supposed fair value.

Your Memorialist would indeed hope that a deviation from the usual practice of the two most civilized nations in the known world in the acquisition of territory from the Aborigines of this continent has in this instance been an oversight on the part of Her Majesty's Provincial Government.

That your Memorialist is aware that your Excellency has but recently entered into the duties of your high office, and that the proceedings of the Provincial Government in reference to the sale of the lands referred to are anterior to your Lordship's arrival to this government.

That your Memorialist has always wished to live and die under that flag which she has been taught to believe waives [sic] with justice and protection over a vast surface of this continent.

That your Memorialist has been made aware of Your Lordship's high and well merited reputation for justice, and would therefore most respectfully draw Your Excellency's attention to this matter, which to Memorialist and family is of the utmost and material consequence. And therefore prays that your Excellency would be pleased to appoint a Commissioner or Commissioners, not interested in the mining companies of the lakes, or by such other mode as in your Excellency's wisdom may seem most meet, to investigate the claims of Memorialist and others interested, as it was their territory [illegible], in order that justice may be rendered your Memorialist in the most prompt and the only efficient and just manner. And that your Excellency would be pleased to order that no further sale of land take place till Memorialist and the several parties interested enter into an arrangement for the final adjustment of this question.

That your Memorialist would also take this [illegible] solemnly but most respectfully nothing is gained [illegible] sales that may have been or are about to be effected by the Provincial Government of any part or parcel of the territory in question till a regular treaty is entered into, and your Memorialist and family indemnified.

[Illegible] in duty bound will ever pray, Charlotte Kattawabidé

Charlotte's 1849 Petition

Petition of Charlotte Kattawabidé, widow of the late Charles Oakes Ermatinger & daughter of an Indian chief, Kattawabidé, praying for a reconsideration of her claims for certain lands on the shores of Lake Superior. [Not dated but considered in Committee 11th August 1849]

[Salutations omitted]

[The petitioner] respectfully submits that on the 7th May 1847 your petitioner forwarded a memorial to your Excellency in reference to certain claims made by her to a certain territory on the north shore of Lake Superior, as well as in her own name as in the name of the tribe of Indians now possessing, and that have been in possession of that territory from time immemorial.

That your petitioner filed this claim as an inherent right derived from her late father Kattawabidé/LeBrocheu, the late hereditary head chief of the tribe of Indians styled Chippeways, Ojibway or Saulteaux, who are still in possession of parts of Lake Huron, River St Mary, the country on both shores of Lake Superior to the headwaters of the Mississippi and embracing the countries bordering on Winnipeg, Leach and Sandy Lakes.

That your petitioner's father was always recognized as such head Chief in those regions up to the time of his decease in 1828.

That your petitioner has the honor to transmit a copy of an extract from a report of the Committee of the Honorable the Executive Council on Matters of State, dated 24th of June 1847, and approved by your Excellency in Council on the same day.

That your petitioner must [illegible] and earnestly protest against the opinions and proceedings of your Excellency's late advisors which, in good faith, determined your Excellency to approve of the decision.

That your Excellency will perceive by the action of the government of the day on this matter that your Excellency's approval was obtained in consequence of the report of the Honorable the Executive Council on Matters of State and from the best information they had been enabled to procure and lay before your Excellency.

But your Excellency could not have been made aware that this information was entirely of an ex parte nature, and that your petitioner was never at any time notified that such an investigation was anticipated, much less actively going on; nor permitted, as is usual in like instances, to be present or to be represented when such was actually pending, and consequently debarred from all possibility of counteracting evidence or of persons, and making good her claim by testimony or otherwise.

That your petitioner is convinced that your Excellency could not have been aware of the means made available by Your Excellency's late advisers and by the Committee of the Honorable Executive Council on Matters of State, in obtaining their best information of this matter. Your petitioner would take this opportunity of filing a copy of a letter from the South St Mary addressed to Charles Oakes Ermatinger Esquire demonstrating clearly that the investigation was carried on by a servant of the Honorable the Hudson's Bay Company, Mr Balenden, acting under instructions from Sir George Simpson, and in what manner will more fully appear by the enclosed letter. Parties most hostile to the interest of petitioner and her children and contesting this same claim with petitioner, were appointed to be arbiters of petitioner's rights in this case, as will be seen on reference to the claims [made?] by Sir George Simpson and others for part and parcel of the same territory.

Your Excellency, from your well known impartiality and justice will thus admit that this was not [illegible], fair or right. Yet such proceedings are [illegible] with the term a state matter [of] investigation, and certainly this was not the mode of obtaining the best evidence of the truth or falsity of a claim of such importance.

Your petitioner has also heard that some portion of the tribe have been induced to come down to [illegible] their claims before Your Excellency and that it is your Excellency's intention to treat with them in sending a Commissioner or Commissioners to [illegible] this question.

Your petitioner would take this opportunity of again solemnly protesting against any arrangement being enterred [sic] into, with any portion of the tribe in question, in which she and her children (viz. Charles Oakes Ermatinger, Frances Ermatinger, William Ermatinger, Anna Maria Ermatinger, and Jane Ermatinger)[1] are not parties agreeing and consenting thereto.

Your petitioner would therefore urge upon the government the expediency of appointing at least three Commissioners not interested either in the mining or Hudson's Bay Companies to enter into this treaty, on this [illegible] it be [illegible] desirable to appoint one of the officers of the Indian Department for this service, that other two persons be named who are not in any way associated with the question, and that they be instructed to hear and investigate the claim of petitioner and her children. And your petitioner therefore prays that Your Excellency would be pleased to reconsider the extract of the report of a Committee of the Honorable the Executive Council on Matters of State, dated 30 June 1847, and approved by Your Excellency in Council on that day.

(Signed) Charlotte Kattawabidé

In Committee, 11 August 1849

The Committee sees no reason to reverse the order of Council of the 24th of June 1847.

Letter from Samuel Atkinson

Sault Ste Marie, 20th May 1847

Charles O. Ermatinger Esquire, Montreal.

Dear Sir, Mr Balenden of the Hon. the Hudson's Bay Co. called on me at my residence this morning and solicited information on the following queries.

Who was the mother of the Ermatinger family of Montreal?

Who the father of Mrs Ermatinger?

Where did he reside?

Was he a chief?

Was he a chief of the whole Chippewa nation?

At what particular part of the country was his authority most respected?

Did he at any time after the boundary line between the United States and Great Britain was established give up his adhesion in any particular manner to the United States' government?

Where did the late Mr Ermatinger marry?

Where were the older part of his family born?

To all of which I gave such information as I possessed.

It appeared in the course of conversation that they were a sett [sic] of interrogatories forwarded by Mr Morris, President of the Executive Council (if I mistake not the title), in relation to some land claim that was about being preferred by the family.

And further, it rather appeared that Mr Balenden was if anything adverse to the claim. Should the above prove of any consequence to you, it is quite at your service. If not, please destroy the record, and believe me, most respectfully, your most Obèdt. servant,

Samuel Atkinson

Appendix C: Two Brothers, Charles and George

John Askin, a storekeeper at St Joseph, Michigan, wrote a letter in 1809 to his father at Detroit introducing Charles Oakes Ermatinger Sr. He was a brother of George Ermatinger, Askin explained, "but a far better man I believe" than George.[1] Though George lived for many years in the American Sault, there is no record of the brothers socializing. Nor does Henry Schoolcraft mention George in all his round of social activities at the Sault. Indeed, the Ermatingers seemed to regard George as something of the family black sheep. His uncle Frederick and his aunt, Mrs Edward Gray, left him the interest on some money, but the capital was to pass on his death to his children. Other relatives were given their legacies with no strings attached.

Trouble between the two Ermatinger brothers first appeared in 1820 when Charles complained that in 1818-19 he had supplied sundry goods to George but had received no payment.[2] Unlike the loving, indulgent father who emerges in Charles' letters to Jemima, these letters show an angry, rebuking brother. These problems arose because he was trustee for the two legacies of which George was a beneficiary. In 1830 Charles complained that his brother had not acknowledged receipt of the previous year's money. Unless he did so, Charles would send him no account next year, nor pay any draft from him. Despite the sharp warning, he remained, "dear George, your affectionate brother."[3]

Then two bills, including board, arrived from Rev. Ferry, who was teaching George's sons. Charles paid the bills, but in future, he told Ferry, he would pay only tuition fees. On the same day, he wrote to a Mr Hulbert, who was holding a draft George had drawn on Charles. George had already overdrawn on his legacy, he told Hulbert. Nevertheless, "I shall however in this instance pay the draft, when due" though this would "greatly reduce his means for a future year."[4] In a third letter, Charles told George he was sorry to hear of his financial embarrassment. He was even sorrier to hear that George had drawn £50 on Charles when he (Charles) had already paid Mr Ferry's bills, Mr Hulbert's bill, and a bill for goods delivered to George at Sault Ste Marie.

In all, his brother owed Charles £209/5/2: "I cannot conceive how you could possibly be induced to draw upon me in the manner you have done." Should he persist in doing so before his annuity fell due, Charles would have to protest the drafts "with all the evil and expense attending such a measure." He hoped his brother could extricate himself from his difficulties. This was "the sincere wish of your affectionate brother."[5]

George's next letter, and it is the only one from him to Charles so far discovered, demanded that he send $24 (New York currency) "for value received on account of my annuity." Brotherly affection was spurned: George signed himself, "I am, sir, your humble servant, George Ermatinger."[6]

By March 1832, Charles was really angry about a letter complaining that he had not paid still more bills from Rev. Ferry. "I am not surprised as to the terms of [the letter]," Charles wrote back, "being precisely in unison with that line of conduct and principle you have ever thought proper to use towards me." The wording shows that the tensions went back a long way, and explains the lack of business co-operation or socializing between the two at the Sault. Again Charles insisted he would pay the annuities only as the money came due. But in the same letter he softened once again. George had drawn $24 on the account. Charles wrote, "Under the impression you could not have received my last letter when the draft was made, I have paid it with a full determination to pay no more" until George's account had the funds from his legacies. That, he said, would not be until June 1833.[7]

In the same letter, Charles denied that "I have written letters to your prejudice. I write it of no man, nor would I be induced under aggravating circumstances to write against a brother." This is a little naïve. Charles' letter to Mr Hulbert mentioning being overdrawn on the inheritance was hardly helpful to his brother. Then Charles counterattacked. Last summer George had written to their sister Jemima for a considerable sum of money to solve his financial problems. He had promised to return it to her out of his inheritances, but George must have known he had already overdrawn his legacies. "How could you attempt to deceive her? Your sister Jemima has little or no money to spare from her income. She does not possess more than barely sufficient to support herself here." Charles claimed he was intervening only because he had been requested to do so.

Despite it all, no record shows Charles ever refusing to pay his brother's bills. Whatever anger he displayed, he seems to have had a soft core when dealing with his family.

Appendix D: Charles Oakes, An Honest Man?

When Governor William Williams took over the Hudson's Bay Company in 1818, Charles, though an independent trader, was supplying the company brigades with goods as they passed through Sault Ste Marie. In July 1819 Williams complained to Charles of the "wasteful expenditure of Goods" by the men in charge of the Montreal canoes. They had "presumed" to give bills on the account of the Hudson's Bay Company with no authority to do so. Because of the dangers of this practice, it would require "a proper degree of understanding between you [Charles] and the agents, that such abuses should not exist in the future."[1]

Graham A. MacDonald, apparently on the basis of the last quoted sentence, interprets the whole letter as a "rather strong rebuke" by Williams of Charles for some possibly shady deals.[2] But the rest of the letter and subsequent correspondence do not support this interpretation. Williams immediately proceeded to ask Charles to undertake *wholly* "any despatches from or to Montreal; as well as obtaining the necessary Provisions for any Brigade, and all persons in charge should be subject to your orders and economical arrangements for which the Agents will always forward letters to you." Williams added, "The respectability and integrity of your character gives me great hopes as to the future management of this but too long existing abuse." Williams was giving authority to Charles to stop the abuses, not accusing him of them.

MacDonald suggests that Williams' reference to Charles' "respectability and integrity of character" was just the normal "note of harmony" that usually ended company letters. But if doubt remains about the identity of the villain(s), on the same day Williams wrote to his Montreal suppliers and accused various Point Meuron and Drummond Island employees by name (*not* Charles) of many "improprieties highly reprehensible." He had, said Williams, written to Mr Ermatinger of Sault Ste Marie asking him "to conduct and undertake *this business wholly* to and from Montreal and in future that all persons on business should be consigned to him, subject to his orders and directions."[3] Clearly, Williams was not just being polite but putting his trust in Charles' "respectability and integrity of character" to correct the abuses.

The following spring Charles told Williams that lack of any system, and extravagance of the men in charge, had caused excessive company expenses in transporting canoes passing through Sault Ste Marie. Charles' attempt to stop this "evil" had caused Hudson's Bay Company employees to take their accounts elsewhere. He assured Williams he would do his best to prevent abuse while at the same time expediting the canoes' passage. Williams was grateful. He wrote to "express my approbation" for Charles' actions. Some thousands of pounds might have been saved had such been adopted at an earlier time. He warned Charles that the next year 100 men would make the journey.[1]

However, one point of tension did arise. Williams complained to both Charles and to his Montreal suppliers that he could not account for a bill for a considerable sum submitted by Charles via James Bird on 14 May. "It appears to me," he told Charles, "only the rolls of Tobacco have been actually received at Point Meuron on account of the Hudson's Bay Company."[5]

This is clearly a misunderstanding by Williams of the 14 May letter to Bird. In it, Charles had told Bird that because he recognized the abuses by some company people, "in many cases I have refused supplying them." As an example, he enclosed copies of orders signed by two persons at different times from the Point Meuron post. "Doubting their having full authority, the orders were not complied with," wrote Charles, "excepting the tobacco in question, say three Rolls. The advances made by me to Louis Nolin do not exceed six or seven pounds, his expenses elsewhere have been too notorious, not to be already fully known to you."[6] Williams apparently thought the copies of the orders submitted to Charles by the Point Meuron post, which Charles had sent to Bird, were demands for payment. But Charles' letter makes it clear that he did *not* claim he had filled the orders, and he was *not* billing for them, other than the tobacco already acknowledged by Williams. Charles had included the correspondence as an example of the dishonesty of company employees. His own honesty remains unchallenged.

CHARLES AND JOHN JOHNSTON

As discussed in Chapter 3, near the end of the War of 1812 an American force attacked Sault Ste Marie and destroyed several buildings, including that of long-time trader John Johnston. Those belonging to Charles were spared. According to MacDonald, Henry Schoolcraft (who was Johnston's son-in-law) hints in his *Memoirs* that Charles somehow betrayed Johnston, leading to the Americans destroying his buildings.[7]

A search of Schoolcraft's *Memoirs* turned up only one relevant passage: "Low minded persons who had been in his [Johnston's] service as clerks, and disliked his pretensions to aristocracy, were the cause of this [destruction], and piloted the detachment up the river."[8] Charles had never been Johnston's clerk, they seem to have remained friendly after the war, and no independent evidence has so far been found to support this charge.

Appendix E: Lawrence and Jemima's Other Children

Lawrence and Jemima Ermatinger had seven children, five sons and three daughters (see Figure 2, p. 16). Their fourth son, Forrest, was born in August 1771 and lived only a few months. Of the daughters, we (regrettably, but as usual) know little. Jemima, the eldest, never married. For some time she lived with her niece, Jemima Cameron, and Jemima's husband in Kingston and York. She inherited money from her aunt, Mrs Edward Gray, and her brother Frederick.[1]

Anna Maria was also known as Margaret.[2] In 1831 when in her sixties she married George Garrett, a British Army surgeon stationed in Montreal. Anna Maria and George Garrett signed a prenuptial agreement under Quebec civil law agreeing to formally renounce the Custom of Paris, meaning there would be no community of property.[3] That is, Anna Maria retained the enjoyment and management of the property she brought into the marriage, while she renounced all dower rights to that of her husband.[4]

In the 1780s, Lawrence sent two of his sons, Lawrence Edward and Frederick William, to London for their education, but when his business failed he had to bring them back to Montreal. After the death of their father, Frederick became the central figure of the Ermatinger family. His life as a businessman in, and sheriff of, Montreal was busy, worthy, and rather dull, though he seemed to have had some doubtful business transactions. He never married. Frederick was very close to his younger brother Charles Oakes, and for many years acted as his Montreal agent.

Lawrence Edward, after a brief spell in Montreal as an adjutant to his uncle Edward Gray, returned to London and by 1805 was in the British Army's commissariat. In this capacity, he served in the Mediterranean.[5] He also served with the disastrous 1810 Walcheren expedition, when 40,000 British troops invaded the Netherlands' Scheldt estuary but failed miserably to destroy Napoleon's launching area for the planned invasion of Britain. The Duke of Wellington described the commissariat as very incompetent with a staff not capable of running anything but a counting house.[6] Lawrence retired on half-pay in 1815 and lived the rest of his life in semi-poverty, boarding with and partly dependent on an old friend. He did return to Montreal in 1817 but, offended by some remarks of Frederick's, left without saying goodbye. Later, when his aunt, Mrs Gray, bequeathed him a small sum, he wrote to Frederick turning the bequest down for unstated reasons, despite his straitened means.[7]

Lawrence had two sons, Francis, known as Frank (1798-1858), and Edward (1797-1876). They came to Canada from England in 1819 as Hudson's Bay Company employees. For many years Frank played a prominent role in the company on the west coast. Despite his deplorable record for treating Indian women (see Introduction), he had courage, generosity, and a sense of humour. He was regarded as a friend by many colleagues and missionaries, and with affection by their wives, despite his reputation. Edward, who left the company after a few years, became a banker and Tory politician in St Thomas, Upper Canada. He also acted as agent for Frank, which sometimes led to tensions between them. Edward became quite close to Charles Oakes and his family, stayed with them on several occasions, and, as mentioned in earlier chapters, a reciprocal correspondence continued over the years.

If Lawrence Edward was the estranged member of the family, George Ermatinger was seen as something of a black sheep and caused constant family arguments by constantly overspending legacies, as discussed in Appendix C. George served as an ensign in the 2nd Battalion of the Canadian Volunteers from 1797 to 1807. In 1800 he was living in Glengarry County, Upper Canada.[8] He married Mary MacDonald and had a son, George. After her death, he married Catherine McKee on 22 November 1803 at York and they had eight children.[9] George finally settled in Sault Ste Marie on the American side of the border, whereas Charles had settled on the Canadian side.

After US laws made it difficult for Canadians to trade south of the Great Lakes, Charles for years worked around the restrictions while remaining a Canadian. George, in contrast, became an American citizen. In 1819, perhaps fifteen years after he moved there, he wrote to the American factor pleading for a licence to trade: "I have purchased goods and engaged men at great price, [a] short delay will put it out of my power to reach the place of my destination." This, he said, would ruin him forever and place his family in distress. The US government had refused him a licence in part because he employed in his business two French Canadians, the Boleaus, contrary to US law. Perhaps, he conceded, that refusal had been just: "They [the Boleaus] will not remain in my employ. What can I do more? … I am an American citizen and must say have always served my country and *still* ready to do so." He hoped to enjoy the privileges of citizenship and added plaintively, "It was [on] your promise I should enjoy them that I made these purchases."[10]

George's will listed nine children by two marriages.[11] This book does not follow their lives. However, James Ermatinger, George's second son, was an Indian trader at James Falls, Wisconsin. His wife, Charlotte, was three-quarters Ojibwa. She spoke Ojibwa and French but never learned to speak English though she lived to age ninety.[12] As discussed in Chapter 7, under the 1926 treaty between the US Government and a Chippewa group, two sections of land were awarded "To the children of George Ermatinger, being of Shawnee extraction."[13] George Sr's two wives were Mary MacDonald and Catherine McKee. Catherine's father, Thomas McKee of Pennsylvania, was half Shawnee.[14] No doubt it was this connection that warranted the land grants. A number of Ermatingers who now live on Walpole Island, in Canada, are presumably descended from the American line of Ermatingers.

Another son to Lawrence and Jemima, Forrest, born in August 1771, lived only a few months. The youngest son, Charles Oakes, his Ojibwa wife, and his family occupy the rest of this book.

Notes

ABBREVIATIONS
AO   Archives of Ontario
HBCA Hudson's Bay Company Archives
LAC   Library and Archives Canada
UWO   University of Western Ontario, J.J. Talman Regional Collection, Papers of the Ermatinger Family

INTRODUCTION

1 John J. Bigsby, *Shoe and Canoe*, vol. 2, 130; LAC, RG 1, L3 182B e-bundle 6, no. 21, Petition of the Undersigned Inhabitants, 21h, 21k.
2 Brown, "Women as Centre," 45.
3 I have generally avoided the terms "half breed" and "mixed blood" because their genetic implications obscure the cultural nature of the discussion. Instead, I prefer such descriptives as "bicultural" defined as "Indian-Canadian," "dual descent," and "Métis," depending on the context. On the other side, I refer to non-Indian individuals (and to urban society) as "Canadian(s)" and to French Canadians as "Canadien(s)/Canadienne(s)."
4 Brown, *Strangers in Blood*, 81-82.
5 Van Kirk, *Many Tender Ties*, 74.
6 Bourgeault, "Indians, Métis and Fur Trade," 55-57.
7 Most of the cases briefly described in this and the following sections occurred between roughly 1800 and 1870. Over this period attitudes towards fur trader marriages with Indians and with Métis changed, as did attitudes towards the education and acceptance of mixed-blood children. Full comparative analysis of the cases would require detailed consideration of these changing attitudes.
8 UWO, microfiche, series 2, no. 81, Francis to Edward Ermatinger, 14 March 1826. Further details concerning Francis, the Indian women, and their children are scattered through this collection. See also McDonald, *Fur Trade Letters*.
9 Brown, "Cameron, Duncan," 137-39.
10 Pannekoek, "Ross, Alexander," 765-68; Van Kirk, *Many Tender Ties*, 41.
11 Van Kirk, *Many Tender Ties*, 124-25.
12 Brown, *Strangers in Blood*, 90ff.
13 Brown, "Diverging Identities," 201.
14 Brown, "Atkinson, George," 32-33.
15 Van Kirk, *Many Tender Ties*, 199, 135.
16 Van Kirk, "What If Mama Is an Indian?" 123-26.
17 Arthur, "Angélique and Her Children," 36.
18 Brown, "Diverging Identities," 188, 201.
19 Brown and Van Kirk, "Barnston, George," 52-53.
20 Brown, *Strangers in Blood*, 195.
21 Zeller and Noble, "Barnston, James," 61-62.

22 Pannekoek, "Ross, Alexander," 765-68.
23 Van Kirk, "What If Mama Is an Indian?" 211.
24 Van Kirk, "Isbister, Alexander Kennedy," 445-46.
25 Cole, ed., *This Blessed Wilderness*, 257-58.
26 Quoted from Schodt, *Native American*, 345.
27 MacDonald, *Ranald MacDonald*, 84, 113-20.
28 Schodt, *Native American*, 376-77.
29 MacDonald, *Ranald Macdonald*, 118. Malcolm MacLeod, part Indian himself and an Ottawa lawyer, ghost-wrote the *Narrative* for his friend Ranald. The Latin phrase suggests that these words are those of the better-educated MacLeod.
30 Francis and Morantz, *Partners in Furs*, 155-56.
31 Peel, "Falcon, Pierre," 276-77.
32 Woodcock, "Grant, Cuthbert," 341-44.
33 Gorham, "Families of Mixed Descent," 37-39, 41.
34 McNeice, *Ermatinger Family*, 61-69.
35 Senior, *British Regulars in Montreal*, 42.

CHAPTER 1: THE URBAN CANADIAN GRANDPARENTS

1 Innis, *Fur Trade in Canada*, 216.
2 LAC, MG 19, A2, series 1, vol. 1, Lawrence to Forrest Oakes, 12 May 1775.
3 McNeice, *Ermatinger Family*, 1.
4 Wallace, *North West Company*, 439.
5 Momryk, "Ermatinger, Lawrence," 262; LAC, MG 19, A2, series 1, vol. 31, file 1, Rules of Agreement, 15 October 1763.
6 "Lawrence Ermatinger and Jemima Oakes," Church of Jesus Christ of Latter-day Saints, Family History Library, http://www.familysearch.org.
7 Wallace, *North West Company*, 489; LAC, MG 23, GII3, Descriptive Record, n.d.
8 LAC, MG 19, A2, series 1, vol. 1, Lawrence to Benjamin Price, c. 23 October 1770; to Thomas Bridges, 19 January and 27 September 1771; to Robert Lister, 13 May 1771; to Henry Taylor, 13 May 1771; to Officer Commanding and others, 6 November 1776; to John Welles, 27 May 1771.
9 LAC, MG 19, A2, series 1, vol. 1, Lawrence to John Welles, 20 February 1772, 13 and 27 April 1772.
10 LAC, MG 19, A2, series 1, vol. 1, Lawrence to Jonas Clarke Minot, 7 September 1772; to Benjamin Price, 9 July 1771; to W. Priestly, 30 September 1771; to Wm. and B. Sampson, 29 September 1773; to John Priestly and Son, 18 February 1775.
11 LAC, MG 19, A2, series 1, vol. 1, Wm. and B. Sampson to Lawrence, c. March 1775.
12 "Forrest Oakes," Church of Jesus Christ of Latter-day Saints, Family History Library, http://www.familysearch.org.
13 Doutre and Lareau, *Droit civil Canadien*, 510.
14 Henry, *Travels and Adventures*, 235. See also Woolworth, "Great Carrying Place," 111. Henry (d. 1814) was sometimes known as Alexander Henry the Elder. His journals covering twenty-three years as a fur trader for the North West Company are much valued for their descriptions of both the fur trade and the Indians.
15 Thorman, "Oakes, Forrest," 585.
16 LAC, MG 19, A2, series 1, vol. 82, Lawrence's Rough Accounts Book, 1764-1771, 30 April 1768.
17 LAC, MG 19, A2, series 1, vol. 1, Lawrence to Forrest Oakes, 11 May 1772, 3 May 1774; Thorman, "Oakes, Forrest," 585.
18 LAC, MG 19, A2, series 1, vol. 1, Edward Chinn to Lawrence, 20 September 1764. Chinn had earlier acted with less than probity. In 1765, the provincial secretary employed him to issue permits to Montrealers to carry fuzees, a type of gun. Only Montrealers who behaved "remarkably well" could get permits, but they were to get them free. "Abuses have been committed and Money exacted" by Chinn, said a report in the *Quebec Gazette* on 20 June 1765. He had to refund the money, but apparently no charges followed. This was in addition to the court martial mentioned earlier.
19 LAC, MG 19, A2, series 1, vol. 1, Lawrence to Randle Meredith, 19 December 1774; to Benjamin Price, 15 November 1771.
20 LAC, MG 19, A2, series 1, vol. 1, Lawrence to Randle Meredith, 15 and 22 June 1772.
21 Innis, *Fur Trade in Canada*, 191.

22 LAC, MG 19, A2, series 1, vol. 1, Lawrence to John Welles, 26 June 1765.
23 Shortt and Dougherty, *Constitutional History of Canada*, 589.
24 LAC, MG 19, A2, series 1, vol. 1, Lawrence to Forrest Oakes, 16 June 1775; to John Wells, 26 June 1775; to Randle Meredith, 12 October 1775; to Swift and Cummings, 12 October 1775.
25 LAC, MG 19, A2, series 1, vol. 1, Lawrence to Thomas Woder, 18 October 1775.
26 Verreau, *Invasion du Canada*, 93.
27 Lanctot, *Canada and the American Revolution*, 127, 130.
28 LAC, MG 19, A2, series 1, vol. 1, Lawrence to Thomas Bridges, 17 October 1775 and 19 July 1776.
29 LAC, MG 19, A2, series 1, vol. 1, Lawrence to John Rowley, 17 October 1776.
30 LAC, MG 19, A2, series 1, vol. 1, Lawrence to Beade and Tate, 13 October 1772.
31 *Quebec Gazette*, 25 September 1783.
32 Armstrong, *Treatise on the Law*, 21.
33 Blackstone, *Commentaries on the Laws*, vol. 2, 433-35; vol. 1, 430.
34 LAC, RG 8 (C series), 1A, vol. 164, no. 60, Court Martial, 10 April 1797.
35 Thorman, "Oakes, Forrest," 585.
36 Lower, "Credit and the Constitutional Act," 123-41.
37 Momryk, "Ermatinger, Lawrence," 262; LAC, MG 19, A2, series 4, vol. 1, file 1, no. 6482, Death Certificate.

CHAPTER 2: THE UPPER COUNTRY OJIBWA GRANDPARENT

1 The Ojibwa are known in the United States as Chippewa. One group were often called Saulteaux because of their relationship to the Sault Ste Marie area. The Dakota were known also as the Sioux.
2 Warren, *History of the Ojibway Nation*, 365-66.
3 Copway, *Traditional History and Characteristic Sketches*, 135ff.
4 Chute, *Legacy of Shingwaukonse*, 99-100.
5 Danziger, *Chippewas of Lake Superior*, 14-15.
6 Warren, *History of the Ojibway Nation*, 459.
7 Though this view of Ojibwa hereditary chiefs seems generally accepted in outline, various writers have suggested modifications. Janet E. Chute, for instance, suggests that, at least among the Sault Ste Marie Ojibwa, the chief had to demonstrate the necessary wisdom and skills to retain his position, and that various subchiefs also had influence. Chute, "Ojibwa Leadership," 157-58.
8 Sandy Lake Band of Ojibwe, "Chief Ka-Ta-Wa-Be-Da (Broken Tooth)."
9 Jones, *History of the Ojebway Indians*, 130; Danziger, *Chippewas of Lake Superior*, 23-24.
10 Cleland, *Rites of Conquest*, 63.
11 Tanner et al., *Atlas of Great Lakes Indian History*, 30-31; LeBlanc, *Compendium of the Anishinabek*, 105.
12 In the discussion of Ojibwa customs above, I have concentrated on the Lake Superior Ojibwa, and tried to avoid material relating to Northern Ojibwa, Southern Ontario Ojibwa, or Plains Ojibwa, unless relevant.
13 Tanner et al., *Atlas of Great Lakes Indian History*, 42-43.
14 MacLeod, "Anishinabeg Point of View," 200.
15 Warren, *History of the Ojibway Nation*, 177. William Whipple Warren (1825-53), an Ojibwa, was an interpreter. He was later elected to the legislature of the territory now known as Minnesota.
16 Warren, *History of the Ojibway Nation*, 477. A group of Ottawa Indians played a game of lacrosse outside the fort, luring the soldiers outside to watch the strange game, then killing them and capturing the fort. Henry, *Travels and Adventures*, 77-78.
17 Schoolcraft, *Historical and Statistical Information*, vol. 5, 150-51; Schoolcraft, *Indian in his Wigwam*, 203. Henry Rowe Schoolcraft (1793-1864) married a part-Indian woman. An ethnologist, he wrote many volumes on Indian customs and language.
18 Danziger, *Chippewas of Lake Superior*, 14.
19 McMillan, *Native Peoples and Cultures*, 99.
20 Landes, *Ojibwa Religion and the Midewiwin*, 8.
21 Schoolcraft, *Historical and Statistical Information*, vol. 5, 151.
22 Copway, *Traditional History and Characteristic Sketches*, 56-57. George Copway (1818-69), or Chief Kah-ge-ga-gah-bowh, was born in Upper Canada. After a chequered career as a missionary, he gained fame as a Native author but later faded into obscurity.
23 Jones, *History of the Ojebway Indians*, 130. Peter Jones (1802-56), or Kahkewaquonaby, son of a Welsh

father and Ojibwa mother, became a missionary to the Ojibwa.

24 Warren, *History of the Ojibway Nation*, 264.

25 Laura Peers sees Ojibwa expansion as fuelled by young men "to fulfil personal and group desires for revenge and status" (*Ojibwa of Western Canada*, 7). Edmund Danziger says social status was accorded to those who could boast of extraordinary exploits on the battlefield (*Chippewas of Lake Superior*, 24). Theresa M. Schenck can understand many of the Ojibwa exploits described by William Warren only through a warrior ethic ("William W. Warren's History," 252). Alan D. McMillan argues that war parties set out to avenge previous deaths and to provide young men with opportunities for glory (*Native Peoples and Cultures*, 100).

26 Barnouw, *Acculturation and Personality*, 30-31, 36, 42, 73-75.

27 Peers, *Ojibwa of Western Canada*, 9.

28 Densmore, *Chippewa Customs*, 33, 37-38.

29 Jones, *History of the Ojebway Indians*, 130-31.

30 The following account is drawn from Warren, *History of the Ojibway Nation*, 223-32. See also Copway, *Traditional History and Characteristic Sketches*, 60-61.

31 Warren, *History of the Ojibway Nation*, 226-27.

32 Ibid., 227-28.

33 Ibid., 229-31.

34 Ibid., 231.

35 Quoted in Trigger, *Natives and Newcomers*, 12, 15.

36 Warren, *History of the Ojibway Nation*, 175-76.

37 Danziger, *Chippewas of Lake Superior*, 11-14; Peers, *Ojibwa of Western Canada*, 64; Ray, *Indians in the Fur Trade*, 175.

38 See White, "Give Us a Little Milk," 186, 192.

39 LAC, RG 10, vol. 32, reel C-11010, Speech by Katawabidai ... at Drummond Island, July 1816.

40 Warren, *History of the Ojibway Nation*, 63.

41 McMillan, *Native Peoples and Cultures*, 99.

42 Densmore, *Chippewa Customs*, 86-87.

43 Peers, *Ojibwa of Western Canada*, 23-24.

44 Schoolcraft, *Historical and Statistical Information*, vol. 5, 151.

45 Danziger, *Chippewas of Lake Superior*, 14.

46 Densmore, *Chippewa Customs*, 61, 46-47.

47 Peers, *Ojibwa of Western Canada*, 56-59, 83.

48 Jenks, *Childhood of Ji-shib*, 43.

49 Talbot, *Five Years' Residence*, vol. 2, 392. Edward Allen Talbot (1801-39) was a British-born author, militia officer, inventor, and schoolteacher.

50 Schoolcraft, *The Indian in His Wigwam*, 74.

51 Van Kirk, *Many Tender Ties*, 28.

52 West, *Substance of a Journal*, 54. John West (1778-1845) was a Church of England missionary in Red River from 1820 to 1822.

53 Schoolcraft, *Historical and Statistical Information*, vol. 2, 160-61.

54 McKenney and Hall, *History of the Indian Tribes*, vol. 2, 39-40. Thomas L. McKenney (1785-1859) was head bureaucrat in the American Indian Affairs department when he visited Sault Ste Marie in June 1823. He kept a diary with paintings of his trip (see also Chapter 5).

55 Schoolcraft, *Historical and Statistical Information*, vol. 2, 160.

56 Schoolcraft, *Personal Memoirs*, 294, 305-06.

57 Schoolcraft, *Historical and Statistical Information*, vol. 2, 160.

58 Pond, "Indian Warfare in Minnesota," 130-34. For Pond, who ministered to the Dakota, the villains were usually the Ojibwa. For Warren, an Ojibwa, the villains were usually the Dakota. At one point after a Dakota had been killed, Rev. Pond in a rather unchristian manner "urged the Indians [Dakota warriors] to kill" the Ojibwa in revenge. They refused (136).

59 LAC, RG 10, vol. 32, reel C-11010, Speech by Katawabidai ... at Drummond Island, July 1816; see also White, "Give Us a Little Milk," 192.

60 This may have been a French flag that Warren reports Katawabidai gave to his son-in-law Charles. Warren, *History of the Ojibway Nation*, 477. This flag reappeared in 1847 in his daughter Charlotte's petition to the government (see Appendix B).

61 McKay may have stated that Katawabidai forgot his flag at the Sault because he was drunk, but here the handwriting of the transcript is very difficult to read.

62 The Red River settlement, founded in 1812, threatened the pemmican supplies of the North West Company. With their Métis allies, the Nor'Wester s retaliated in 1815 by encouraging most of the settlers to quit the place with threats and promises. Finally the Nor'Westers burned the settlement.

63 Schoolcraft, *Historical and Statistical Information*, vol. 2, 161.

64 Chute, *Legacy of Shingwaukonse*, 278, n 72.

65 Kugel, *To Be the Main Leaders*, 24.

66 Schoolcraft, *Historical and Statistical Information*, vol. 2, 161.

CHAPTER 3: CHARLES SR'S FUR TRADE CAREER

1 This company had been formed to compete with the longer established and dominant North West Company.

2 See especially George Nelson's comments on Charles, at the end of Chapter 4.

3 LAC, MG 19, B1, vol. 1, nos. 51-52, Alexander Mackenzie to McTavish, Frobisher and Co., 4 June 1799.

4 Coues, *New Light on the Early History*, vol. 1, 488-89.

5 LAC, MG 19, B1, vol. 1, nos. 51-52, Alexander Mackenzie to McTavish, Frobisher and Co., 4 June 1799. The only Papin found in fur trade records is Joseph Papin, still alive in 1804 so obviously not Charles' colleague. Coues, *New Light on the Early History*, vol. 2, 993.

6 LAC, MG 19, B1, vol. 1, no. 89, Alexander Mackenzie to John Sayer, 9 August 1799.

7 From Charlotte's death certificate, LAC, MG 19, A2, series 4, vol. 1, file 1, no. 6493.

8 Van Kirk, *Many Tender Ties*, 44. George Nelson (1786-1859) worked for the North West and Hudson's Bay Companies before retiring to Sorel in 1823 with his wife and family. His letters and journals are a valuable source of information about Indian life. They are held in the Baldwin Room of the Toronto Reference Library, as the collected *Nelson Journals*.

9 Ens, *Homeland to Hinterland*, 13.

10 LAC, MG 19, B1, vol. 1, no. 88, Alexander Mackenzie to John Sayer, 9 August 1899; no. 132, William McGillivray to T. Pothier, 13 July 1800.

11 Wallace, *North West Company*, 157. Frederick, Charles' older brother, was at that time assistant to their uncle, Edward Gray, sheriff of Montreal.

12 LAC, MG 19, B1, vol. 3, no. 56, "Rearrangements of Departments for 1806."

13 Victor P. Lytwyn, cited in Bishop, review of *The Fur Trade of the Little North*, 147.

14 Toronto Reference Library, Baldwin Room, *Nelson Journals*, "Letters to Parents 1811-12," 11.

15 Ibid., "Journal 1805," 2 September 1805; and "Journal, Reminiscences 1825-36," 73.

16 Ibid., "Journal," September 1807, 190; and "Journal, Reminiscences 1825-36," 73-74.

17 Ibid., "Journal, Reminiscences 1825-36," 8, 20, 28-32.

18 Wallace, *North West Company*, 211. In the end, the company found it impossible to enforce the edict.

19 Peers, *Ojibwa of Western Canada*, 35.

20 Momryk, "Ermatinger, Charles Oakes," 236.

21 LAC, MG 19, A2, series 3, vol. 32, file 2, no. 266, Invoice, 27 July 1808.

22 LAC, MG 19, A2, series 3, vol. 35, file 1, no. 1712, Invoice, 8 May 1817.

23 Sneakers, "Michigan Voyageurs"; LAC, MG 19, A2, series 3, vol. 40, file 2, no. 4810, Petition of Charles Sr to Sir Peregrine Maitland, 1825-26.

24 Lord Selkirk, *Collected Writings*, 60; Higgins, *Whitefish Lake Ojibwa Memories*, 52. Since 1837, Michilimackinac Island has been known as Mackinac Island. Heritage Quest, "Michilimackinac," http://www2.heritagequest.com; see also Early Chicago Encyclopedia, "Michilimackinac," http://www.earlychicago.com/encyclopedia.

25 LAC, MG 19, A2, series 3, vol. 40, file 2, no. 4810, Petition of Charles Sr to Sir Peregrine Maitland, 1825-26.

26 Gilpin, *War of 1812*, 88-91.

27 Cruikshank, *Documents Relating to the Invasion of Canada*, 66, 112.

28 Franchère, *Voyage to the North West Coast*, 274-75. Gabriel Franchère (1786-1863), though Canadian-born, was for many years the Montreal and then Sault Ste Marie agent for the American Fur Company. He travelled across Canada between 1811 and 1814.

29 Capp, *Story of Baw-a-Ting*, 146-47.

30 For rumours about why Charles' property was spared and Johnston's burned, see Appendix D. John

Johnston (c. 1762-1828), an Irishman, traded on the south shore at Sault Ste Marie for many years. He married an Ojibwa woman.

31 Lavender, *Fist in the Wilderness*, 277-78.
32 HBCA, B.194/e/1-8, Angus Bethune, 1825 Report.
33 Schoolcraft, *Personal Memoirs*, 294, 305-6.
34 LAC, MG 19, A2, series 3, vol. 37, file 5, no. 3847, Deed of Bargain and Sale, Jean Baptiste Nolin Sr, 14 August 1821.
35 LAC, RG 10, vol. 32, reel C-11010, "Speech by Katawabidai … at Drummond Island," July 1816; AO, MS 23, Speech of Cai-tai-wau-bi-tai [Katawabidai] at Drummond Island, 9 June 1822. See also Schoolcraft, *Personal Memoirs*, 305, 294; Warren, *History of the Ojibway Nation,* 477ff.
36 Gilman, *Where Two Worlds Meet*, 46.
37 HBCA, B.194/b/1-16, Angus Bethune to William Smith, 5 September 1824; LAC, MG 19, A2, series 3, vol. 35, file 1, nos. 1908-1950, Charles Sr to Frederick re Bills, August-October 1817; LAC, MG 19, A2, series 3, vol. 188, Sales to Henry and Bethune, 14 December 1820.
38 Schoolcraft quoted in Chute, *Legacy of Shingwaukonse*, 39-40.
39 LAC, MG 19, A2, series 3, vol. 192, file 1, Invoices, 1 May 1822.
40 HBCA, B.194/b/1-16, Angus Bethune to [illegible], 3 and 21 July 1826.
41 HBCA, B.194/c/1, William A. Aitkin to Angus Bethune, 3 August 1829.
42 Thomas Douglas Selkirk, fifth earl of Selkirk (1771-1820), was a major shareholder in the company.
43 LAC, MG 19, E1, vol. 6, no. 1967, Charles Sr to Miles MacDonnell, 2 January 1816; no. 2054, Charles Sr to Selkirk, 12 February 1816; vol. 7, no. 2211, Selkirk to Charles Sr, 16 April 1816; vol. 7, no. 2846, 29 August 1816.
44 Lord Selkirk, *Collected Writings*, 132.
45 LAC, MG 19, E1, vol. 15, no. 5185, Selkirk to Charles Sr, 2 July 1818; Amos, *Report of the Trials*, xiv.
46 LAC, MG 19, E1, vol. 17, no. 5963, Selkirk to Charles Sr, 27 February 1819.
47 Franchère, *Voyage to the North West Coast*, 276; LAC, MG 19, A2, series 3, vol. 40, file 2, no. 4810, Petition of Charles Sr to Sir Peregrine Maitland, 1825-26.
48 HBCA, B.194/b/1-16, Angus Bethune to McGillivray, Thain and Co., 20 October 1824; B.194/a/1-9, Angus Bethune Journal, 13 September 1824.
49 Schoolcraft, *Personal Memoirs,* 97-98; Bryce, *Remarkable History*, 310.
50 HBCA, B.194/b/1-16, George Keith to Angus Bethune, 11 January 1828.
51 HBCA, B.194/b/1-16, Angus Bethune to J. Haldan, 2 October 1824; Angus Bethune to J. MacIntosh, 27 April 1828.
52 LAC, R6435-0-8-E, M-57, no. 300, Robert Stuart to Charles Sr, 5 July 1822; MG 19, A2, series 3, vol. 41, file 1, no. 5294, Invoice, 1827.
53 HBCA, B.194/e/1-8, Angus Bethune, 1825 and 1826 Reports.
54 LAC, RG 8 (C series), 1A, vol. 515, no. 108, Permission to build, signed by Maj. James Winniet, 27 June 1816.
55 Quoted in Phillips, *Fur Trade*, vol. 2, 370.
56 LAC, MG 19, A2, series 3, vol. 37, Land Deed signed by James Winniet, 4 November 1821 (cited in McNeice, *Ermatinger Family,* 45).
57 LAC, MG 19, A2, series 3, vol. 40, file 2, no. 4810, Petition of Charles Sr to Sir Peregrine Maitland, 1825-26. During the War of 1812 the British commonly awarded prize money to the regular army, the militia, and Indians, as well as to navy personnel, for the capture of enemy equipment, stores, and vessels. On 29 May 1814, the governor general authorized the first payment of the prize money from the sale of property captured from the enemy at Michilimackinac by "the Detachment of Troops and Volunteers under the command of Captain Roberts." This first payment amounted to £10 for each private, but what the officers and gentlemen volunteers received was not recorded. Why Charles did not claim his share of the prize money is not known. LAC, RG 8 (C series), 1 XX, Prize Money: First dividend of prize goods captured at Michilimackinac by Capt. Roberts, 10th Royal Battalion, Adjt.-Gen. Boynes, Montreal, 29 May 1814, 276.
58 Quoted in McNeice, *Ermatinger Family,* 55.
59 LAC, MG 19, A2, series 4, vol. 2, no. 1, Charles Sr to Edward Ermatinger, 1 June 1821.
60 LAC, MG 19, A2, series 3, vol. 188, Receipt, 3 June 1820.
61 It has been said that William Aitkin, a Scot working for the American Fur Company in 1818, married Madeleine, or Striped Cloud, alleged daughter of Charles Ermatinger (Aitkin Festival of Adventures, "William Aitkin: Legendary Figure of Minnesota's Fur Trade Era," 2006, http://www.aitkin.com/fest/wmait).

htm). This information was probably taken from *Short Sketches of Some Fur Traders of Morrison County,* by another fur trader of the time, Clement H. Beaulieu. Unfortunately no copy of *Short Sketches* can be traced. Late in the progress of writing this book, research revealed the family tree of Chief Joseph Osaugie, also claiming that Aitkin's wife, Striped Cloud, was Charles's daughter. It adds that she was one of eleven children. Such family tree lists, however, very often run counter to what is known of Charles's children. The information for Chief Joseph Osaugie can be found at http://familytreeinfo.familytreeguide. com; McNeice, *The Ermatinger Family,* appendix 2, 2,6,4.

The family tree claims that Jemima (b. 1800), Frances (b. 1804), George (b. 1805), William (b. 1808), and Madeline (b. 1808) were all born at the Red River settlement. Whatever was meant by the Red River Settlement in the first decade of the 1800s, by 1808 the family was in Sault Ste Marie, making the alleged location of the last two births most unlikely.

As well, the family tree claims that Charles Jr was born in 1801 in Sault Ste Marie, Michigan, suggesting that there may be a confusion here with George's family. This is strengthened by the claim that James Rough was born in 1808 in Michilmackinac. James, son of Charles Oakes, was born in 1815 at Lake of Two Mountains. No documents have been found giving him the middle name Rough, but George Ermatinger had a son called James Rough, born in 1805.

In short, none of the references to Madeline/Striped Cloud are documented. Confusion exists between the two Ermatinger families of Sault Ste Marie. And no mention of another daughter has been found in the papers of the Canadian family.

CHAPTER 4: CHARLES AND CHARLOTTE IN MONTREAL

1 LAC, MG 19, A2, series 3, vol. 202, file 1, Washing Book; MG 19, A2, series 3, vol. 41, file 3, nos. 5631, 5635, 5640, 5648, 5657, and 5687, Sundry Bills, 21 August 1828.

2 LAC, MG 19, A2, series 3, vol. 41, file 3, Receipts, nos. 5685, 10 August 1828; 5689, 18 August 1828; 5602, 20 August 1828; 5612, 2 September 1828; 5717, September-October 1828; 5691-5724, December 1828.

3 LAC, MG 19, A2, series 3, vol. 42, file 2, no. 5881, Charles Sr to Jemima, 2 January 1832.

4 Henry, *Travels and Adventures,* x-xi.

5 LAC, MG 19, A2, series 1, vol. 1, Lawrence to Thomas Woder, 19 January 1771.

6 LAC, MG 19, A2, series 3, vol. 42, file 3, nos. 6063 and 6695, Montreal Library Subscriptions, 1829 and 1834; MG 19, A2, series 3, vol. 42, file 1, no. 5780, Library Receipt, 1 August 1834; MG 19, A2, series 3, vol. 42, file 1, no. 5766, Church Receipt, n.d.

7 LAC, MG 19, A2, series 3, vol. 42, file 1, nos. 5737-43, Power of Attorney, 5 November 1829; MG 19, A2, series 3, vol. 42, file 3, nos. 6090-6107, Legal Opinion.

8 LAC, MG 19, A2, series 2, vol. 1, part 2, John Clowes to Edward Ermatinger, 20 February 1830.

9 Act to Incorporate certain persons therein mentioned under the name of President, Director and Company of the Bank of Montreal, Lower Canada, *Statutes (of Lower Canada),* 1821, c. 25.

10 Lower Canada, *Journals of the House of Assembly, 1832,* vol. 42, app. U, "List of Stockholders of the Bank of Montreal, 1 June 1832 and 1st December 1832," 16; app. W, "List of Stockholders in the Quebec Fire Assurance Co.," 1.

11 LAC, MG 19, A2, series 4, vol. 2, no. 8, Charles Jr to Edward Ermatinger, 22 August and [added later] 20 September 1831.

12 LAC, MG 19, A2, series 3, vol. 42, file 2, no. 6152, Public Notice, 18 May 1830.

13 LAC, MG 19, A2, series 3, vol. 41, file 2, nos. 5409-12, Notification, 7 February 1828.

14 LAC, MG 19, A2, series 3, vol. 42, file 1, no. 5840, Charles Sr v. Handyside, 20 April 1829; MG 19, A2, series 3, vol. 42, file 2, nos. 5873-74, Charles Sr to John D. Campbell, 25 July and 12 October 1831; MG 19, A2, series 3, vol. 203, file 1, Sundry Items.

15 Biographer McNeice describes Charles as a somewhat shadowy figure since he left no journals and, she says, few letters. McNeice, *Ermatinger Family,* 71. Presumably these letters and Charles' letters to his brother George (in Appendix C), all in Library and Archives Canada, were not known to her.

16 LAC, MG 19, A2, series 3, vol. 42, file 2, no. 5869, Charles Sr to Jemima, 20 April 1831.

17 LAC, MG 19, A2, series 3, vol. 42, file 2, no. 5890, Charles Sr to Jemima, n.d.; no. 6561, Charles Sr to Jemima, 3 December 1832.

18 LAC, MG 19, A2, series 3, vol. 42, file 2, no. 5890, Charles to Jemima, n.d.

19 LAC, MG 19, A2, series 3, vol. 33, file 4, no. 987, [name illegible] to Frederick.

20 Ontario Genealogical Society, Norfolk County Branch, Oakwood Cemetery, book 1, 2 May 1890-11 March 1932.

21 McLean, *John McLean's Notes*, 11. John McLean (c. 1799-1890) worked for the Hudson's Bay Company from 1820 to 1846.
22 LAC, MG 19, A2, series 4, vol. 1, file 1, no. 6491, Baptismal Certificate, Anne, 18 August 1815; no. 6485, Baptismal Certificate, Charles Jr., 20 July 1815; no. 6492, Baptismal Certificate, Frances, 18 August 1815; no. 6484, Baptismal Certificate, George, 20 July 1815; no. 6490, Baptismal Certificate, Jemima, 18 August 1815; no. 6447, Death Certificate, John, 1 May 1817.
23 McNeice, *Ermatinger Family*, appendix 1, Will of Charles Sr, 12 May 1815.
24 LAC, MG 19, A2, series 3, vol. 41, file 1, nos. 5249-50, Samuel Gale to Charles Sr, 5 March 1827. Gale's fears were justified in 1886, when Chief Justice Ramsey ruled that country-style marriages were not valid in law. See Van Kirk, *Many Tender Ties*, 203-5.
25 LAC, MG 19, A2, series 4, vols. 1-3, file 1, nos. 74-82, Will of Charles Sr, 4 July 1831.
26 LAC, MG 19, A2, series 4, vol. 1, file 1, no. 6488, Marriage Certificate.
27 Jenkins, *Montreal, Island City*, 261-62.
28 LAC, MG 19, A2, series 4, vol. 1, file 1, nos. 59-64, Deed of Tutorship, 17 September 1833. Charles' eldest daughter, Anne, had died aged seventeen in 1817. The youngest, often referred to in family documents as Anne, was actually named Anna Maria.
29 Bigsby, *Shoe and Canoe*, vol. 2, 127. See Chapter 6 for a full discussion of John Bigsby and his visit.
30 McKenney, *Sketches of a Tour*, 191, 182.
31 Toronto Reference Library, Baldwin Room, *Nelson Journals*, "Journal Reminiscences 1825-26," 73.
32 LAC, MG 19, A2, series 3, vol. 42, file 2, no. 6562, Charles Sr to Jemima, 3 December 1832; no. 5869, Charles Sr to Jemima, 10 April 1831; no. 5881, Charles Sr to Jemima, 2 January 1832; no. 6560, Charles Sr to Jemima, 3 August 1832.
33 LAC, MG 19, A2, series 4, vol. 2, no. 10, Charles Sr to Edward Ermatinger, 9 March 1832; MG 19, A2, series 2, vol. 3, pt. 1, Edward Ermatinger to Frank Ermatinger, 26 April 1830.
34 Van Kirk, "What If Mama Is an Indian?" 211.
35 LAC, MG 19, A2, series 4, vol. 1, file 1, no. 6493, Death Certificate, Charlotte, 9 July 1850.
36 See, for instance, Brown. "Demographic Transition," 66-67.
37 LAC, MG 19, A2, series 3, vol. 42, file 2, no. 5879, Charles Sr to Jemima, 1830.
38 LAC, MG 24, D84, nos. 79-82, Jemima to Edward Ermatinger, 21 February 1831.
39 LAC, MG 19, A2, series 3, vol. 42, file 2, no. 5864, Charles Sr to C. Yorke, 3 August 1830; MG 19, A2, series 3, vol. 42, file 2, no. 5880, Charles Sr to Louis Gugy, 25 November 1831.
40 LAC, MG 19, A2, series 4, vol. 1, file 1, no. 6494, Death Certificate, Charles Sr; no. 6493, Death Certificate, Charlotte, 9 July 1850.
41 LAC, MG 19, A2, series 2, vol. 3, pt. 1, Edward Ermatinger to Frank Ermatinger, 26 April 1830; MG 19, A2, series 4, vol. 2, no. 31, Charles Jr to Edward, 14 October 1833.
42 LAC, MG 19, E1, vol. 6, Selkirk to John Askin, 27 July 1816.
43 Toronto Reference Library, Baldwin Room, *Nelson Journals*, "Journal, Reminiscences 1825-36," 73.
44 McNeice, *Ermatinger Family*, 75-76.
45 Schoolcraft, *Personal Memoirs*, 326.
46 Bigsby, *Shoe and Canoe*, vol. 2, 126-27.

CHAPTER 5: A WILD MAN'S LAND AND A WORLD OF VIRGIL

1 Reid, *Mansion in the Wilderness*, 5.
2 Henry, *Travels and Adventures*, 61-62.
3 HBCA, B.194/a/1-9, Angus Bethune Journal, 16 October 1824.
4 Reid, *Mansion in the Wilderness*, 5.
5 Henry, *Travels and Adventures*, 63.
6 Garry, "Diary of Nicholas Garry," 110-11.
7 Catlin, *Letters and Notes*, vol. 2, 162. American George Catlin (1796-1872) spent years travelling and painting in North and South America.
8 Bigsby, *Shoe and Canoe*, vol. 2, 130, 123-24. Dr John Bigsby (1792-1881), a noted English geologist and physician, wrote a report on the geology of Upper Canada. He was later British secretary and medical officer to the Canada-US Boundary Commission.
9 Gorham, "Families of Mixed Descent," 37.
10 Toronto Reference Library, Baldwin Room, *Nelson Journals*, "Journal Reminiscences, 1825-26," 373.
11 LAC, MG 19, A2, series 3, vol. 192, file 1, Invoice, 1 May 1823.

12 Toronto Reference Library, Baldwin Room, *Nelson Journals,* "Journal Reminiscences, 1825-26," 373.

13 Bigsby, *Shoe and Canoe,* vol. 1, 163.

14 Ibid., vol. 2, 127-28. Actually, Bigsby writes, "In 1824, I remained three weeks a guest at the North-west Company's post, enjoying the great kindness of Mr. Siveright, the superintendent." This is puzzling for two reasons. By 1824, the North West Company had been subsumed under the Hudson's Bay Company, which had taken over the North West Company post. With the takeover only the year before, however, it is possible the post was still known locally by its familiar North West Company name. Second, Siveright had been transferred from Sault Ste Marie in 1823. No record has been found of an 1824 trip by Bigsby to the Sault. It is probable that either he or his typesetters got the date wrong and that he was, in what follows, expanding on his 1822 visit.

15 Ibid., 131, 128, 129-30; LAC, RG 18-G, vol. 3320, file 127, North West Mounted Police medical certificate, C.H. Ermatinger.

16 Bigsby, *Shoe and Canoe,* vol. 2, 130. The Seven Oaks massacre of 1816, six years earlier. The phrase "then recent" presumably comes from the perspective of 1850 when the book was published, that is, twenty-eight years after Bigsby's visit.

17 Ibid., 128-29.

18 Ibid., 129. This observation was prescient. Fifteen years later, William was a cavalryman in Spain wearing a most impressive uniform (see Chapter 9).

19 Bigsby, *Shoe and Canoe,* vol. 2, 129.

20 Glazebrooke, *Hargrave Correspondence,* 6, John Siveright to James Hargrave, 3 September 1821. John Siveright (1779-1856), fur trader, was over the years a member of the XY Company, the North West Company, and the Hudson's Bay Company. He was in charge of the Sault Ste Marie post from 1816 to 1823.

21 Reid, *Mansion in the Wilderness,* 1.

22 Catlin, *Letters and Notes,* opposite p. 162.

23 Bigsby, *Shoe and Canoe,* vol. 2, 127.

24 McKenney, *Sketches of a Tour,* 191.

25 McNeice, *Ermatinger Family,* 43.

26 AO, MU 4549, PR.MSS, envelope 2: "Ermatinger Genealogy."

27 Bigsby, *Shoe and Canoe,* vol. 2, 126.

28 Schoolcraft, *Personal Memoirs,* 134-5, 144, 149, 151-53.

29 Glazebrooke, *Hargrave Correspondence,* 6, John Siveright to James Hargrave, 10 May 1823.

30 Elaborate entertaining seems to have been a family trait. In 1821, Nicholas Garry, deputy governor of the Hudson's Bay Company, was passing through Montreal when he noted one Saturday, "With Mr Armitringer [sic], very agreeable Party and most excellent dinner." This would have been Charles' brother Frederick. Garry, "Diary of Nicholas Garry," 90.

31 Toronto Reference Library, Baldwin Room, *Nelson Journals,* "Journal Reminiscences, 1825-26," 73.

32 Unless otherwise noted, ages for school attendance in Montreal are deduced from dates in Frederick W. Ermatinger's cash and invoice books for board and supplies. LAC, MG 19, A2, series 3, vol. 187, Invoices, 17 March, 18 May, and 30 November 1816, [?] November 1818; MG 19, A2, series 3, vol. 188, Invoices, 10 July 1821, 28 July 1825.

33 McNeice, *Ermatinger Family,* appendix 1, Will of Frederick, 25 November 1826.

34 Ibid., 51; LAC, MG 19, A2, series 3, vol. 187, Receipt, 10 July 1819; MG 19, A2, series 3, vol. 38, file 1, nos. 3321-24, Cash, 30 June 1821; MG 19, A2, series 3, vol. 192, file 1, Invoice, 1 May 1822.

35 LAC, MG 19, A2, series 3, vol. 37, cited in McNeice, *Ermatinger Family,* 51.

36 LAC, MG 19, A2, series 3, vol. 34, file 1, nos. 1209 and 1211, Invoices, 25 February to 30 June 1815; MG 19, A2, series 3, vol. 187, Invoice, 30 November 1818; MG 19, A2, series 3, vol. 189, Invoice, April 1819; MG 19, A2, series 3, vol. 38, file 1, nos. 3321-24, Cash, 30 June 1821; MG 19, A2, series 3, vol. 190, Invoices, 25 June 1823, 6 December 1825, and 25 August 1825 to 17 May 1826.

37 LAC, MG 19, A2, series 3, vol. 188, Invoice, 30 October 1830; MG 19, A2, series 3, vol. 34, file 1, nos. 1209 and 1211, Invoices, 25 February to 30 June 1815; MG 19, A2, series 3, vol. 38, file 5, no. 3814, Invoice, 1822; MG 19, A2, series 3, vol. 42, file 3, no. 6278, Invoice, November 1830.

38 Van Kirk, *Many Tender Ties,* 198-99.

39 LAC, MG 19, A2, series 3, vol. 39, file 3, no. 4286, Invoice, 28 July 1824; MG 19, A2, series 3, vol. 43, file 2, Invoices, no. 6699, 1833; no. 6702, 8 April 1833; no. 6651, 13 February 1833; no. 6803, 1833; MG 19, A2, series 3, vol. 44, file 4, no. 7329, Invoice, October 1837; MG 19, A2, series 3, vol. 44, file 1, no. 7059, Invoice, November 1835.

40 LAC, MG 19, A2, series 3, vol. 209, Exercise Book, 1818.

41 LAC, MG 19, A2, series 4, vol. 2, no. 1, Charles Sr to Edward Ermatinger, 1 June 1821.

42 LAC, MG 19, A2, series 3, vol. 43, file 2, no. 6561, Charles Sr to Jemima, 3 December 1832.

CHAPTER 6: FARMER AND CAVALRYMAN

1 McNeice, *Ermatinger Family,* 55.

2 LAC, MG 24, D84, nos. 79-82, Jemima to Edward Ermatinger, 21 February 1831.

3 LAC, MG 19, A2, series 4, vol. 2, no. 8, Charles Jr to Edward Ermatinger, 22 August and 20 September 1831.

4 LAC, MG 19, A2, series 3, vol. 40, file 4, no. 5092, Marriage Agreement, 20 September 1826; LAC, MG 19, A2, series 4, vol. 1, file 1, no. 6499, Death Certificate, Anna Maria.

5 LAC, MG 19, A2, series 4, vol. 2, no. 17, Charles Jr to Edward Ermatinger, 11 April 1832.

6 LAC, MG 19, A2, series 3, vol. 43, file 2, no. 6695, Montreal Library Subscription, 1834; no. 6697, Montreal Music Society, 1833; MG 19, A2, series 3, vol. 44, file 3, nos. 7183 (for annual membership) and 7208 (for annual dinner), German Society, March 1836; no. 7168, Montreal Turf Club, March 1836.

7 Montreal *Transcript,* 20 May 1841.

8 *Gazette* (Montreal), 5 April 1848.

9 "Incompatibility of temper between Mrs E. and myself has been the chief cause of much misery to both of us," Edward wrote. UWO, microfiche, series 1, file 9, no. 236, Memoirs of Edward Ermatinger.

10 LAC, MG 19, A2, series 4, vol. 2, no. 17, Charles Jr to Edward Ermatinger, 11 April 1832.

11 LAC, MG 19, A2, series 3, vol. 206, file 1, Estate Journal, 1822-23, no. 32, Bank of Montreal stock, 1 June 1833.

12 LAC, MG 19, A2, series 4, vols. 1-3, file 1, nos. 74-82, Will of Charles Sr, 4 July 1831.

13 LAC, MG 19, A2, series 4, vol. 2, no. 31, Charles Jr to Edward Ermatinger, 14 October 1833.

14 LAC, MG 19, A2, series 3, vol. 205, no. 169, Cash Expenditures, 1834.

15 LAC, MG 19, A2, series 3, vol. 44, file 4, Notes Due, 1837.

16 LAC, MG 19, A2, series 3, vol. 44, file 5, no. 7432, Nonpayment protested by Louis Compte; MG 19, A2, series 3, vol. 44, file 5, Invoice, William Adams, January 1838; MG 19, A2, series 3, vol. 44, file 4, no. 7432, Note, James Carswell; MG 19, A2, series 3, vol. 44, nos. 7282, 7403-4, and 7498, Invoices, Bank of Montreal, 15 February 1837, 20 October 1837, 28 October 1837, and 18 September 1838.

17 LAC, MG 19, A2, series 3, vol. 43, file 2, no. 6657, Receipt, 5 August 1833; MG 19, A2, series 3, vol. 44, file 1, no. 6938, Receipt, 17 June 1834; MG 19, A2, series 3, vol. 44, file 1, no. 7164, Receipt, 31 June 1837; MG 19, A2, series 3, vol. 43, file 1, no. 7613, Award of Damages, 1834; MG 19, A2, series 3, vol. 44, file 5, no. 7296, Receipt, 4 April 1837.

18 LAC, MG 19, A2, series 3, vol. 43, file 2, no. 6474, Statement by S. Gale, 29 March 1832; MG 19, A2, series 3, vol. 44, file 1, no. 6850, Invoice, 1835; MG 19, A2, series 3, vol. 44, file 3, no. 7328, Invoice, April 1838; MG 19, A2, series 3, vol. 44, file 1, no. 6885, "To a set of plans," 29 March 1834; MG 19, A2, series 3, vol. 43, file 1, no. 7620, Sale of Land, 1832-33; MG 19, A2, series 3, vol. 44, file 5, no. 7343, Invoice, 6 June 1837.

19 LAC, MG 19, A2, series 3, vol. 42, file 1, no. 5750, Letter of Attorney, 5 November 1829.

20 McNeice, *Ermatinger Family,* 39.

21 Reid, *Mansion in the Wilderness,* 10, 12.

22 LAC, MG 19, A2, series 4, vol. 2, no. 51, John Ballenden to Charles Jr, 6 January 1844.

23 Canku Ota, *Interesting Sidelights on the History of the Early Fur Trade Industry,* issue 90, part 8, (28 June 2003), Martin McLeod diary excerpts, http://www.turtletrack.org.

24 Quoted in Arthur, "General Dickson," 151-52.

25 LAC, MG 19, A2, series 3, vol. 44, file 3, no. 7171, copy of scroll.

26 *Gazette* (Montreal), 19 July and 6 September 1836.

27 McLeod, "Diary of Martin Mcleod," 371f. McLeod made further reference to visiting "Mr. E.," whom the diary's editor, Grace L. Nute, identifies as Charles. However, Charles Sr had died several years earlier.

28 Canku Ota, *Interesting Sidelights on the History of the Early Fur Trade Industry,* issue 85, part 3, (19 April 2003), from George Ermatinger to James Ermatinger, 5 October 1836, http://www.turtletrack.org; AO, MU 4549, PR.MSS, envelope 4, Correspondence, Catherine Ermatinger to James Ermatinger, 14 September 1836. See also Nute, "Notes and Documents," 77. Dickson and party met James at Onatonagon on 9 October 1836 on the way to Red River. Martin McLeod, "The Diary of Martin McLeod," *Minnesota Quarterly* 4, 7-8 (1922): 374.

29 M. Elizabeth Arthur, "General Dickson and the Liberating Army," 151-53.

30 LAC, MG 19, A2, series 4, vol. 2, no. 9, Charles to Edward Ermatinger, 22 August 1831, with an addition on 20 September 1831.

31 Cited in Senior, *Redcoats and Patriotes,* 13.

32 Atherton, *Montreal,* vol. 2, 146.

33 *Gazette* (Montreal), 9 January 1836.

34 LAC, RG 8 (C series), 1A, vol. 217, no. 7, Maj. E.D. David to Lt.-Col. McCord, 12 February 1838. The account of what followed is based on LAC, MG 8, A25, "Les Événements de 1837 et 1838," Depositions nos. 50-70; LAC, MG 24, B25, IIA, Sydney Bellingham, "A Memoir," 80-81, 86; *Gazette* (Montreal), 18 and 21 November 1837; "Narrative of the Rebellion," *Gazette* (Montreal), 29 March 1838; *Le Canadien,* 20 and 22 November 1837; Gérard Filteau, *Histoire des Patriotes,* vol. 2, 235-39; Joseph-François Davignon in Fortin, *La Guerre des Patriotes,* 30-33; Rumilly, *Papineau et ses temps,* 499-502; David, *Les Patriotes de 1837-38,* 25-27; Christie, *History of the Late Province,* vol. 4, 511, 448; Lysons, *Early Reminiscences,* 69-70; Senior, "Provincial Cavalry," 7; Jodoin and Vincent, *Histoire de Longueuil,* 336-38; Greer, *Patriots and the People,* 301-2. All translations are my own.

35 Bonaventure Viger (1804-77), a legendary figure in Quebec, was briefly exiled to Bermuda for his role in the rebellion. He was later acquitted of murder during the rebellion.

36 LAC, RG 8 (C series), 1A, vol. 217, no. 9, Charles Jr to Lt.-Col. McCord, 12 February 1838.

37 Glenelg, *Correspondence Relative to the Affairs,* 111, Earl of Gosford to Glenelg, 22 November 1837, enclosure 3 in no. 51.

38 Davignon (1807-67) escaped to a life of exile in the United States. He was not pardoned, as many others were, and died there. Demarais (1798-1854) was also exiled but returned to become politically active, and later, mayor of St Jean. He wished at his death to be buried wearing his shackles. Fortin, *La Guerre des Patriotes,* 146-47, 151.

39 Choquette, *Les Ribaud,* 163 (my translation).

40 LAC, RG 8 (C series), 1A, vol. 217, no. 5, Charles Jr to Lt.-Col. McCord, 12 February 1838.

41 Christie, *History of the Late Province,* vol. 4, 490.

42 Bellingham, *Some Personal Recollections,* 14.

43 "Narrative of the Rebellion (cont.)," *Gazette* (Montreal), 3 April 1838.

44 Senior, "Provincial Cavalry," 10.

45 LAC, MG 24, B25, IIA, Sydney Bellingham, "A Memoir," 98. Bellingham (1808-1900) was born in Ireland but immigrated to Upper Canada, near Peterborough, when he was fifteen. He became a farmer, politician, soldier, businessman, and author.

46 LAC, MG 19, A2, series 3, vol. 42, file 2, nos. 5854-6, Charles Sr to George Ermatinger, 1 May 1829.

47 LAC, MG 19, A2, series 3, vol. 44, file 4, no. 7364, George Ermatinger to Charles Jr, 19 July 1837.

48 Ramsay Crooks to John R. Livingston, 27 June 1842, quoted in "Letter from Fur Company Officer."

49 AO, MU 4549, PR.MSS, envelope 3, Interview of Annie Ermatinger by Hugh MacMillan, 8.

50 *Gazette* (Montreal), 6 April 1839.

51 LAC, MG 24, B17, Quebec, 7 November 1838, General Orders No. 2 and 3; RG 8 (C series), 1A, vol. 1303, no. 91, Brook Taylor to Charles Jr, 1 May 1845; RG 8 (C series), 1A, vol. 1003, no. 77, Charles Jr to Lt.-Col. Taylor, 19 February 1842; RG 8 (C series), 1A, vol. 918, nos. 10-13, Charles to Military Secretary, 11 August 1845; RG 8 (C series), 1A, vol. 989, nos. 62 and 67-71, Charles Jr to Lt.-Col. S.D. Pritchard, 7 November 1849; RG 8 (C series), 1A, vol. 1003, no. 78, Capt. Taylor to Military Secretary, 20 February 1852.

52 LAC, RG 8 (C series), 1A, vol. 802, no. 176, Capt. Walter Jones to Col. Pritchard, 12 February 1848; RG 8 (C series), 1A, vol. 801, no. 139, Charles Jr to Col. Pritchard, January 1848.

CHAPTER 7: OJIBWA CHIEF AND MONTREAL POLICE OFFICER

1 Chute, *Legacy of Shingwaukonse,* 72-73, 81, 99-100.

2 LAC, RG 10, vol. 163 (reel C-11501), no. 94932, William to T.E. Campbell, 7 May 1847.

3 Chute, *Legacy of Shingwaukonse,* 99-100.

4 LAC, RG 1, L-3, vol. 279, Canada Land Petitions, K bundle 5, 1848-50, no. 13½, Petitions of Charlotte, 1847 and 1849.

5 "Treaty with the Chippewa, 5 August 1826," in *Indian Affairs,* ed., Kappler, 273.

6 William Penn (1644-1718), a Quaker, founded what became the state of Pennsylvania. Whether in fact he signed a Great Treaty at the village of Shackamaxon in 1682 is open to doubt, as the treaty has never been found. But he and his agents bought land from the Delaware, whom he saw as its rightful "owners."

7 "Treaty with the Ottawas, etc., 28 March 1836," in *Indian Affairs,* ed., Kappler, 455.

8 Barnouw, *Acculturation and Personality,* 37.

9 Blackbird, *History of the Ottawa,* 51-52.

10 LAC, RG 1, L-3, vol. 279, Canada Land Petitions, K bundle 5, 1848-50, no. 13½i.

11 LAC, MG 13, WO1, vol. 563, nos. 51-54 and 69, Reports by Capt. A.P. Cooper, 3 and 16 December 1849.

12 William B. Robinson (1797-1873) was a Tory politician and member for Simcoe. He had trading posts in the Muskoka district, which gave him much influence with the Indians there.

13 Robinson, "Report to Indian Affairs," 17-20. These individuals possibly included Allan MacDonell (1808-88), a lawyer who helped the Ojibwa pressure the government for compensation. Swainson, "MacDonell, Allan," vol. 11, 553.

14 LAC, RG 8 (C series), 1A, vol. 80, no. 94, Certificate as magistrate to the Rifle Brigade at Sault Ste Marie.

15 Province of Canada, LAJA, 1851, vol. 10, app. II, "Réponse à une addresse distribué aux sauvages du Lac Superior." Papasainse was a signatory to the Lake Huron Treaty.

16 LAC, RG 8 (C series), 1A, vol. 163 (reel C-11501), no. 94932, William to T.E. Campbell, 7 May 1847; RG 8 (C series), 1A, vol. 500, nos. 92-95, Charles Jr, "Memorial to Lord Elgin," 8 November 1850.

17 AO, MS 4, W.B. Robinson, Transcription of Diaries, Sault Ste Marie, 29 April and 1 May 1850.

18 Robinson, *Copy of the Robinson Treaty*, 3-8. See also Henderson, "Indian Treaties," in *The Canadian Encyclopedia*, vol. 2, 873-74.

19 Robinson, "Report to Indian Affairs," 20.

20 LAC, RG 1, L3, 182B, e-bundle 6, no. 21, Petition of the Undersigned Inhabitants, n.d., 21e-21f.

21 Ibid., Petition of 16 [four] Undersigned Chiefs, 21h-21i.

22 LAC, RG 1, L3, 182B, e-bundle 6, no. 3, Memorial of the Undersigned Chiefs, 10 September 1850, 3a-3b.

23 LAC, RG 1, L3, 182B, e-bundle 6, no. 21, Commissioner of Crown Lands, John Rabb to the Governor-General, 29 November 1850, 21, 21a, 21b.

24 Ingram, *Views of the Sault*, 101; Sneakers, "Pim Family."

25 McNab, "Métis Participation," 74.

26 Morris, *Treaties of Canada*, 18 and note.

27 Royal Commission on Aboriginal Peoples, *Final Report*, vol. 2, 4.3 "Failure of Alternative Economic Options," Opening Statement, 486-87, 491-92.

28 Senior, "Provincial Cavalry," 22-23. With the arrival of responsible government in Lower Canada, the Tories lost their political domination and flirted with the idea of joining the United States.

29 Alexander, *L'Acadie*, vol. 1, 47; Senior, "Provincial Cavalry," 2.

30 *Gazette* report quoted in *Daily News* (Kingston), 30 June 1866.

31 LAC, RG 8 (C series), 1A, C-500, nos. 92-95, "Memorial to Lord Elgin," 8 November 1850.

32 Evidence by Charles given at the "Inquest on the Bodies of the Sufferers of the 9th of June," *Transcript* (Montreal), 15 June 1853.

33 Ibid.; "Inquest on the Bodies of the Sufferers of the 9th of June," *Transcript* (Montreal), 11 June 1853.

34 Evidence by Charles, 15 June 1853.

35 Rumilly, *Histoire de Montréal*, vol. 2, 347. Wolfred Nelson (1791-1863) was a brother of George Nelson, Charles Sr's friend of the North West Company days.

36 "Obituary," *Transcript* (Montreal), 10 January 1857.

37 "Funeral of Captain Ermatinger," *Transcript* (Montreal), 13 January 1857.

38 "Obituary," *Transcript* (Montreal), 10 January 1857; "Funeral of the Late Captain Charles O. Ermatinger," *Gazette* (Montreal), 13 January 1857.

39 "Funeral of Captain Ermatinger," *Transcript* (Montreal), 15 January 1857.

CHAPTER 8: SOLDIER, CLERK, AND A LAST ADVENTURE

1 LAC, MG 24, D84, nos. 79-82, Jemima to Edward Ermatinger, 21 February 1831.

2 LAC, MG 19, A2, series 4, vol. 2, nos. 24 and 27, Charles Sr to Edward, 1 July and 4 August 1833.

3 LAC, MG 19, A2, series 4, vol. 2, no. 31, Charles Jr to Edward, 14 October 1833.

4 Williams, "Reminiscences of Samuel Williams," 64.

5 UWO, microfiche, series 1, file 3, no. 61, Gazette, 1 June 1838; LAC, RG 9, 1B1, vol. 34, file "Middlesex, 1839," Roster St Thomas Cavalry, nos. 1-2, 1 January 1838.

6 "Despatches," *Gazette* (Montreal), 8 March 1838.

7 Williams, "Reminiscences of Samuel Williams," 67.

8 The following description of the battle is drawn from Williams, "Reminiscences of Samuel Williams," and Tomlinson, "Reminiscences of Roswell Tomlinson."

9 "Saturday Evening," *Gazette* (Montreal), 10 March 1838.

10 Read, *Rising in Western Upper Canada*, 146-47.

11 Ermatinger, *Talbot Regime*, 220; LAC, MG 13, WO13, no. 3711, St Thomas Troop of Cavalry.

12 LAC, MG 19, A2, series 2, vol. 3, District Order, 9 March 1838.

13 Tomlinson, "Reminiscences of Roswell Tomlinson," 61; Williams, "Reminiscences of Samuel Williams," 69.

14 LAC, RG 8, 1B1, vol. 29, file "Middlesex, 1838," James to Maj.-Gen. George Arthur, August 1838.

15 St John's Anglican Church, Parish Register, 1830-1851, 1885-1948, 35, Marriage Record; Ontario Genealogical Society, Oakwood Cemetery, Book 1, 2 May 1890-11 March 1932, Mary E. Fraser.

16 Hughes, *St John's Anglican Church*, 35; Reid, *Marriage Notices of Ontario*, 161; Yeager, *Norfolk County Marriage Records*.

7 Mutrie, *1852 Census of Simcoe Town*.

18 LAC, MG 26-A, Political Papers, Letter Books, vol. 516, part 3, no. 616, Sir John A. Macdonald to William McDougall, 27 November 1869.

9 LAC, RG 1, L3, 182B, no. 21, Petition of the Undersigned Inhabitants of Sault Ste Marie, 21j.

20 Eva Brook Donly Museum, Norfolk County Council Records, box 1, 3rd Special Session of the Norfolk County Council, 29 October 1856.

21 Eva Brook Donly Museum, Norfolk County Council Records, box 1, 1st Regular Session of the Norfolk County Council, 1857; box 11, Post Card, 19 July 1886.

22 Norfolk County Council, By-Law No. 124, To appropriate certain sums of money to improve certain county roads, CIHM microfiche, series no. 542558.

23 LAC, MG 26-A, Political Papers, Letter Books, vol. 516, part 3, no. 616, Sir John A. Macdonald to William McDougall, 27 November 1869. Presumably Macdonald referred to the 1849 treaty negotiations at Sault Ste Marie where James was present. Chippewaian/Chipewyan refers to the Athapaskan people of the northern provinces and subarctic (and their language).

24 Canada, House of Commons, *Sessional Papers, 1871*, vol. 5, no. 44, "Statement of Claims Made on the Dominion Government Consequent Upon the Insurrection in the North West Territories," 6-8, E.A. Meredith to James, 31 December 1869; A. Walsh to E.A. Meredith, 16 February 1870; Joseph·Howe to James, 16 February 1870; James to Joseph Howe, 5 March 1870; E.A. Meredith to James, 17 March 1870.

25 Canada, House of Commons, *Sessional Papers, 1870*, vol. 5, no. 12, "Correspondence and Papers Connected with Recent Occurrences in the North West Territories," 83, James to Joseph Howe, 20 December 1869 and reply.

26 "House Had Ties with Red River Tragedy," *Sault Daily Star*, 18 June 1970, 3.

27 LAC, MG 26-A, Political Papers, Letter Books, vol. 517, part 1, no. 185, Prime Minister's Office to James 30 June 1870.

28 Thomson, *Men and Meridians*, vol. 2, 85-86.

29 LAC, MG 19, A2, series 2, vol. 3, Report of Touchwood Hills Survey; Canada, House of Commons, *Sessional Papers, 1872*, vol. 7, no. 33, "Progress Report on the Canadian Pacific Railway," 6. The report in the Ermatinger files starts with no introduction at a page numbered 142. The date is 24 November 1871, when the survey expedition was in the Touchwood Hills. The report ends equally abruptly at page 166 on 22 December 1871 at Rat Creek, south of Fort Garry. Clearly this is part of a larger document that has not yet been found.

30 "For explorations or preliminary examinations in advance of regular surveys, the barometer was used to ascertain altitude. Horizontal distances were computed on the basis of time elapsed in passing from one place to another." Thomson, *Men and Meridians*, vol. 2, 86.

31 Canada, Senate, *Journals*, 1877, app. 1, "Minutes of Evidence," 3, 49-50.

32 LAC, MG 26-A, Political Papers, Letter Books, vol. 523, no. 220, John A. Macdonald to James, 29 May 1873.

33 Williams, "Reminiscences of Samuel Williams," 69; LAC, RG 9, vol. 34, file "Middlesex, July-December," James to Maj.-Gen. George Arthur, n.d.

34 UWO, microfiche, series 1, file 11, nos. 132-34, James to Edward Ermatinger, 30 May 1863 and 27 July 1864.

35 Glazebrooke, *History of Transportation*, vol. 1, 115-16.

36 LAC, MG 19, A2, series 2, vol. 3, part 2, Assistant to Secretary of State for War to James, 26 February 1856.

37 Gilkison, *Visit of the Governor-General*, 8.

38 LAC, RG 31, 1871 Census, file "Norfolk 14," no. 89.

39 Canada, *Manual Containing the Census Act*, chapter 5 (Directions Concerning the Separate Schedules), schedule no. 1, "Nominal Return of the Living," 23, column 13.

40 *Census of Canada, 1881*, Town of Simcoe, Ontario.

41 Ontario Genealogical Society, Oakwood Cemetery, Book 1, 2 May 1890-11 March 1932; "The Late Capt.

Ermatinger," *Norfolk Reformer*, 18 December 1890.

42 "The Late Capt. Ermatinger," *Norfolk Reformer*, 18 December 1890.

CHAPTER 9: DANDY TURNED HERO

1 UWO, microfiche, series 2, Letters, no. 87, Frank Ermatinger to Edward Ermatinger, 4 December 1827.

2 LAC, MG 19, A2, series 3, vol. 42, file 3, no. 6258, Invoice, Gibbs & Co., 16 July 1832.

3 LAC, MG 19, A2, series 3, vol. 37, file 3, no. 3019, Invoice, Gibbs and Kollinger, 21 October 1820.

4 LAC, MG 24, D84, nos. 79-82, Jemima to Edward Ermatinger, 21 February 1831.

5 LAC, MG 19, A2, series 3, vol. 43, file 1, no. 6315, Bill, 28 April 1831.

6 LAC, MG 25, G38, clipping from *Evening Telegraph* (Montreal), n.d.; MG 19, A2, series 4, vol. 2, no. 10, Charles Sr to Edward Ermatinger, 9 March 1832.

7 Lower Canada, *Journals of the House of Assembly, 1832-33*, vol. 42, app. M, "Copies of Official Communications and Reports ... re ... Occurrences which took place in Montreal on 21st May, 1832," Evidence of A. Carlisle Buchanan.

8 At that time, and for many years, British regiments were stationed in Montreal and stood to in times of crisis.

9 LAC, MG 19, A2, series 3, vol. 41, file 2, no. 5493, Receipt, Gibbs & Co., 1) December 1828.

10 Marshall-Cornwall, "British Aid in the Carlist Wars," 180.

11 Holt, *Carlist Wars in Spain*, 83-93.

12 Somerville, *History of the British Legion*, 186, 209, 226.

13 Marshall-Cornwall, "British Aid in the Carlist Wars," 185-86.

14 Great Britain, War Office, *Army Lists of the British Auxiliary Legion Spain, 1835-37*, National Army Museum, London.

15 *Gazette* (Montreal), 25 August and 29 September 1836.

16 Richardson, *Personal Memoirs*, 101-5. R.C. de La Saussaye was later a marshal in the Austrian army (Roy, *La Famille Juchereau Duchesnay*, 353). John Richardson (1796-1882), a colourful soldier, historian and novelist, was born in Queenstown, Upper Canada, and died, poverty stricken, in New York. He was perhaps Canada's first English-language novelist. Some years after the duelling incident, he and William policed labour riots on Canada's growing canal system, Richardson at Welland, and William at Lachine and Beauharnois (see next chapter).

17 Henderson, *Soldier of Three Queens*, vol. 2, 7-8.

18 Somerville, *History of the British Legion*, appendix, "British Legion of Spain."

19 Marshall-Cornwall, "British Aid in the Carlist Wars," 186.

20 Quoted in Holt, *Carlist Wars in Spain*, 160.

21 Holt, *Carlist Wars in Spain*, 164.

22 Carman, "Lancers of the British Auxiliary," 65.

23 LAC, MG 19, A2, series 3, vol. 43, file 4, nos. 7282 and 7403-4, Bills.

24 Carman, "Lancers of the British Auxiliary," 65-67.

25 Holt, *Carlist Wars in Spain*, 163.

26 *Gazette* (Montreal), 5 May 1838.

27 MacMunn, *Always into Battle*, 115.

28 Evans, *Memoranda of the Contest*, 122. Colonel La Saussaye's name was misspelled even more egregiously than William's surname.

29 Public Records Office, Kew, UK, FO 72 514, nos. 26, 9, William Wylde to Viscount Palmerston, 7 December 1838. Lt.-Col. William Wylde, Royal Artillery, was British commissioner at the Spanish Army headquarters at the time he wrote this account.

30 Thomas, "Chronology."

31 Holt, *Carlist Wars in Spain*, 191-92.

32 MacMunn, *Always into Battle*, 113; Burgess, "Evans and the British Legion," 268.

33 LAC, MG 25, G38, clipping from *Evening Telegraph* (Montreal), n.d.

34 LAC, MG 25, G38, Judge C.O. Ermatinger, "Incomplete Narrative History of the Ermatinger Family"; Roy, *La Famille Juchereau Duchesnay*, 353. Prince Baldomero Espartero (1793-1879) was commander in chief of the Christino forces. He opened the negotiations that led to the Convention of Vergara (1839) and effectively ended the civil war. Unfortunately, the legion list in Nicholas Carlisle's book, *A Concise Account of the Several Foreign Orders*, finishes just before William joined the force, so the title he received can't be confirmed.

35 Cole, *This Blessed Wilderness*, 257.

Chapter 10: Suppressing Riots in Montreal

1 *Gazette* (Montreal), 27 March 1838.
2 LAC, MG 25, G 38, *Evening Telegraph* (Montreal), n.d.
3 Province of Canada, LAJA, 1843, vol. 3, app. T, "Report of the Commissioners to Enquire into the Disturbances [at the] Beauharnois and Lachine Canals." See also Province of Canada, Legislative Assembly, *Debates*, 1844-45, vol. 4, 1460.
4 *Transcript* (Montreal), 4 March 1843.
5 Ibid.
6 Dominick Daly (1798-1868) allied with the Reformers till 1843, when he supported Governor General Metcalfe against the Reformers in their fight for responsible government.
7 Province of Canada, LAJA, 1843, vol. 3, app. T, no. 30, Copie des Instructions ... D. Daly, 25 March 1843.
8 Ibid., no. 32, Deposition of Laviolette.
9 LAC, MG 24, SL-3, vol. 22, no. 1361, William K. McCord to William, 11 May 1850.
10 Province of Canada, LAJA, 1843, vol. 3, app. T, no. 39, Deposition de Benjamin Seaton.
11 Ibid., no. 32, Deposition of Laviolette.
12 Senior, *Constabulary*, 64; Province of Canada, LAJA, 1843, vol. 3, app. T, "Report of the Commissioners to Enquire into the Disturbances [at the] Beauharnois and Lachine Canals." The report refers to William as "Colonel England," though it is quite clear he is meant.
13 An Ordinance to Incorporate the City and Town of Quebec, Province of Canada, *Revised Acts and Ordinances of Lower Canada, 1845*, 3 & 4 Vict., c. 35, ss. 2, 3, 42. The Act says that the sections in the Quebec Ordinance concerning the police are also to apply to Montreal.
14 Senior, *Constabulary*, 68.
15 Province of Canada, LAJA, 1843, vol. 3, app. A, B3, "Statements of Warrants Issued on the Receiver-General"; Province of Canada, LAJA, 1851, vol. 10, app. BBB, "Return to an Address and Copy of the Commission appointing Messrs McCord and Ermatinger Inspectors and Superintendents of Police at Quebec and Montreal," 210.
16 Province of Canada, LAJA, 1854-55, vol. 13, app. XX, "Report of Commission Appointed to Investigate and Report upon the Best Means of Reorganizing the Militia of Canada ... and to Report upon an Improved System of Police."
17 LAC, RG 4, B10, vol. 2, Letters Patent, no. 362, William appointed Inspector and Superintendent of Police for Montreal with the duties of a Justice of the Peace, 1 January 1843; no. 372, Ralph B. Johnson appointed jointly with William as Inspector and Superintendent, 17 November 1849; nos. 374-75, William commissioned to act as magistrate, if required, 17 December 1849; nos. 576-77, appointment of Johnson revoked, William continued, 23 June 1853; LAC, RG 8, series 1, vol. 80, no. 10, Bartholomew Conrad Augustus Gugy appointed jointly with William to the same post, 8 October 1853; no. 52, Appointments of both William and Gugy revoked, 4 November 1853.
18 *Gazette* (Montreal), 13, 18, 20, and 23 April 1844, including extracts from the *Montreal Courier*.
19 Province of Canada, LAJA, 1846, vol. 5, app. EEE, "Report of Select Committee ... [re] ... Municipal Election for the city of Montreal, March 1846, St James Ward," Evidence of William.
20 Roy, *La Famille Juchereau*, 353.
21 Cole, *This Blessed Wilderness*, 257-58.
22 LAC, RG 10, vol. 163 (reel C-11501), nos. 94933-35, William Ermatinger, attorney for Charlotte Kattawabide, 7 May 1847.
23 "Meeting of the Parliament: A Stormy Debate," *Pilot* (Montreal), 27 April 1849.
24 LAC, RG 4, C1, vol. 254, file 1592, William to James Leslie, "Report on the Late Occurrences," 10 May 1849.
25 Province of Canada, Legislative Assembly, *Debates*, 1849, vol. 8, part 3, 2055. The political career of Francis Hincks (1807-85) ran from the LaFontaine-Baldwin Reform years starting in 1848 until he joined MacDonald's first post-Confederation ministry in 1869 and then finally quit politics in 1874.
26 The two Reform leaders Louis-Hippolyte LaFontaine (1807-64) of Lower Canada and Robert Baldwin (1804-58) of Upper Canada, as attorneys general east and west, were joint heads of the first responsible government in United Canada.
27 LAC, RG 4, C1, vol. 254, file 1592, William to James Leslie, "Report on the Late Occurrences," 10 May 1849.
28 "Meeting of the Parliament: A Stormy Debate," *Pilot* (Montreal), 27 April 1849.
29 Province of Canada, Legislative Assembly, *Debates*, 1849, vol. 8, part 3, 2085. Gugy (1796-1876), a soldier,

seigneur, Tory politician, and eccentric, was bitterly opposed to the Liberals.

30 *Gazette* (Montreal), 30 April and 3 May 1849; Province of Canada, Legislative Assembly, *Debates,* 1849, vol. 8, part 3, 2130.

31 LAC, RG 4, C1, vol. 254, file 1592, William to James Leslie, "Report on the Late Occurrences," 10 May 1849.

32 Ibid.

33 Ibid. For Hincks's claim of a 7:00 p.m. meeting with William, see Province of Canada, Legislative Assembly, *Debates,* 1849, vol. 8, part 3, 2055. John Young (1811-78) was a businessman and Liberal politician heavily involved in canal construction and the Montreal harbour operations. Unfortunately, the letter William mentions is no longer attached to the report.

34 LAC, RG 4, C1, vol. 254, file 1592, William to James Leslie, "Report on the Late Occurrences," 10 May 1849.

35 LAC, RG 8 (C series), vol. 80, mfm C-2644, no. 10, Secretary Leslie to Maj. T.E. Campbell re Capt. Wetherall, 30 April 1849; no. 23, Appointment of William and Wm King McCord as magistrates, 26 May 1849; no. 52, William to act as magistrate, 1 December 1849.

36 Province of Canada, *Papers Relating to the Removal of the Seat of Government and to the Annexation Movement,* enclosure 4, signed by C. Wetherall, William K. McCord, and William Ermatinger.

37 LAC, MG 24, SL-3, vol. 22, no. 1361, William K. McCord to William, 11 May 1850.

38 For a view of the 1849 Montreal riots from a different angle, see Stewart, *A Life on the Line,* 35-43.

39 Province of Canada, LAJA, 1850, vol. 9, app. NNN, I, "Extracts from a Report of a Committee of the Honourable Executive Council ... 26 September 1849."

40 Dent, "Honourable John Young," 197.

41 An Act for Defraying the Expenses of the River Police of Montreal, Province of Canada, *Statutes,* 1851, c. 24.

42 Province of Canada, LAJA, 1854, vol. 13, app. G, no. 5, Montreal Police; no. 6, Montreal Water Police.

43 LAC, MG 24, SL-3, vol. 21, no. 1356, William McCord to William, 26 June 1846 (McCord's emphasis).

44 Evidence by William given at the "Inquest on the Bodies of the Sufferers of the 9th of June," reported in the *Transcript* (Montreal), 13 June 1853.

45 Ibid.

46 Evidence by Capt. Cameron given at the "Inquest on the Bodies of the Sufferers of the 9th of June," reported in the *Transcript* (Montreal), 15 June 1853.

47 Evidence by Charles given at the "Inquest on the Bodies of the Sufferers of the 9th of June," reported in the *Transcript* (Montreal), 15 June 1853.

48 Evidence by William, 13 June 1853.

49 Evidence by Charles, 15 June 1853.

50 Evidence by William, 13 June 1853.

51 Ibid.

52 Ibid., and Evidence by Charles, 15 June 1853.

53 Evidence by Dr Crawford given at the "Inquest on the Bodies of the Sufferers of the 9th of June," reported in the *Transcript* (Montreal), 11 June 1853.

54 Elinor Senior, *British Regulars in Montreal,* 141.

55 Evidence by William, 13 June 1853; Evidence by Dr MacDonell given at the "Inquest on the Bodies of the Sufferers of the 9th of June," reported in the *Transcript* (Montreal), 13 June 1853.

56 Evidence by William, 13 June 1853.

57 Evidence by Mayor Wilson given at the "Inquest on the Bodies of the Sufferers of the 9th of June," reported in the *Transcript* (Montreal), 13 June 1853.

58 Evidence by Col. Hogarth given at the "Inquest on the Bodies of the Sufferers of the 9th of June," reported in the *Transcript* (Montreal), 13 June 1853.

59 Evidence by William, 15 June 1853; Evidence by Dr MacDonell, 13 June 1853.

60 Evidence by William, 13 June 1853.

61 Evidence by Lieut. Quarterly and by William Palmer given at the "Inquest on the Bodies of the Sufferers of the 9th of June," both reported in the *Transcript* (Montreal), 15 June 1853.

62 Evidence by Col. Hogarth, 13 June 1853.

63 Evidence by Mayor Wilson, 16 June 1853; Evidence by H.L. Routh given at the "Inquest on the Bodies of the Sufferers of the 9th of June," reported in the *Transcript* (Montreal), 13 June 1853.

64 Evidence by Lieut. Quarterly, 15 June 1853.

65 Evidence by Robert S. Oliver given at the "Inquest on the Bodies of the Sufferers of the 9th of June," reported in the *Transcript* (Montreal), 5 July 1853.

66 Evidence by Margaret Brown, widow, given at the "Inquest on the Bodies of the Sufferers of the 9th of

June," reported in the *Transcript* (Montreal), 8 July 1853.

67 Evidence by William, 13 June 1853.
68 Evidence by Lieut. Quarterly, 15 June 1853.
69 Evidence by Dr MacDonell, 13 June 1853.
70 "Coroner's Jury Reports," in the *Transcript* (Montreal), 11 July 1853.
71 *Transcript* (Montreal), 20 June 1853.

CHAPTER 11: MURDER, MILITIA, AND MILITARY INTELLIGENCE

1 LAC, RG 8, series 1, vol. 80, no. 52, Appointments of both William and Bartholomew Conrad Augustus Gugy revoked, 4 November 1853.
2 This section is based on *Quebec Morning Chronicle*, 9, 11-16, and 19 February, 4, 11-15, 18, 20, 25-26, and 29 March, 9 and 11 April 1856; Province of Canada, LAJA, 1856, vol. 14, app. 42, "Return to an Address ... re the Murder in Sylvestre de Lotbinière"; LAJA, 1857, vol. 15, app. 45, "Report of Commission ... re the Murder in Sylvestre de Lotbinière"; LAJA, 1858, vol. 16, app. 48, "Final Report of the Commissioners ... re the murder in Sylvestre de Lotbinière."
3 Dunbar Ross (1800-65) replaced Dominic Daly as the member for Mégantic. A Reformer, he yet managed to work with several Conservative governments.
4 Province of Canada, LAJA, 1848, vol. 7, app. O, "Return to Two Addresses ... re the Dismissal of A.B. Papineau, 2 July 1847."
5 LAC, MG 24, B25, IIA, Sydney Bellingham, "A Memoir," 193.
6 Province of Canada, LAJA, 1849, vol. 8, app. EEE, no. 11, Evidence of Hugh Brereton.
7 Province of Canada, LAJA, 1855, vol. 13, app. AAA, "Statistics Shewing the Number of Persons, Male and Female, Brought before William Ermatinger ... 1 January 1849 to 30 November 1854."
8 Province of Canada, LAJA, 1851, vol. 10, app. QQ, Evidence of James Court, 280 and 294.
9 LAC, MG 25, G38, clipping from *Evening Telegraph* (Montreal), n.d.
10 LAC, MG 24, G55, Maj. John Boomer to William, 24 February 1857; MG 24, SL-3, vol. 22, no. 10270, Lt.-Col. Christopher Dunkin to William, 1 September 1857; no. 10123, Capt. Thomas Burns to William, 15 April 1857.
11 LAC, MG 24, G55, Charles Nelson to William, 17 October 1862. Brown and Brightman, in *The Orders of the Dreamed*, assert, "Of eight children born to Nelson and his Ojibwa wife, Mary Ann, between 1809 and 1829 only one daughter survived past 1831 into adulthood" (20). Unless Nelson married again, it is possible that a son of Mary Ann also survived.
12 Province of Canada, LAJA, 1859, vol. 17, app. 46, "Extrait du rapport d'inspection de l'officier inspecteur."
13 LAC, MG 24, SL-3, vol. 22, no. 10332, William to [unknown], 31 March 1856.
14 After the Fenian crisis, the adjutant general found that the militia lacked provincial magazines; that equipment of the cavalry corps and the field batteries was "in a very unsatisfactory" condition with the harnesses of the field batteries "falling to pieces from age and rottenness"; that the force needed a "uniform system for clothing"; that experts in gun repair should be permanently employed; that the lack of drill sheds greatly disadvantaged the force; that better training for the gunners was urgently needed; and that many commanding officers failed to provide systematic target practice. Most were problems William had reported on earlier. Province of Canada, LAJA, 1866, vol. 2, app. 4, "Report, Adjutant General (Colonel P.L. McDougall)."
15 LAC, MG 24, G55, George Hunt to William, 23 July 1859, 4 and 25 February 1862, 10 March 1862. I have been unable to decipher this phrase or to discover what it refers to, but it seems to have been some sort of wetlands or marsh, perhaps dotted with clumps of grass – at any rate, dangerous.
16 "Harrison Stephens," in *Canadian Biographical Dictionary and Portrait Gallery of Eminent and Self-Made Men: Quebec and the Maritime Provinces*, vol. 2: *Quebec* (Toronto and Chicago: H.C. Cooper Jr, 1881), 348.
17 LAC, MG 24, G55, George Hunt to William, 4 February 1862.
18 LAC, MG 25, G38, clipping from *Evening Telegraph* (Montreal), n.d.
19 Canada, House of Commons, *Sessional Papers, 1869*, vol. 6, no. 75, "Return to Address of the House of Commons, 26 April 1869," 25, Attorney General Cartier to Governor General Monck, 30 September 1864.
20 *Transcript* (Montreal), 21 October 1864.
21 Winks, *Civil War Years*, 301.
22 *Irish Canadian* (city?), 1 February 1865.
23 Canada, House of Commons, *Sessional Papers, 1869*, vol. 6, no. 75, "Return to Address of the House of

Commons, 26 April 1869," 55, Governor General Monck to J.H. Burnley, 20 December 1864. Viscount Charles Stanley Monck (1819-94) was governor general from 1861 to 1868. His skills as a diplomat helped keep Britain out of war with America, and later did much to bring about Confederation.

24 *Transcript* (Montreal), "Over the Border," 17 December 1864, and "The Border Troubles," 20 December 1864.

25 *Globe and Mail*, 9 February 1865.

26 Canada, House of Commons, *Sessional Papers, 1869*, vol. 6, no. 75, "Return to Address of the House of Commons, 26 April 1869," 74-75, Order-in-Council, 27 June 1865; Attorney General Cartier to William, 27 July 1865. Gilbert McMicken (1813-91) was at various times a businessman, spy, land speculator, politician, magistrate, and policeman. In later life he was very influential in Manitoba politics.

27 Quoted from MacDonald, "Canada's Secret Police," *Beaver* 71, 3 (June-July 1991): 46; Carl Betke, "McMicken, Gilbert," *Dictionary of Canadian Biography*, vol. 12, 676.

28 LAC, MG 27, IJ2A, List of Expenses Incurred by the Men of the Water Police ... , October 1864-April 1866; Sundry Cash Advances, 4 January 1867-27 February 1869.

29 LAC, MG 24, G55, A. Campbell to William, 11 January 1867.

30 LAC, MG 26-A, *Political Papers, Correspondence*, vol. 56, nos. 22450-53, "Fenians, Burns Report," 20 November 1865.

31 LAC, MG 25, G38, clippings from *Evening Telegraph* (Montreal), n.d.; *Globe and Mail*, 13 January 1866.

32 LAC, MG 26-A, *Political Papers, Correspondence*, vol. 157, nos. 22646-49, "Fenians, Activities," 1 to 7 February 1866; vol. 237, no. 103288, "Fenians, Malone Surveillance," 5 March 1866.

33 LAC, MG 53, B27, vol. 54, J.F.M. DesRivières to William, 8 February 1866.

34 Senior, *Last Invasion of Canada*, 52.

35 *Evening Times* (Hamilton), 18 April 1866 (reprinted from *The Leader*, Cornwall).

36 Stacey, "Michael Murphy," 146-52; Senior, *From Royal Township*, 219.

37 LAC, MG 26-A, *Political Papers, Correspondence*, vol. 237, no. 104036, "Fenians, Vermont Frontier," 9 June 1866.

38 Canada, *Correspondence Respecting the Recent Fenian Aggression, 27-29; Daily News* (Kingston), 27 June 1866, quoting the *Gazette* (Montreal).

39 This was the first body of troops in Canada to be armed with breech-loading weapons. Campbell, *Fenian Invasions of Canada*, 27. At trial, two prisoners were found guilty but the case against the rest was dropped.

40 Campbell, *Fenian Invasions of Canada*, 25-27.

41 LAC, MG 26-A, *Political Papers, Correspondence*, vols. 240-41, nos. 106427-29, "Fenians, Activity, Montreal," 5 February 1868.

42 LAC, MG 26-A, *Political Papers, Letter Books*, vol. 11, no. 579, "Ermatinger, W, Secret Enquiry," 12 March 1868; MG 26-A, *Political Papers, Correspondence*, vols. 240-41, nos. 106549-52, "Fenians, Activities," 12 March 1868; nos. 106619-21, "Surveillance," 26 March 1868.

43 LAC, MG 26-A, *Political Papers, Correspondence*, vols. 240-41, no. 106947-48, "Fenians, St Armand Report," 23 May 1868; nos. 107013-17, "Fenians, Activity, Boston," 2 June 1868.

44 LAC, MG 26-A, *Political Papers, Correspondence*, vols. 240-241, nos. 107177-80, "Fenians – Arms and Munitions," 3 June 1868; nos. 107049-50, "Fenians – Activities – St Albans," 6 June 1868.

45 LAC, MG 27, IJ2A, List of Expenses Incurred by the Men of the Water Police ... Sundry Cash Advances, 4 January 1867 to 27 February 1869. After William's death, Joseph Coursol replaced him as head of the Water Police. The Frontier Police force was finally disbanded in January 1869 (LAC, MG 27, IJ2A, no. 19, sundry cash advances, January 27, 1869). The *Evening Pilot* bitterly regretted the loss of this "trustworthy, energetic and intelligent body of men – a terror to evil doers" (19 January 1869).

46 LAC, MG 25, G38, clipping from *Evening Telegraph* (Montreal), n.d.

47 Winks, *Civil War Years*, 335.

48 LAC, RG 13, A2, vol. 21, no. 638, R. Campbell to John A. Macdonald, 1 May 1869.

49 LAC, MG 19, A2, series 4, vol. 1, file 1, no. 6510, Death Certificate, William.

50 LAC, MG 25, G38, clipping from *Evening Telegraph* (Montreal), n.d.; Cloutier, *Mt. Royal Cemetery Records*, by letter.

51 *Montreal News*, 25 January 1869.

52 LAC, MG 25, G38, clipping from *Evening Telegraph* (Montreal), n.d.

53 "Death of Late Col. Ermatinger," *Montreal Herald*, 25 January 1869.

54 *Le Nouveau Monde*, 25 January 1869; *La Minerve*, 25 January 1869 (author's translations).

55 LAC, Shakespeare Dramatic and Literary Club (Montreal), *Annual Report, 1846-47* and *List of Members*,

25 May 1847; *Gazette* (Montreal), 12 March 1844.

56 *Montreal Herald*, 29 August 1863 and 25 June 1864.

CHAPTER 12: "THE GIRLS HAVE TURNED OUT TO BE FINE WOMEN"

1 LAC, MG 19, A2, series 3, vol. 42, file 1, nos. 5768-70, Marriage Contract, Jemima and Lieut. T.C. Cameron, 1829.

2 McNeice, *Ermatinger Family*, appendix 1, Will of Frederick William, 25 November 1826.

3 LAC, MG 19, A2, series 4, vols. 1-3, file 1, nos. 74-82, Will of Charles Sr, 4 July 1831.

4 McNeice, *Ermatinger Family*, 69.

5 LAC, MG 19, A2, series 3, vol. 42, file 2, no. 5857, Statement of Accounts, 1 April 1829; MG 19, A2, series 3, vol. 204, file 1, no. 103, Estate Ledger, May 1830; MG 19, A2, series 3, vol. 43, file 2, nos. 5871 and 5879, Charles Sr to Jemima, 20 April 1831 and 23 November 1831.

6 LAC, MG 19, A2, series 3, vol. 42, file 2, nos. 5861-62, Charles Sr to Jemima, 25 November 1830.

7 Ibid.; MG 19, A2, series 3, vol. 43, file 1, nos. 5869-72, Charles Sr to Jemima, 20 April 1831.

8 LAC, MG 19, A2, series 3, vol. 42, file 2, nos. 5882 and 5887, Charles Sr to Lieut. Cameron, March 1832 and 30 April 1832; no. 5888, Charles Sr to Jemima, 30 April 1832; LAC, MG 19, A2, series 3, vol. 43, file 2, no. 5889, Charles Sr to J.T. Billing, York, 22 June 1832.

9 McNeice, *Ermatinger Family*, 69.

10 LAC, MG 19, A2, series 3, vol. 202, file 1, Washing Book.

11 LAC, MG 19, A2, series 4, vols. 1-3, file 1, nos. 74-82, Will of Charles Sr, 4 July 1831.

12 UWO, microfiche, series 1, file 11, nos. 132-34, James to Edward Ermatinger, written between 30 May 1863 and 27 July 1864.

13 *Montreal Herald*, 25 May 1872.

14 McNeice, *Ermatinger Family*, 69.

15 *Transcript* (Montreal), 18 February 1841.

16 LAC, MG 19, A2, series 4, vol. 1, file 1, no. 6502, Death Certificate, Anna Maria.

17 UWO, microfiche, series 2, no. 87, Francis to Edward Ermatinger, 4 December 1827. Casual insults of this sort are not unusual in the letters of Frank Ermatinger.

18 McKenney, *Sketches of a Tour*, 191.

19 Glazebrooke, *Hargrave Correspondence*, 6 and 8, Siveright to James Hargrave, 3 September 1821. Dr Hoskins may have remained on friendly terms with the family. In 1822 in Montreal a Dr Hoskins ordered a variety of medicines for an unnamed Ermatinger child. LAC, MG 19, A2, series 3, vol. 38, file 5, no. 3924, Invoice, 14 September 1822.

20 Schroder, *Marriages, 1766-1850*; LAC, MG 24, D84, nos. 79-82, Jemima to Edward Ermatinger, 21 February 1831.

21 LAC, MG 19, A2, series 4, vol. 2, no. 8, Charles Jr to Edward Ermatinger, 22 August 1831; LAC, MG 19, A2, series 4, vol. 2, no. 19, Charles Sr to Edward Ermatinger, 9 November 1832.

22 Cloutier, *Mt. Royal Cemetery Records*, by letter; McNeice, *Ermatinger Family*.

23 Bullock, *Beautiful Waters*, vol. 2, 115-16; Reid, *Mansion in the Wilderness*, 10.

24 McNeice, *Ermatinger Family*, appendix 1, Will of Frederick William, 25 November 1826.

25 LAC, MG 19, A2, series 4, vols. 1-3, file 1, nos. 74-82, Will of Charles Sr, 4 July 1831.

26 LAC, MG 19, A2, series 4, vol. 2, no. 42, Annie Ermatinger to Judge C.O. Ermatinger, 5 May 1909.

27 UWO, microfiche, series 1, file 11, no. 135, Frances to Edward Ermatinger, 11 February 1874.

28 Canada, House of Commons, *Sessional Papers, 1893*, vol. 9, no. 16a, "The Civil List of Canada," 67.

29 LAC, MG 19, A2, series 2, vol. 1, part 2, no. 393, [April 1874]. Edward died in 1876, and this was probably written just before his death. The previous document in the file (John Todd to Edward) is dated April 1874.

30 Cloutier, *Mt Royal Cemetery Records*, by letter.

31 Roy, *La Famille Juchereau Duchesnay*, 356-57. A Kingston Historical Society paper says, "A newspaper of 1846 announces the birth of a son to the lady of Colonel Ermatinger at Bellevue Terrace" and adds that the house was soon after occupied by Sir John A. Macdonald. This must have been the birth of William Roch Daly, though just what William and Caroline were doing in Kingston at that time is not known. Angus, "Some Old Kingston Houses and Who Lived in Them," 10.

32 Canada, House of Commons, *Sessional Papers, 1872*, vol. 7, no. 38, "Statement of Names, Origin, Creed, etc.," 35; Roy, *La Famille Juchereau Duchesnay*, 356; LAC, MG 19, A2, series 4, vol. 2, no. 39, M. Thibodeau to C.O.Z. Ermatinger, 15 April 1909.

33 LAC, MG 19, A2, series 4, vols. 1-3, file 1, nos. 74-82, Will of Charles Sr, 4 July 1831.

34 LAC, RG 13, A2, vol. 21, no. 638, Office of Secy. of State, 1869, Widow of late F.W. Ermatinger … for relief, 30 April 1869. The senator was probably Elzéar Henri Juchereau Duchesnay (1809-71), a politician, lawyer, and landowner related to Caroline.

35 LAC, RG 13, A2, vol. 21, no. 639, Caroline to Sir John A. Macdonald, 22 June 1869; LAC, MG 26-A, *Political Papers, Letter Books*, vol. 13, no. 954, Sir John A. Macdonald to Caroline, 9 July 1869.

36 Canada, House of Commons, *Sessional Papers, 1869*, vol. 6, no. 75, "Return to Address of the House of Commons, 26 April 1869," Memorandum from the Adjt.-Gen. of Militia, P.L. MacDougall, 18 August 1866; Order-in-Council, 2 January 1867.

37 Canada, House of Commons, *Sessional Papers, 1869*, vol. 6, no. 75, "Return to Address of the House of Commons, 26 April 1869," 156 and 161, Abstract of Claims to Pensions.

38 LAC, MG 26-A, *Political Papers, Letter Books*, vol. 13, no. 650, John A. Macdonald to Edward, 4 March 1869. Alexander Campbell (1822-92) was a lawyer, businessman, politician, and a father of Confederation.

39 LAC, MG 26-A, *Political Papers, Letter Books*, vol. 14, nos. 56 and 87, John A. Macdonald to Caroline, 7 and 9 August 1869; no. 355, John A. Macdonald to Edward, 1 November 1869; MG 26-A, *Political Papers, Letter Books*, vol. 15, no. 1018, John A. Macdonald to Caroline, 7 July 1871.

40 AO, MU 472, file 23, John A. Macdonald to Alexander Campbell, 28 November 1872.

41 Canada, House of Commons, *Sessional Papers, 1872*, vol. 7, no. 38, "Statement of Names, Origin, Creed, etc.," 35.

42 *Le Franc-Parleur*, 28 March 1872 and 23 September 1873.

43 Roy, *La Famille Juchereau Duchesnay*, 356.

44 LAC, RG 18-G, vol. 3320, file 127, Toussaint A.R. Laflamme to the Hon R.W. Scott, 22 March, 24 April, 4 May, and 7 May 1878.

45 LAC, RG 18-G, vol. 3320, file 127, North West Mounted Police medical certificate, C.H. Ermatinger.

46 Roy, *La Famille Juchereau Duchesnay*, 356; LAC, MG 19, A2, series 4, vol. 2, no. 43, R. Campbell to C.O. Ermatinger, 20 April 1909; nos. 38-39, M. Thibadeau to C.O. Ermatinger, 15 April 1909.

47 LAC, MG 26 A, *Political Papers, Correspondence*, vols. 440-41, no. 217888 and no. 218041, P.T.H. [Hildebrand] Ermatinger to John A. Macdonald, 26 and 29 March 1887. The correspondence is signed "P.T.H. Ermatinger."

48 Roy, *La Famille Juchereau Duchesnay*, 356.

49 LAC, MG 25, G38, clipping from *Evening Telegraph* (Montreal), 1892.

50 *Le Franc-Parleur*, 28 March 1872.

51 "Edward Ermatinger," Church of Jesus Christ of Latter-day Saints Family History Library, http://www.familysearch.org.

52 Roy, *La Famille Juchereau Duchesnay*, 356.

53 LAC, MG 26-A, *Political Papers, Correspondence*, vols. 472-74, nos. 235157-59 and 235293-94, Caroline to John A. Macdonald, 24 April and 7 May 1889.

54 Roy, *La Famille Juchereau Duchesnay*, 356.

55 "Old Stone House," *Sault Daily Star*, 18 June 1970, 4.

Chapter 13: A Lost Past, a Future Unattained

1 Berger, *Writing of Canadian History*, 268, 271.

2 Stueber, "Psychological Basis of Historical Explanation," 37.

3 Toronto Reference Library, Baldwin Room, *Nelson Journals*, "Journal Reminiscences 1825-26," 73; Bigsby, *Shoe and Canoe*, vol. 2, 128-31.

4 Carr, "Place and Time," 165-66.

5 Bigsby, *Shoe and Canoe*, vol. 2, 127.

6 Harriet Gorham, "Families of Mixed Descent," 50-51 (emphasis added).

7 Brown, "Diverging Identities," 204.

8 Canada, House of Commons, *Sessional Papers, 1870*, vol. 5, no. 12, "Correspondence and Papers Connected with Recent Occurrences in the North West Territories," 83, James to Joseph Howe, 20 December 1869 and reply.

9 LAC, MG 19, A2, S4, vol. 2, no. 17, Charles Jr to Edward Ermatinger, 11 April 1832.

10 Schoolcraft, *Historical and Statistical Information*, vol. 2, 62, his translation.

Appendix A: Extract from John Bigsby's Journal

Source: Bigsby, *Shoe and Canoe*, vol. 2, 122-31.

APPENDIX B: PETITIONS OF CHARLOTTE KATAWABIDAI
Source: LAC, RG 1, L-3, vol. 279, Canada Land Petitions, K Bundle 5, 1848-50, no. 13½, Petitions of Charlotte, 1847 and 1849.
1 For some reason, James' name was not included, though it was in the 1847 petition.

APPENDIX C: TWO BROTHERS, CHARLES AND GEORGE
1 Quaife, *John Askin Papers*, vol. 2, 645.
2 LAC, MG 19, A2, series 3, vol. 34, file 2, nos. 1482-3, George Ermatinger to Charles, [1820].
3 LAC, MG 19, A2, series 3, vol. 42, file 2, no. 5859, Charles Sr to George Ermatinger, 1 June 1830.
4 LAC, MG 19, A2, series 3, vol. 43, file 2, no. 5878, Charles Sr to Rev. Ferry, 7 November 1831; no. 5875, Charles Sr to Hulbert, 7 November 1831.
5 LAC, MG 19, A2, series 3, vol. 43, file 2, no. 5875, Charles Sr to George Ermatinger, 7 November 1831.
6 LAC, MG 19, A2, series 3, vol. 42, file 1, no. 6443, George Ermatinger to Charles Sr, 10 December 1831. This is the only example we have of George's letters to Charles.
7 LAC, MG 19, A2, series 3, vol. 43, file 2, nos. 5883-86, Charles Sr to George Ermatinger, 14 March 1832.

APPENDIX D: CHARLES OAKES, AN HONEST MAN?
1 HBCA, Governor's Records, D.1/1-10, Governor Williams to Charles Sr, 2 January 1819 and 17 July 1819. William Williams (?-1837), a somewhat cantankerous man, did not have a successful career with the Hudson's Bay Company and died in poverty in London.
2 MacDonald, "Commerce, Civility, and Old Sault Ste Marie," 19-25 and 52-59.
3 HBCA, Governor's Records, D.1/1-10, Governor Williams to Messrs. Maitland, Garden, and Auldy, 17 July 1819 (emphasis added).
4 HBCA, Governor's Records, D.1/13, Charles Sr to Governor Williams, #58-60, 14 May 1820; D.1/1-10, Governor Williams to Charles Sr, 28 July 1820.
5 HBCA, Governor's Records, D.1/1-10, Governor Williams to Charles Sr, 28 July 1820; Governor Williams to Messrs. Maitland, Garden, and Auldy, 23 July 1820.
6 HBCA, Governor's Records, D.1/13, Charles Sr to Governor Williams, #58-60, 14 May 1820.
7 MacDonald, "Commerce, Civility and Old Sault Ste Marie," 52-29.
8 Schoolcraft, *Personal Memoirs*, 314.

APPENDIX E: LAWRENCE AND JEMIMA'S OTHER CHILDREN
1 LAC, MG 19, A2, series 3, vol. 39, file 3, no. 4401, Extracts from the last will of Mrs Margarette Gray, 14 November 1824; McNeice, *Ermatinger Family*, app. 1, Will of Frederick William Ermatinger, 25 November 1826.
2 McNeice, *Ermatinger Family*, appendix 2, lists Margaret (1766-?) and Ann Mary/Anna Maria (1766-1836) as sisters. (She also lists George as born in 1766, manifestly impossible for all three without at least twins.) No birth certificate for Anna Maria and no death certificate for Margaret have been found, with Anna Maria's birthdate deduced from her age and date of death. In papers at the Ermatinger Stone House, Sault Ste Marie, family historian A. Eugene Ermatinger sometimes refers to "Margaret aka Anna Maria," sometimes to two sisters, Margaret and Anna Maria ("The Ermatinger Saga," manuscript held at the Old Stone House, Sault Ste Marie, 18). The former seems most plausible since, while the marriage agreement mentioned below names Anna Maria and George Garrett, the death certificate for "Margaret" says her husband was George Garrett.
3 LAC, MG 19, A2, series 3, vol. 40, file 4, no. 5092, Articles of Marriage, 20 September 1826.
4 She could not sell her property without her husband's agreement, however, since that would be "opposed to the dependence in which the wife is placed by nature and law with respect to her husband." Armstrong, *Treatise on the Law*, 14.
5 Public Records Office, Kew, UK, WO 61, no. 1, List of Clerks Employed in the Commissariat as of 12 May 1810, 27, 72.
6 Glover, *Peninsula Preparation*, 272; Wellington to Col. Gordon, 19 December 1810, quoted in ibid., 256.
7 LAC, MG 19, A2, series 2, vol. 2, file 1, John Clowes to Edward Ermatinger, 10 March 1829; UWO, microfiche, series 1, file 9, Memoirs of Edward Ermatinger, no. 236; LAC, MG 19, A2, series 3, vol. 40, file 4, nos. 5102-9, Lawrence Edward to Frederick, 14 September 1826.
8 MacDonnell, *Early Settlement of Glengarry*; LAC, RG 9, IB2, vol. 29, no. 239.
9 McNeice, *Ermatinger Family*, appendix 2.

10 George Ermatinger to Col. Boyd, 3 August 1819, quoted in Thwaites, "The Fur Trade in Wisconsin," 119.

11 A. Eugene Ermatinger, "The Ermatinger Saga" (manuscript held at the Old Stone House, Sault Ste Marie).

12 AO, MU 4549, PR.MSS, envelope 1, Fur Trade Lore of the Chippewa Valley, 97-98.

13 "Treaty with the Chippewa, 5 August 1826," in *Indian Affairs*, ed., Kappler.

14 Rykhus, "Letter from Willis A. Gorman to James Ermatinger."

Bibliography

ARCHIVAL SOURCES

Archives of Ontario, Toronto
MS 4, John Beverley Robinson Family Fonds
MS 23, T.G. Anderson Papers, 1814-22
MU 4549, PR.MSS: Ermatinger Family Papers (1833-69)
MU 472, file 23: Alexander Campbell Fonds

Church of Jesus Christ of Latter-day Saints
Family History Library, http://www.familysearch.org

Eva Brook Donly Museum, Simcoe, ON
Norfolk County Council Records

Hudson's Bay Company Archives, Winnipeg
B.194/a/1-9: Post Journals, Sault Ste Marie, 1824-36
B.194/b/1-16: Correspondence Books, Sault Ste Marie, 1824-53
B.194/c/1: Correspondence Inward, Sault Ste Marie, 1824-61
B.194/e/1-8: Reports on Districts, Sault Ste Marie, 1825-35
Governor's Records, William Williams, D.1/1-10: Correspondence Outward, 1818-1826
Governor's Records, William Williams, D.1/13: Correspondence Inward, 1818-1820
Sault Ste Marie Post, List of Post Managers

Library and Archives Canada
CO42 (previously Q series): Board of Trade Papers
MG 8, A25: Les Evénements de 1837 et 1838 (reel 8259)
MG 13, WO1: War Office Fonds, Canada, In Letters and Papers
MG 13, WO13: Muster Books and Pay Lists, Militia and Volunteers
MG 18, H44: Collection de la famille Aubert de Gaspé, Série 5, Divers
MG 19, A2, series 1: Lawrence Ermatinger
MG 19, A2, series 2: Edward Ermatinger
MG 19, A2, series 3: Jacobs/Ermatinger Estate
   vol. 28-44, F.W. Ermatinger's Estate Papers, 1822-38
   vol. 45, Notes of C.O. (Z.) Ermatinger on Francis and Edward Ermatinger
   vol. 187-90, F.W. Ermatinger's Cash Books, 1816-23
   vol. 192, C.O. Ermatinger's Invoice Book, 1823-24
   vol. 202, Washing Book
   vol. 203, Samuel Gale Account Book
   vol. 204, Estate Ledger, 1829-33

vol. 205, Blotter Book
vol. 206, file 11: Estate Journal, 1822-23
vol. 209, Exercise Book, 1818
MG 19, A2, series 4: Miscellaneous
MG 19, B1: North West Company Fonds
MG 19, E1: Selkirk Papers (Calendar)
MG 23, GII3: Edward William Gray Fonds
MG 24, B17: Sir Allan Napier McNab Fonds
MG 24, B25, IIA: Sydney Bellingham, "A Memoir," annotated version, vol. 2
MG 24, D84: Colin H. Bayley Fonds, Miscellaneous Correspondence
MG 24, G55: William Ermatinger Fonds, Correspondence and Related Papers
MG 24, SL-3: Baby Collection, Correspondence
MG 25, G38: Ermatinger Family Fonds
MG 26-A: Sir John A. Macdonald Fonds
MG 27, IJ2A: Government Constabulary for Frontier Service Fonds
MG 53, B27: Lawrence Montague Lande Collection
RG 1, L3
    vol. 182B, Upper Canada and Canada Land Petitions, E-Bundle (1847-52)
    vol. 279, Canada Land Petitions, K-Bundle (1848-50)
RG 4, B10: Lower Canada East, Provincial Secretary's and Registrar Letters Patent
RG 4, C1: Provincial Secretary's Office, Canada East, Numbered Correspondence
RG 8 (C series), 1A: Correspondence of the Military Secretary of the Commander of the Forces
RG 9, 1B1: Adjutant-General's Office, Upper Canada Fonds: Correspondence, Letters Received
RG 9, 1B2: Adjutant-General's Office, Upper Canada Fonds: Nominal Rolls
RG 10: Indian Affairs, series 3B
RG 13, A2: Department of Justice Fonds, Numbered Central Registry Files
RG 18-G: Royal Canadian Mounted Police Fonds, Personnel Records
RG 31: 1871 Census File Norfolk
R6435-0-8-E: American Fur Company Fonds, Michilimackinac and Sault Ste Marie Records 1803-38

Old Stone House, Sault Ste Marie
Ermatinger, A. Eugene. The Ermatinger Saga: 15th Century to the Present. Typed document

Ontario Genealogical Society, Norfolk County Branch
Oakwood Cemetery Book 1

Public Records Office, Kew, UK
FO 72 514: Correspondence, WO 61, No. 1, List of clerks employed by the Commissariat, 12 May 1810

St John's Anglican Church, Woodhouse, ON
Parish Registers, 1830-51, 1885-1948

Toronto Reference Library, Baldwin Room
Nelson, George. *Nelson Journals.* "Journals"; "Journals and Reminiscences (1825-26)"; "Letters to Parents"

University of Western Ontario Archives, London, ON
J.J. Talman Regional Collection, Papers of the Ermatinger Family
    microfiche series 1: General
    microfiche series 2: Letters of Francis to Edward Ermatinger

GOVERNMENT PUBLICATIONS

Canada, 1867-
Canada. *Correspondence Respecting the Recent Fenian Aggression upon Canada.* [London? 1867?]. CIHM microfiche series no. 34299.

—. *Manual Containing the Census Act ... 1871.* CIHM microfiche series no. 53661.

Royal Commission on Aboriginal Peoples. *Final Report*, vol. 2: *Restructuring the Relationship.* Ottawa, 1996.

Senate. *Journals,* 1877, app. 1. "Report and Minutes of Evidence taken before the select committee of the Senate appointed to enquire into and report on the route of the Canadian Pacific Railway from Keewatin Westward."

House of Commons Sessional Papers

1869   Vol. 6, no. 75: "Return to Address of the House of Commons, 26 April 1869."

1870   Vol. 5, no. 12: "Correspondence and Papers Connected with Recent Occurrences in the North West Territories."

1871   Vol. 5, no. 44: "Statement of Claims Made on the Dominion Government Consequent Upon the Insurrection in the North West Territories."

1872   Vol. 7, no. 33: "Progress Report on the Canadian Pacific Railway."

1872   Vol. 7, no. 38: "Statement of Names, Origin, Creed, Position, Pay of All the Employees of the Dominion Government, 1872."

1893   Vol. 9, no. 16a: "The Civil List of Canada: Post Office Dept., Outside Service, Sherbrooke."

Great Britain

Colonial Office. *Papers Relating to the Removal of the Seat of Government and to the Annexation Movement.* Presented to both Houses of Parliament by command of Her Majesty, 15 April 1850. London: W. Clowes, 1850. CIHM microfiche series no. 34019.

War Office. *Army Lists of the British Auxiliary Legion Spain, 1835-37* London: National Army Museum.

—. *A List of All Officers of the Army and Royal Marines on Full and Half Pay and a List of Officers in the Army and Marines on Half Pay, also with an Index.* London, 1812-14, 1831.

Lower Canada, 1791-1840

Statutes (of Lower Canada), 1821, c. 25, Act to Incorporate ... Bank of Montreal.

Appendices to Journals of the House of Assembly

1832   Vol. 42, app. U: "List of Stockholders of the Bank of Montreal, 1 June 1832 and 1st December 1832."

Vol. 42, app. W: "List of Stockholders in the Quebec Fire Assurance Co."

1832-33 Vol. 42, app. M: "Copies of Official Communications and Reports ... re ... Occurrences which took place in Montreal on 21st May, 1832."

Norfolk County Council

By-Law No. 124, To appropriate certain sums of money to improve certain county roads. CIHM microfiche series no. 542558.

Province of Canada, 1841-67

Legislative Assembly. *Debates,* 1849.

Province of Canada. *Report of the Commissioners Appointed to Enquire into the Conduct of the Police Authorities on the Occasion of the Riot at Chalmers Church (Quebec) on 6th June 1853.* [Quebec? 1854?]. CIHM microfiche series no. 63000.

Revised Acts and Ordinances of Lower Canada, 1845, 3 & 4 Vict., c. 35, An Ordinance to Incorporate the City and Town of Quebec.

Statutes, 1851, c. 24, An Act for Defraying the Expenses of the River Police of Montreal.

Appendices/Sessional Papers of Journals of the Legislative Assembly

1843   Vol. 3, app. A, B3: "Statements of Warrants Issued on the Receiver-General."

1843   Vol. 3, app. T: "Report of the Commissioners to Enquire into the Disturbances [at the] Beauharnois and Lachine Canals."

1846   Vol. 5, app. EEE: "Report of Select Committee ... [re] ... Municipal Election for the city of Montreal, March 1846, St James Ward."

1848   Vol. 7, app. O: "Return to Two Addresses ... re the Dismissal of A.B. Papineau, 2 July 1847."

1849   Vol. 8, app. EEE: "Immigration Report for 1848."
1850   Vol. 9, app. NNN, I: "Extracts from a Report of a Committee of the Honourable Executive Council ... 26 September 1849."
1851   Vol. 10, app. II: "Réponse à une addresse distribué aux sauvages du Lac Superior."
1851   Vol. 10, app. QQ: "Report of Commissioners of Enquiry into the Montreal Provident and Savings Bank, 21 June 1851."
1851   Vol. 10, app. BBB: "Return to an Address and Copy of the Commission appointing Messrs McCord and Ermatinger Inspectors and Superintendents of Police at Quebec and Montreal."
1854   Vol. 13, app. G: "List of Witnesses Examined before the Commission," no. 5, Montreal Police; no. 6, Montreal Water Police.
1854-55 Vol. 13, app. XX: "Report of Commission Appointed to Investigate and Report upon the Best Means of Reorganizing the Militia of Canada ... and to Report upon an Improved System of Police."
1855   Vol. 13, app. AAA: "Statistics Shewing the Number of Persons, Male and Female, Brought before William Ermatinger ... 1 January 1849 to 30 November 1854."
1856   Vol. 14, app. 42: "Return to an Address ... re the Murder in Sylvestre de Lotbinière."
1857   Vol. 15, app. 45: "Report of Commission ... re the Murder in Sylvestre de Lotbinière."
1858   Vol. 16, app. 48: "Final Report of the Commissioners ... re the Murder in Sylvestre de Lotbinière."
1859   Vol. 17, app. 46: "Extrait du rapport d'inspection de l'officier inspecteur ..."
1866   Vol. 2, app. 4: "Report, Adjutant General (Colonel P.L. McDougall)."
1866   Vol. 3, app. 20: "Return to an Address ... for Statement of Expenses for Militia Forces Sent to the Frontier, 10 August 1865."

OTHER SOURCES

Aitkin Festival of Adventures. "William Aitkin: Legendary Figure of Minnesota's Fur Trade Era." 2006. http://www.aitkin.com/fest/wmait.htm.

Alexander, Sir James Edward. *L'Acadie, or Seven Years Exploration in British America.* 2 vols. London: H. Colburn, 1849.

Amos, Andrew. *Report of the Trials in the Courts of Canada Relative to the Destruction of the Earl of Selkirk's Settlement on the Red River.* London: J. Murray, 1820.

Angus, Margaret. "Some Old Kingston Houses and the Families Who Lived in Them." In Kingston Historical Society, *Reports and Proceedings,* ed. Richard A. Preston, no. 4 (1955): 3-13.

Armstrong, James. *A Treatise on the Law Relating to Marriage in Lower Canada.* Montreal: John Lovell, 1857.

Arthur, Elizabeth M. "Angélique and Her Children." *Papers and Records* (Thunder Bay Historical Museum Society) 6 (1978): 30-40.

—. "General Dickson and the Liberating Army." *Ontario History* 62, 3 (1970): 151-62.

Atherton, William H. *Montreal, 1535-1914.* 2 vols. Montreal: S.J. Publishing Company, 1914.

Bailey, Lt.-Col. John R. *Mackinaw, Formerly Michilimackinac.* Lansing, MI: Darius D. Thorp, 1896.

Barkwell, Lawrence. *Resources of Métis Researchers.* Winnipeg: Louis Institute of Manitoba Métis Federation, 1999.

Barnouw, Victor. *Acculturation and Personality among the Wisconsin Chippewa.* American Anthropological Association, 1950. Reprint, Millwood, NY: Kraus, 1974.

Beaulieu, Clement H. *Short Sketches of Some Fur Traders of Morrison County.* N.p., n.d.

Bellingham, Sydney. *Some Personal Recollections of the Rebellion of 1837 in Canada.* Dublin: Browne and Nolan, 1902.

Berger, Carl. *The Writing of Canadian History: Aspects of English Canadian Historical Writing since 1900.* 2nd ed. Toronto: University of Toronto Press, 1987.

Betke, Carl. "McMicken, Gilbert." *Dictionary of Canadian Biography.* Vol. 12, 675-79. Toronto: University of Toronto Press, 1990.

Bigsby, John J. *The Shoe and Canoe, or, Pictures of Travel in the Canadas, Illustrative of Their Scenery and of Colonial Life with Facts and Opinions on Emigration, State Policy and Other Points of Public Interest.* 2 vols. London: Chapman and Hall, 1850.

Bishop, Charles A. *The Northern Ojibwa and the Fur Trade.* Toronto: Holt, Rinehart and Winston of Canada, 1974.

—. Review of *The Fur Trade of the Little North: Indians, Peddlers and Englishmen East of Lake Winnipeg,*

1760-1821, by Victor P. Lytwyn. *Native Studies Review* 3, 2 (1987): 145-48.

Blackbird, Andrew J. *History of the Ottawa and Chippewa Indians of Michigan*. Ypsilanti, MI: Ypsilanti Job Printing House, 1887.

Blackstone, William Sir. *Commentaries on the Laws of England*. 4 vols. Oxford: Clarendon Press, 1765.

Bond, Gordon C. *The Grand Expedition: The British Invasion of Holland in 1809*. Athens: University of Georgia Press, 1979.

Bourgeault, Ron. "The Indians, the Métis and the Fur Trade." *Studies in Political Economy* 12 (Fall 1983): 45-80.

Brown, Jennifer S.H. "Atkinson, George." In *Dictionary of Canadian Biography*. Vol. 4, 32-33. Toronto: University of Toronto Press, 1979.

—. "Cameron, Duncan." In *Dictionary of Canadian Biography*. Vol. 7, 137-39. Toronto: University of Toronto Press, 1983.

—. "A Demographic Transition in the Fur Trade Country." *Western Canadian Journal of Anthropology* 6, 1 (1976): 61-71.

—. "Diverging Identities: The Presbyterian Métis of St Gabriel Street, Montreal." In *The New Peoples: Being and Becoming Métis in North America*, ed. Jacqueline Peterson and Jennifer S.H. Brown, 1195-206. Winnipeg: University of Manitoba Press, 1985.

—. "Métis, Half Breeds and Other Real People." *History Teacher* 27, 1 (Spring 1993): 19-26.

—. "Northern Algonquians from Lake Superior and Hudson's Bay to Manitoba in the Historic Period." In *Native Peoples: The Canadian Experience*, ed. R. Bruce Morrison and C. Roderick Wilson, 96-100. Toronto: McClelland and Stewart, 1995.

—. *Strangers in Blood: Fur Trade Company Families in Indian Country*. Vancouver: UBC Press, 1980.

—. "Women as Centre and Symbol." *Canadian Journal of Native Studies* 3, 1 (1983): 39-46.

Brown, Jennifer S.H., and Robert Brightman. *The Orders of the Dreamed: George Nelson on Cree and Northern Ojibwa Religion and Myth*. Winnipeg: University of Manitoba Press, 1988.

Brown, Jennifer S.H., and Sylvia Van Kirk. "Barnston, George." In *Dictionary of Canadian Biography*. Vol. 8, 61-62. Toronto: University of Toronto Press, 1985.

Bryce, George. *Remarkable History of the Hudson's Bay Co. Including That of the French Traders of North Western Canada and of the North-West, XY, and Astor Fur Companies*. Toronto: W. Briggs, 1900.

Bullock, William B. *Beautiful Waters Devoted to the Memphremagog Region*. 2 vols. Newport, VT: Memphremagog Press, 1926.

Burgess, Drummond E. "Evans and the British Legion, 1835-38." MA thesis, McGill University, 1966.

Burt, Alfred Leroy. *The Old Province of Quebec*. 2 vols. Toronto: McClelland and Stewart, 1968.

Campbell, Francis Wayland. *Fenian Invasions of Canada of 1866 and 1870, and the Operations of the Montreal Militia in Connection Therewith*. Montreal: J. Lovell and Son, 1904.

Capp, Edward H. *The Story of Baw-a-ting, being the Annals of Sault Ste Marie*. Sault Ste Marie: Sault Star Presses, 1904.

Carlisle, Nicholas. *A Concise Account of the Several Foreign Orders of Knighthood, and Other Marks of Honourable Distinction, Especially of Such As Have Been Conferred upon British Subjects, Together with the Names and Achievements of Those Gallant Men, Who Have Been Presented with Honorary Swords, or Plate, by the Patriotic Fund Institution*. London: J. Hearne, 1839.

Carman, W.Y. "The Lancers of the British Auxiliary in Spain." *Journal of the Society for Army Historical Research* 63, 254 (Summer 1985): 63-67.

Carr, David. "Place and Time: On the Interplay of Historical Points of View." *History and Theory: Studies in the Philosophy of History* 40, 4 (December 2004): 153-67.

Carter, Sarah. *Aboriginal People and Colonizers of Western Canada*. Toronto: University of Toronto Press, 1999.

Catlin, George. *Letters and Notes on the Manners, Customs and Conditions of the North American Indians Written during Eight Years of Travel (1832-39) amongst the Wildest Tribes of Indians in North America, 1832-39*. 2 vols. Self-published, 1844. Reprint, New York: Dover Publications, 1973.

Choquette, Ernest. *Les Ribaud: Une idylle de 37*. Montreal: Eusèbe Senécal, 1890.

Christie, Robert. *History of the Late Province of Lower Canada, Parliamentary and Political, from the Commencement to the Close of Its Existence as a Separate Province*. 6 vols. Montreal: Richard Worthington, 1866.

Chute, Janet. *The Legacy of Shingwaukonse*. Toronto: University of Toronto Press, 1998.

—. "Ojibwa Leadership during the Fur Trade Era at Sault Ste Marie." In *New Faces of the Fur Trade:*

Selected Papers of the Seventh North American Fur Trade Conference, Halifax, Nova Scotia, 1995. East Lansing: Michigan State University Press, 1998.

Cleland, Charles E. *Rites of Conquest: The History and Culture of Michigan's Native Americans.* Ann Arbor: University of Michigan Press, 1992.

Cloutier, Myriam. *Mt. Royal Cemetery Records.* Montreal: Friends of the Mount Royal Cemetery, n.d.

Cole, Jean Murray, ed. *This Blessed Wilderness: Archibald McDonald's Letters from the Columbia, 1822-44.* Vancouver: UBC Press, 2001.

Copway, George. *Traditional History and Characteristic Sketches of the Ojibway Nation.* [Toronto]: Coles Publishing, 1972.

Coues, Elliott, ed. *New Light on the Early History of the Greater Northwest: The Manuscript Journals of Alexander Henry, Fur Trader of the North West Company, and of David Thompson, Official Geographer and Explorer of the Same Company, 1799-1814; Exploration and Adventure among the Indians on the Red, Saskatchewan, Missouri, and Columbia Rivers.* 2 vols. Minneapolis, MN: Ross and Haines, 1965.

Cox, Bruce Alden. *Native People, Native Land: Canadian Indians, Inuit and Métis.* Ottawa: Carleton University Press, 1991.

Cruikshank, Ernest A. *Documents Relating to the Invasion of Canada and the Surrender of Detroit, 1812.* Ottawa: Government Printing Bureau, 1912.

Damphouse, Patricia. *Legislative Assembly of the Province of Canada, An Index to the Journal Appendices and Sessional Papers, 1841-46.* London, ON: E. Phelps, 1974.

Danziger, Edmund Jefferson Jr. *The Chippewas of Lake Superior.* Norman: University of Oklahoma Press, 1978.

David, L.-O. *Les Patriotes de 1837-38.* Montreal: Eusèbe Senécal, 1884.

Densmore, Frances. *Chippewa Customs.* Bulletin 86. Washington, DC: Bureau of American Ethnology, 1929.

Dent, John Charles. "Honourable John Young," In *Canadian Portrait Gallery,* vol. 3, 197. Toronto: J.B. Magnum, 1881.

Dorge, Lionel. "Bruneau, François-Jacques." In *Dictionary of Canadian Biography.* Vol. 9, 94-95. Toronto: University of Toronto Press, 1976.

Doutre, Gonsalve, and Edmond Lareau. *Le Droit civil Canadien suivant l'ordre établi par les codes: Précédé d'une histoire général du droit Canadien.* Montréal: A. Doutre, 1872.

Elliott, Bruce S., Dan Walker, and Fawne Stratford-Devai. *Men of Upper Canada: Militia Nominal Rolls 1828-1829: Return of the Men of the 3rd Regiment Glengarry Militia from 19-39 Years of Age Inclusive.* Toronto: Ontario Genealogy Society, 1995.

Ens, Gerhard J. *Homeland to Hinterland: The Changing World of the Red River Métis in the 19th Century.* Toronto: University of Toronto Press, 1996.

Ermatinger, C.O.Z. *The Talbot Regime or the First Half-Century of the Talbot Settlement.* St Thomas, ON: Municipal World, 1904.

Evans, Sir George de Lacy. *Memoranda of the Contest in Spain.* London: J. Ridgeway, 1840.

Filteau, Gérard. *Histoire des Patriotes.* 3 vols. Montreal: Éditions de l'A. C.-F, 1938-42.

Fortin, Réal. *La Guerre des patriotes.* Saint-Jean-sur-Richelieu, QC: Société nationale des Québécois Richelieu-Saint-Laurent, 1988.

Franchère, Gabriel, *Voyage to the North West Coast of North America during the Years 1811-1814,* ed. M.M. Quaife. Chicago: Lakeside Press, 1954.

Francis, Daniel, and Toby Morantz. *Partners in Furs: A History of the Fur Trade in Eastern James Bay, 1600-1870.* Montreal: McGill-Queen's University Press, 1983.

Garry, Nicholas. "The Diary of Nicholas Garry, Deputy Governor of the Hudson's Bay Company from 1822 to 1825." *Proceedings and Transactions of the Royal Society of Canada,* 1900. Series 2, vol. 6, section 2, 73-204.

Gilkison, J.T. *Visit of the Governor-General and the Countess of Dufferin to the Six Nation's Indians: August 25, 1874.* Available at Early Canadiana Online, http://www.canadiana.org/ECO.

Gilman, Caroline. *Where Two Worlds Meet: The Great Lakes Fur Trade.* St Paul: Minnesota Historical Society, 1982.

Gilpin, Alec Richard. *The War of 1812 in the Old North West.* Toronto: Ryerson Press, 1958.

Glazebrooke, George P. DeT. *The Hargrave Correspondence, 1821-43.* Toronto: Champlain Society, 1938.

—. *A History of Transportation in Canada.* 2 vols. Toronto: McClelland and Stewart, 1964.

Glenelg, Baron Charles Grant. *Correspondence Relative to the Affairs of Canada.* London, 1849.

Glover, Richard. *Peninsula Preparations: The Reform of the British Army, 1795-1809*. Cambridge: Cambridge University Press, 1963.

Gorham, Harriet. "Families of Mixed Descent in the Western Great Lakes Region." In *Native People, Native Lands: Canadian Indians, Inuit and Métis*, ed. Bruce Alden Cox, 37-55. Ottawa: Carleton University Press, 1991.

Greer, Allan. *The Patriots and the People: The Rebellion of 1837 in Rural Lower Canada*. Toronto: University of Toronto Press, 1993.

"Harrison Stephens." In *Canadian Biographical Dictionary and Portrait Gallery of Eminent and Self-made Men: Quebec and the Maritime Provinces*. Vol. 2: *Quebec*, 347-48. Toronto and Chicago: H.C. Cooper Jr, 1881.

Henderson, Capt. R. *The Soldier of Three Queens: A Narrative of Personal Adventure*. 2 vols. London, 1866.

Henderson, William B. "Indian Treaties." In *The Canadian Encyclopedia*, vol. 2, 872-73. Edmonton: Hurtig Publishing, 1985.

Henry, Alexander. *Travels and Adventures in Canada and the Indian Territories between the years of 1760 and 1776*, ed. James Bain. Edmonton: M.G. Hurtig, 1969.

Henry, Alexander, the Younger. *The Journal of Alexander Henry the Younger*. 2 vols. Toronto: Champlain Society, 1988-92.

Higgins, Edwin G. *Whitefish Lake Ojibwa Memories*. Cobalt, ON: Highway Book Shop, 1982.

Holt, Edgar. *The Carlist Wars in Spain*. London: Putnam, 1967.

Hughes, John, ed. *St John's Anglican Church, Woodhouse, Ont.: 150 Years of Service, 1821-1971*. N.p., 1971.

Ingram, Heather. *Views of the Sault*. Burnstown, ON: General Store Publishing House, 1995.

Innis, H.A. *The Fur Trade in Canada: An Introduction to Canadian Economic History*. Rev. ed. Toronto: University of Toronto Press, 1956.

Jenkins, Kathleen. *Montreal, Island City of the St Lawrence*. Garden City, NJ: Doubleday, 1966.

Jenks, Albert Ernest, *The Childhood of Ji-shib, the Ojibway and Sixty-four Pen Sketches*. Madison, WI: American Thresherman, 1900.

Jodoin, Alex[andre], and J.L. Vincent. *Histoire de Longueuil et de la famille Longueuil*. Montreal: Impr. Gebhardt-Berthiaume, 1889.

Jones, Peter. *History of the Ojebway Indians with Especial Reference to their Conversion to Christianity. With a Brief Memoir of the Writer*. London: A.W. Bennett, 1861.

Josephy, Alvin M. Jr. *The Indian Heritage of America*. New York: Knopf, 1968.

Kappler, Charles Joseph, ed. *Indian Affairs: Laws and Treaties*, vol. 2: *Treaties*. Washington, DC: Government Printing Office, 1904.

Kugel, Rebecca. *To Be the Main Leaders of Our People: A History of Minnesota Ojibwe Politics, 1825-1898*. East Lansing: Michigan State University Press, 1998.

Lanctot, Gustav. *Canada and the American Revolution, 1774-1783*. Toronto: Clark Irwin, 1967.

Landes, Ruth. *Ojibwa Religion and the Midewiwin*. Madison, Milwaukee, and London: University of Wisconsin Press, 1968.

Lavender, David Rosenblum. *The Fist in the Wilderness*. New York: Doubleday, 1964.

LeBlanc, Larry C. *A Compendium of the Anishinabek: An Overview of the Anishinabek with Special Reference to the Historical Three Fires Confederacy*. M'Chigeeng First Nation, ON: Kenjgewin Teg Educational Centre, 2003.

"Letter from Fur Company Officer." In "Interesting Sidelights on the History of the Early Fur Trade Industry, Part 3," reprinted from *Eau Claire Leader*, 10 June 1925. *Canku Ota (Many Paths)*, 19 April 2003, http://www.turtletrack.org.

Lower, A.R.M. "Credit and the Constitutional Act." *Canadian Historical Review* 6, 2 (June 1925): 123-41.

Lysons, Sir Robert Daniel. *Early Reminiscences*. London: John Murray, 1896.

MacDonald, Cheryl. "Canada's Secret Police." *Beaver* 71, 3 (June-July 1991): 44-49.

MacDonald, Graham A. "Commerce, Civility and Old Sault Ste Marie." Pts. 1 and 2. *Beaver* 61, 2 (Autumn 1981): 19-25; 61, 3 (Winter 1981): 52-59.

MacDonald, Ranald. *Ranald MacDonald: The Narrative of His Early Life on the Columbia under the Hudson's Bay Company Regime ...*, ed. William S. Lewis and Naojiro Murakami. Spokane: Eastern Washington State Historical Society, 1923.

MacDonnell, J.A. *Sketches Illustrating the Early Settlement of Glengarry*. Glengarry: Foster W., 1893.

MacLeod, Peter B. "The Anishinabeg Point of View: The History of the Great Lakes Region to 1800 in Nineteenth Century Mississauga, Odawa and Ojibway Historiography." *Canadian Historical Review*

77, 2 (June 1992): 194-210.

MacMunn, Lt.-Gen. Sir George. *Always into Battle: Some Forgotten Sagas.* Aldershot, UK: Gale and Polden, 1952.

Marshall-Cornwall, Sir James. "British Aid in the Carlist Wars." *History Today* 1, 1 (March 1976): 179-87.

McDonald, Lois Halliday. *Fur Trade Letters of Francis Ermatinger, Written to His Brother Edward during His Service with the Hudson's Bay Company, 1818-1853.* Glendale, CA: A.H. Clark, 1980.

McKenney, Thomas L. *Sketches of a Tour to the Lakes.* Minneapolis, MN: Ross and Haines, 1959.

McKenney, Thomas L., and James Hall. *History of the Indian Tribes of North America: With Biographical Sketches and Anecdotes of the Principal Chiefs. Embellished with One Hundred Portraits from the Indian Gallery in the War Department at Washington.* 2 vols. Philadelphia: Rice, Rutler, 1860.

McLean, John. *John McLean's Notes of a Twenty-Five Year's Service in the Hudson's Bay Territory,* ed. William S. Wallace. 2 vols. Toronto: Champlain Society, 1932.

McLeod, Martin. "The Diary of Martin McLeod." *Minnesota History* 4, 7-8 (August-November 1922): 351-439.

McMillan, Alan D. *Native Peoples and Cultures of Canada: An Anthropological Overview.* Vancouver: Douglas and McIntyre, 1988.

McNab, David T. "Métis Participation in the Treaty Making Process." *Native Studies Review* 1, 2 (1985): 57-79.

McNeice, Gladys. *The Ermatinger Family of Sault Ste Marie.* Sault Ste Marie: Sault Ste Marie and 49th Field Regiment RCA Historical Society, 1984.

Momryk, M. "Ermatinger, Charles Oakes." In *Dictionary of Canadian Biography.* Vol. 6, 236-37. Toronto: University of Toronto Press, 1987.

—. "Ermatinger, Frederick William." In *Dictionary of Canadian Biography.* Vol. 6, 237-39. Toronto: University of Toronto Press, 1987.

—. "Ermatinger, Lawrence." In *Dictionary of Canadian Biography.* Vol. 4, 262-63. Toronto: University of Toronto Press, 1979.

—. "Gray, Edward William." In *Dictionary of Canadian Biography.* Vol. 5, 382-84. Toronto: University of Toronto Press, 1966.

Morris, Alexander. *The Treaties of Canada with the Indians of Manitoba and the North-West Territories, Including the Negotiations on Which They Were Based, and Other Information Relating Thereto, 1826-1889.* Toronto: Belfords, Clarke, 1880.

Mutrie, R. Robert. *1852 Census of Simcoe Town, Norfolk County, Canada West.* Ridgeway, ON: Log Cabin Publishing, 1993.

Nute, Grace L. "Notes and Documents: The Dickson Filibuster." *Minnesota History* 8, 1 (1927).

Pannekoek, Frits. "Ross, Alexander." In *Dictionary of Canadian Biography.* Vol. 8, 765-68. Toronto: University of Toronto Press, 1985.

Peel, Bruce. "Falcon, Pierre." In *Dictionary of Canadian Biography,* Vol. 9, 276-77. Toronto: University of Toronto Press, 1976.

Peers, Laura. *The Ojibwa of Western Canada, 1789 to 1870.* Winnipeg: University of Manitoba Press, 1994.

Peterson, Jacqueline. "The Indians and the Fur Trade: A Review of Recent Literature." *Manitoba History* 10 (Autumn 1985): 10-18.

Peterson, Jacqueline, and Jennifer S.H. Brown, eds. *New Peoples: Being and Becoming Métis in North America.* Winnipeg: University of Manitoba Press, 1995.

Phillips, Paul C. *The Fur Trade.* 2 vols. Norman: University of Oklahoma Press, 1961.

Pond, Rev. S.W. "Indian Warfare in Minnesota." In *Minnesota Historical Society Collections.* Vol. 3, 1870-80, 128-38. St Paul: Minnesota Historical Society, 1880.

Provost, Honorius. "Juchereau Duchesnay, Elzéar Henri." In *Dictionary of Canadian Biography.* Vol. 10, 388-89. Toronto: University of Toronto Press, 1972.

Quaife, Milo M., ed. *The John Askin Papers.* 2 vols. Detroit: Detroit Library Commission, 1928-31.

Ray, Arthur J. *Indians in the Fur Trade: Their Role as Hunters, Trappers and Middlemen in the Lands South-East of Hudson Bay.* Toronto: University of Toronto Press, 1997.

Read, Colin. *The Rising in Western Upper Canada 1837-38: The Duncombe Revolt and After.* Toronto: University of Toronto Press, 1974.

Reid, C.S. (Paddy). *Mansion in the Wilderness: The Archeology of the Ermatinger House.* Toronto: Ontario Ministry of Culture and Recreation, Historical Planning and Research Branch, 1977.

Reid, William D. *Marriage Notices of Ontario, 1813-1854.* Lambertville, NJ: Hunterdon House, 1980.

Richardson, Maj. John. *Personal Memoirs of Major Richardson as Connected with the Singular Oppression of that Officer While in Spain by Lieutenant General Sir de Lacy Evans*. Montreal: Armour and Ramsay, 1838.

Robinson, W.B. *Copy of the Robinson Treaty: Made in the Year 1850 With the Ojibwa Indians of Lake Huron Conveying Certain Lands to the Crown*. Reprinted from the Edition of 1939 by Roger Duhamel, F.R.S.C. Queen's Printer and Controller of Stationery Ottawa, 1964. Cat. No. Ci 72-1264.

—. "Report to Indian Affairs, 24 September 1850." In *The Treaties of Canada with the Indians of Manitoba and the North-West Territories, Including the Negotiations on Which They Were Based, and Other Information Relating Thereto, 1826-1889*, ed. Alexander Morris, 17-21. Toronto: Belfords, Clarke, 1880.

Rosenblum, Thomas. "Pelts and Patronage." In *Rendezvous: Selected Papers of the Fourth North American Fur Trade Conference, 1981*, ed. Thomas C. Buckley, 63-72. St Paul, MN, North American Fur Trade Conference, 1984.

Roy, Pierre-Georges. *La Famille Juchereau Duchesnay*. Lévis, QC, 1903.

Rumilly, Robert. *Histoire de Montréal*. 5 vols. Montreal: Fides, 1970-74.

—. *Papineau et ses temps, 1791-1838*. Montreal: Fides, 1977.

Rykhus, John. "Letter from Willis A. Gorman to James Ermatinger." Term paper, 22 May 2004, University of Wisconsin, Eau Claire. http://www.uwec.edu/Library/archives/exhibits/goldsmith/Rykhus.pdf.

Sandy Lake Band of Ojibwe. "Chief Ka-Ta-Wa-Be-Da (Broken Tooth)." http://www.sandylakeojibwe.org/katawabe.htm.

Schenck, Theresa M. *The Voice of the Crane Echoes Afar: The Sociopolitical Organization of the Lake Superior Ojibwa, 1640-1855*. New York: Garland Publications, 1997.

—. "William W. Warren's History of the Ojibway People." In *Reading beyond Words: Contexts for Native History*, ed. Jennifer S.H. Brown and Elizabeth Vibert, 242-60. Peterborough, ON: Broadview Press, 2003.

Schoolcraft, H.R. *Historical and Statistical Information Respecting the History, Conditions and Prospects of the Indian Tribes of the United States, Collected and Prepared under the Direction of the Bureau of Indian Affairs*. 6 vols. Philadelphia: Lippincott, Grambo, 1851-59.

—. *The Indian in His Wigwam, or Characteristics of the Red Race of America*. Buffalo, NY: Derby and Hewson, 1848.

—. *Personal Memoirs of a Residence of Thirty Years with Indian Tribes on the American Frontiers, with Brief Notices of Passing Events, Facts and Opinions, 1812-1842*. Philadelphia: Lippincott, Grambo, 1851.

Schodt, Frederik L. *Native American in the Land of the Shogun*. Berkeley, CA: Stonebridge Press, 2003.

Schroder, Gary. *Marriages, 1766-1850, Christ Church Cathedral, Montreal, Quebec*. Pointe Claire: Quebec Family History Society, 1991.

Selkirk, Lord (Thomas Douglas, Baron Daer and Shortcleuch, 5th Earl of Selkirk). *The Collected Writings of Lord Selkirk, 1810-1820*. Winnipeg: Manitoba Record Society, 1984.

Senior, Elinor Kyte. *British Regulars in Montreal: An Imperial Garrison, 1832-54*. Montreal: McGill-Queen's University Press, 1981.

— "Ermatinger, (Frederick) William." In *Dictionary of Canadian Biography*. Vol. 9, 242-43. Toronto, University of Toronto Press, 1976.

—. *From Royal Township to Industrial City*. Belleville, ON: Mika, 1983.

—. "The Influence of the British Garrison on the Development of the Montreal Police, 1832-1853." In *Lawful Authority: Readings in the History of Criminal Justice in Canada*, ed. R.C. MacLeod. Toronto: Copp Clark Pitman, 1988.

—. "The Provincial Cavalry in Lower Canada." *Canadian Historical Review* 77, 1 (March 1976): 1-24.

—. *Redcoats and Patriotes: The Rebellions in Lower Canada*. Stittsville, ON: Canada's Wings, 1985.

Senior, Hereward. *The Constabulary: The Rise of Police Institutions in Britain, the Commonwealth and the United States*. Toronto: Dundurn Press, 1997.

—. *The Last Invasion of Canada*. Toronto: Dundurn Press, 1991.

Shakespeare Club (Montreal). *Annual Report, 1846-47 and List of Members*, 25 May 1847. Montreal: N.p., 1845-48.

Shortt, A., and A.G. Dougherty. *Documents Relating to the Constitutional History of Canada, 1759-1791*. Ottawa: Canadian Archives, 1907.

Sneakers. "Michigan Voyageurs, from the Notary Book of Samuel Abbott, Mackinac Island, 1807-1817." http://www3.sympatico.ca/sneakers/abbottlist.htm.

—. "Pim Family." http://www3.sympatico.ca/sneakers/Pimfamily.htm.

Somerville, Alexander. *History of the British Legion and War in Spain, from Personal Observations and Other Authentic Sources, Containing a Correct Detail of the Events of the Expedition under General Evans ...*

With an Appendix, Containing every Officer's name, rank, and service ... London: James Paltie, 1839.

Stacey, C.P. "Michael Murphy: A Fenian Interlude." *Canadian Historical Review* 15, 2 (June 1934): 133-54.

Stewart, W. Brian. *A Life on the Line: Commander Pierre-Etienne Fortin and His Times.* Ottawa: Carleton University Press, 1997.

Stueber, Karsten R. "The Psychological Basis of Historical Explanation." *History and Theory: Studies in the Philosophy of History* 41, 1 (February 2002): 25-42.

Swainson, Donald. "Campbell, Sir Alexander." In *Dictionary of Canadian Biography.* Vol. 12, 150-54. Toronto: University of Toronto Press, 1988.

—. "MacDonell, Allan." In *Dictionary of Canadian Biography.* Vol. 11, 552-55. Toronto: University of Toronto Press, 1982.

Talbot, Edward Allan. *Five Years' Residence in Canada Including a Tour through Parts of the United States in the Year 1823.* 2 vols. East Ardsley, NY: S.R. Publishers, 1968.

Tanner, Helen Hornbeck. *The Ojibwas: A Critical Bibliography.* Bloomington: Published for the Newberry Library by Indiana University Press, 1976.

Tanner, Helen Hornbeck, Adele Hast, Jacqueline Peterson, Robert J. Surtees, and Miklos Pinther, eds. *Atlas of Great Lakes Indian History.* Norman: Published for the Newberry Library by University of Oklahoma Press, 1987.

Thomas, Steven. "Chronology: 1833-40 First Carlist War." http://www.balagan.org.uk/war/iberia/1833/chronology1833.htm.

Thomson, Donald W. *Men and Meridians: The History of Survey and Mapping in Canada.* 3 vols. Ottawa: Information Canada, 1966-67.

Thorman, George E. "Oakes, Forrest." In *Dictionary of Canadian Biography.* Vol. 4, 585-86. Toronto: University of Toronto Press, 1979.

Thwaites, Reuben G., ed. "The Fur Trade in Wisconsin." *Wisconsin Historical Collections* 20 (1911).

Tomlinson, Roswell. "Reminiscences of Roswell Tomlinson." The Elgin Historical and Scientific Institute, reprinted in *London Free Press,* June 1891.

Trade Goods. "Ermatinger." http://www.usinternet.com/users/dfnels/ermatinger.htm.

—. "Biauswah." http://www.usinternet.com/users/dfnels/biauswah.htm.

Trigger, Bruce G. *Natives and Newcomers: Canada's "Heroic Age" Reconsidered.* Montreal: McGill-Queen's University Press, 1985.

Tulchinsky, G., and Brian J. Young. "Young, John." In *Dictionary of Canadian Biography.* Vol. 10, 722-27. Toronto: University of Toronto Press, 1972.

Van Kirk, Sylvia. "The Custom of the Country, An Examination of Fur Trade Marriage Practices." In *Essays in Western History,* ed. Lewis H. Thomas, 49-70. Edmonton: University of Alberta Press, 1976.

—. "Isbister, Alexander Kennedy." In *Dictionary of Canadian Biography.* Vol. 11, 445-46. Toronto: University of Toronto Press, 1982.

—. *Many Tender Ties: Women in Fur Trade Society in Western Canada, 1670-1870.* Winnipeg: Watson and Dwyer, 1999.

—. "What if Mama Is an Indian? The Cultural Ambivalence of the Alexander Ross Family." In *The New Peoples: Being and Becoming Métis in North America,* ed. Jacqueline Peterson and Jennifer S.H. Brown. Winnipeg: University of Manitoba Press, 1985.

Van Kirk, Sylvia, and Jennifer S.H. Brown. "Nelson, George." In *Dictionary of Canadian Biography.* Vol. 8, 652-53. Toronto: University of Toronto Press, 1985.

Verreau, H.A.B. *Invasion du Canada: Collection des mémoirs.* Montreal: Eusèbe Senécal, 1873.

Wallace, W. Stewart, ed. *Documents Relating to the North West Company.* Toronto: Champlain Society, 1934.

Warren, William W. *History of the Ojibway Nation.* Minneapolis: Ross and Haines, 1957.

West, John. *The Substance of a Journal during a Residence at the Red River Colony, British North America; and Frequent Excursions among the North-West American Indians in the Years 1820, 1821, 1822, and 1823.* London: L.B. Seeley and Son, 1824.

White, Bruce M. "'Give Us a Little Milk': The Social and Cultural Significance of Gift Giving in the Lake Superior Fur Trade." In *Rendezvous: Selected Papers of the Fourth North American Fur Trade Conference, 1981,* ed. Thomas C. Buckley, 185-96. St Paul, MN: North American Fur Trade Conference, 1984.

Williams, Samuel. "Reminiscences of Samuel Williams." The Elgin Historical and Scientific Institute, reprinted in *London Free Press,* June 1891.

Winks, Robin W. *The Civil War Years: Canada and the United States.* 4th ed. Montreal: McGill-Queen's University Press, 1998.

Woodcock, George. "Grant, Cuthbert." In *Dictionary of Canadian Biography*. Vol. 4, 310. Toronto: University of Toronto Press, 1979.

Woolworth, Alan R. "The Great Carrying Place: Grand Portage." In *Where Two Worlds Meet: The Great Lakes Fur Trade,* ed. Caroline Gilman, 110-15. St Paul: Minnesota Historical Society, 1982.

Yeager, William R. *Norfolk County Marriage Records, 1795-1870.* Simcoe, ON: Norfolk Historical Society, 1978.

Zeller, Suzanne E., and John H. Noble. "Barnston, James." In *Dictionary of Canadian Biography*. Vol. 8, 61-62. Toronto: University of Toronto Press, 1985.

Index

Printed and bound in Canada by Friesens
Set in Fairfield by Blakeley
Copy editor: Sarah Wight
Proofreader: Gail Copeland
Cartographer: Eric Leinberger
Indexer: Nancy Mucklow